New Casebooks

MIDDLEMARCH

New Casebooks

New Casebooks

MIDDLEMARCH

GEORGE ELIOT

EDITED BY JOHN PECK

St. Martin's Press   New York

First published in the United States of America in 1992

Printed in Hong Kong

ISBN 0–312–07567–7

Library of Congress Cataloging-in-Publication Data
available from the publisher

Contents

v

Acknowledgements

The editor and publishers wish to thank the following for permission to use copyright material:

Gillian Beer, extract from *George Eliot* (1986), by permission of Harvester-Wheatsheaf and Indiana University Press;

Katherine Blake, extract from *Love and The Woman Question in Victorian Literature* (1983), by permission of Harvester-Wheatsheaf and Barnes and Noble Books;

Terry Eagleton, extract from *Criticism and Ideology*, New Left Books (1976), by permission of Verso;

Suzanne Graver, extract from *George Eliot and Community: A Study in Social Theory and Fictional Form* (1984). Copyright © 1984 the Regents of the University of California, by permission of the University of California Press;

David Lodge, essay, '*Middlemarch* and the Idea of the Classic Realist Text', by permission of Curtis Brown on behalf of the author;

Kerry McSweeney, extracts from *Middlemarch: Art, Ideas, Aesthetics* (1984), by permission of Unwin Hyman Ltd;

D. A. Miller, extract from *Narrative and Its Discontents: Problems of Closure in the Traditional Novel* (1981). Copyright © 1981 Princeton University Press, by permission of Princeton University Press;

J. Hillis Miller, 'Optic and Semiotic in *Middlemarch*' in *The Worlds of Victorian Fiction*, ed. Jerome H. Buckley (1975), Harvard University Press. Copyright © 1975 by the President and

Fellows of Harvard College, by permission of Harvard University;

Sally Shuttleworth, extract from *George Eliot and Nineteenth-Century Science* (1984), by permission of Cambridge University Press.

Every effort has been made to trace all the copyright holders but if any have been inadvertently overlooked the publishers will be pleased to make the necessary arrangement at the first opportunity.

General Editors' Preface

The purpose of this series of Casebooks is to reveal some of the ways in which contemporary criticism has changed our understanding of commonly studied texts and writers and, indeed, of the nature of criticism itself. Central to the series is a concern with modern critical theory and its effect on current approaches to the study of literature. Each New Casebook editor has been asked to select a sequence of essays which will introduce the reader to the new critical approaches to the text or texts being discussed in the volume and also illuminate the rich interchange between critical theory and critical practice that characterises so much current writing about literature.

The focus of the New Casebooks is on modern critical thinking and practice, with the volumes seeking to reflect both the controversy and the excitement of current criticism. Because much of this criticism is difficult and often employs an unfamiliar critical language, editors have been asked to give the reader as much help as they feel is appropriate, but without simplifying the essays or the issues they raise.

The project of New Casebooks, then, is to bring together in an illuminating way those critics who best illustrate the ways in which contemporary criticism has established new methods of analysing texts and who have reinvigorated the important debate about how we 'read' literature. The hope is, of course, that New Casebooks will not only open up this debate to a wider audience, but will also encourage students to extend their own ideas, and think afresh about their responses to the texts they are studying.

John Peck and Martin Coyle
University of Wales, Cardiff

Introduction

JOHN PECK

The essays in this collection were all published within fifteen years of each other, and yet they reveal extraordinary changes in the critical response to *Middlemarch*. This is not a case of its reputation as a novel rising or falling, but rather a matter of new readings and new ways of looking at the novel. What has prompted this activity has been the development of modern critical theory, and especially the influence of structuralist, deconstructive, Marxist, New Historicist and feminist thinking. The impact of such thinking has been felt in discussions of every kind of literature, but has been particularly prominent in discussions of the novel. In these discussions, no novel has been referred to more frequently than *Middlemarch*, partly at least because it seems to carry representative status as the central Victorian text and also the most ambitious English-language realistic novel. This should be apparent in the essays that follow, where many of the critics see themselves as engaged in something more complicated than just constructing an original reading of *Middlemarch*; they see themselves as engaged in a continuing debate about the novel as a genre, a debate about history, and, indeed, in a debate about the nature and function of criticism itself. In this sense the essays not only present new readings of *Middlemarch* but also represent a major contribution to current critical and cultural theory.

I

This is not to say, of course, that the essays included here invalidate past criticism of *Middlemarch*. Indeed, the strength of traditional criticism seems the necessary point at which to begin a survey of critical responses: at the same time, we do need to identify the assumptions that informed and dictated its emphases. Inevitably, such a survey involves a good measure of simplification. The truth is that traditional criticism is far more varied and complex than is sometimes suggested, and yet, looked at from the present day, there does seem a certain uniformity about the views that prevailed in the 1950s and '60s. (For the earlier critical history of the novel, see the original *Casebook*, edited by Patrick Swinden.[1]) There is always an assured grasp of the central areas of thematic concern in George Eliot's novel: her subject-matter is seen to be individuals, and their relationships with other individuals and with society as a whole. Her mode is realistic: she offers a substantial picture of society and a psychologically convincing portrayal of the characters. There is a well-defined pattern in the novel connecting the characters, so that Dorothea and Lydgate, for example, are both seen as idealists, but idealists whose dreams are destroyed as they come up against the harsh realities of daily existence. As such, they are twin studies in defeated aspiration. But as well as idealists, her central characters are also egoists: a much discussed episode is the sequence (in chapters 77 to 80) in which Dorothea discovers Rosamond and Ladislaw alone together and, after a sleepless night of reflection, realises how self-absorbed she has been. It is a move from immaturity to maturity, from selfishness to a sense of life beyond the self, which is common in Victorian fiction, and frequently focused upon in traditional critic- ism.

Critics have always understood the anxieties that underlie George Eliot's use of such a narrative pattern. As Barbara Hardy notes, Eliot was 'concerned with the problems of a humanity without a provi- dence'.[2] The loss of her religious faith had disturbing social implica- tions for Eliot, for it seemed to remove the foundations of morality; *Middlemarch* can be seen as attempting to construct a new secular morality, built on an idea of social obligation. For many critics (and readers) this is the central feature of George Eliot's art, that her novels do seem to offer a sense of how society can be reformulated. The intellectual background to this, in which the influence of Feuerbach's writings on George Eliot is of central importance, is explored in two indispensable books: U. C. Knoepflmacher's *Reli- gious Humanism and the Victorian Novel*,[3] and Bernard J. Paris's *Experiments in Life: George Eliot's Quest for Values*.[4] Neither Knoepflmacher nor Paris, however, is directly concerned with Eliot's art as a novelist. Outstanding in this latter respect are W. J. Harvey's *The Art of George Eliot*,[5] and Barbara Hardy's *The Novels of*

George Eliot.[6] Both concentrate on the form of George Eliot's fiction, and offer a clear stance on the problem at the heart of discussions of *Middlemarch*: the relationship between the novel's realism, that is its creation of a truthful impression of life, and the moral pattern that is developed in the text. Criticism returns again and again to this relationship and to the question of the kind of control that George Eliot exercises in the novel.

For some critics, including Knoepflmacher, realism and Eliot's moral vision are at odds. Harvey and Hardy set out to counter this view. They both accept the notion of a morally instructive novel, but argue that artistic complexity is compatible with a moral scheme. To quote Barbara Hardy again:

> In *Middlemarch* ... we feel the pressure of an enormous number of human beings, similar and dissimilar, modifying the doctrines of the novelist as well as contributing to them. George Eliot has a simple and not very varied moral scheme but her novels are never schematic or rigid in their generalizations about human beings. The human examples are always variations of the theme rather than examples which fit it perfectly.[7]

Such a view emphasises Eliot's poise and control, her ability to understand a complex world. It is a view which chimes with the feelings of many readers of *Middlemarch* – a sense of George Eliot as a steady, perceptive and authoritative guide to the vividly realised world she presents – and it is a view which many critics continue to endorse. Indeed, the first essay in this book, by Kerry McSweeney, begins by discussing George Eliot's loss of faith, and the kind of humanised Christianity she wished to construct in its place. McSweeney then focuses on the problem of egoism and the need for a sense of human fellowship. This leads him on to the danger Eliot's art runs of becoming too diagrammatically moral, a danger, he argues, which is countered by the use of the narrator in *Middlemarch*, who is particularly successful in penetrating beneath the surface of the subject-matter. This view of the balanced nature of George Eliot's achievement might seem non-contentious, yet it is just such a view that a great deal of recent criticism rejects and reacts against.

II

The most obvious challenge to the traditional view of *Middlemarch* comes from those critics who question the kind of control George

Eliot establishes in her novel. At its simplest, this amounts to an objection to novels which rely on an intrusive and omniscient narrator. More recently, however, the objection has been to the stance and ideology of the narrative voice rather than to the mere fact of its presence. Such a view began to gain currency in the 1970s, but the essence of the case had been anticipated by Arnold Kettle in his chapter on *Middlemarch* in *An Introduction to the English Novel*.[8] Kettle criticises Eliot for her lack of a sense of a larger historical process of change, for the way in which she conceives of the world as made up of individuals existing within a static society. The patronising tone of Kettle's writing, his confidence in his own convictions as he rejects Eliot's convictions, makes it hard to sympathise with his view, but this should not obscure the force of Kettle's case that Eliot is a rather blinkered thinker who accepts and works within a limited ideological position. Looked at from Kettle's viewpoint, the standard claims about George Eliot's insight and wisdom do start to crumble, and the enthusiasm of some critics for her liberal values of toleration, sympathy and understanding can start to seem little more than an echo of their own political assumptions.

The unsympathetic view of George Eliot's position finds its most forceful expression in Terry Eagleton's *Criticism and Ideology*, an extract from which appears as the second essay in this anthology. In a complex argument, Eagleton touches on a great many issues, but the two most relevant to the broader debate about Eliot's fiction are his discussion of division and conflict within *Middlemarch*, and his view of how George Eliot manages to reconcile seemingly incompatible positions. Eagleton argues that 'Eliot's work attempts to resolve a structural conflict between two forms of mid-Victorian ideology: between a progressively muted Romantic individualism ... and certain "higher" corporate ideological modes'.[9] This might seem merely to point up the tensions between the individual and society which critics have always recognised as central in Eliot's work, but Eagleton's argument is rather that the novel is caught in a socio-political divide that cannot be bridged. Consequently, what we find in the novel is George Eliot attempting to recast 'historical contradictions into ideologically resolvable form'.[10] When this resolution cannot be achieved, when the claims of individualism cannot be accommodated within the corporate society, George Eliot's resort is to pull everything together in her self. The 'ethical' position in the novel becomes a way of getting out of difficult situations; what cannot be resolved is countered by a moralising of the issues.

Whereas Harvey and Hardy see openness and breadth in George Eliot's narrative voice, Eagleton sees that voice as deflecting attention away from problems by its moral discourse. Essentially, social and political problems are reduced to interpersonal terms, and solutions expressed in interpersonal terms. A broadly similar view is expressed by Raymond Williams. He argues that there is a sense in which George Eliot never really engages with the reality of the society in which she lives. 'Value', he argues, 'is in the past, as a general retrospective condition, and is in the present only as a particular and private sensibility, the individual moral action.'[11]

Marxist critics, such as Kettle, Eagleton and Williams, are sometimes challenged on the grounds that they themselves write from a specific ideological position, but the importance of what they say cannot be dismissed this glibly, especially as they contribute to our sense of *Middlemarch* as a book grounded in a historical period which demands to be seen as the product of particular material conditions. What they draw attention to is how George Eliot reveals the very real divisions of Victorian society, even if they do expose her answers as limited and artificial. To draw attention to such matters is not necessarily to find fault with her novels; on the contrary, it can be a good position from which to analyse the options open to a novelist in the period. As such, it might appeal more as a critical approach than that which seems to invest George Eliot with an almost superhuman ability to transcend the contradictions of her age. The most obvious point, however, is that we seem to have arrived at an *impasse*: on one side is a group of critics with almost unqualified respect for the achieved balance of George Eliot's art, on the other a group of critics who draw attention to the limits of her vision. If there is to be a way out of this *impasse*, it will have to be found by critics who discover different ways of talking about the control that George Eliot exercises in *Middlemarch*.

III

The best way of approaching this question of new ways of reading *Middlemarch* is by way of some brief remarks of Colin MacCabe in his book *James Joyce and the Revolution of the Word*.[12] As his title suggests, MacCabe is chiefly interested in Joyce, but he uses George Eliot's novels to define the alternative (and, for him, more interesting) tradition in which Joyce works. Central to his case is his description of *Middlemarch* as a 'classic realist text'.[13] Such a novel, he argues, works on a deception, the deception that it is offering us a true, transparent view of the world; the text refuses to acknowledge its own status as writing or construct. This means that 'the narrative discourse functions simply as a window on reality',[14] that the text purports to offer us a picture of the world beyond itself. But no novel can give us the whole world; some sort of dominance has to be imposed. In the classic realist text the world is read, in fact, on the terms the author wishes to impose, and MacCabe suggests that in *Middlemarch* the terms are fairly narrow.

A critic exploring similar issues to MacCabe is Catherine Belsey in *Critical Practice*.[15] She shares his interest in the deceptive nature of a realistic text, the way in which it encourages us to believe that it is presenting a truthful picture of the world, to the extent that generations of readers have come to feel that Dorothea has a life beyond the pages of the novel. But in addition to this, Belsey argues: 'The experience of reading a realistic text is ultimately reassuring, however harrowing the events of the story, because the world evoked in the fiction, its patterns of cause and effect, of social relationships and moral values, largely confirms the patterns of the world we seem to know'.[16] Both MacCabe and Belsey are interested in looking at the wider implications of the existence of, and popularity of, realistic fiction. They are interested in seeing how a certain form of writing served, and might still serve, an ideological purpose: how it inscribed and maintained particular ideas of what was normal and acceptable. A novel such as *Middlemarch* might seem to offer a sensitive exploration of the fate of the individual, but inherent in the nature of realism, it can be argued, is a strong bias towards the socially conservative, towards conformity. (For a discussion of how George Eliot's kind of representational narrative is constructed and functions, it is well worth looking at the linguistic criticism of Geoffrey N. Leech and Michael H. Short in *Style in Fiction*,[17] and Roger Fowler in *Linguistics and the Novel* and *Literature as Social Discourse*.[18])

IV

In the responses of MacCabe and Belsey Marxism combines with structuralism, or, more strictly, poststructuralism. It is of no small interest, therefore, that the principal rejoinder to MacCabe comes from another critic who has been closely associated with structuralist thinking: David Lodge. His essay '*Middlemarch* and the Idea of the Classic Realist Text', which follows Eagleton's in this collection, is included for two reasons: first, it is an important contribution to *Middlemarch* criticism, moving beyond the kind of hostility to George Eliot which is found in some structuralist and poststructuralist criticism; and, second, because it offers an incisive analysis of the issues at work in contemporary criticism. The essay starts by defining the difference between structuralism, which is concerned with 'the purely formal, semiological analysis of literary texts and genres,'[19] and poststructuralist criticism, which follows through structuralist ideas about language and emphasises the gap between language and the world. One effect of this is that poststructuralist criticism tends to favour a novelist such as Joyce who delights in the free play of language, and be critical of a realistic novelist such as George Eliot who apparently offers a univocal interpretation of experience.

Lodge himself is not interested in trying to return to the stance of traditional criticism, where George Eliot's realism was considered as 'timeless truthfulness to human experience'.[20] What he is interested in is what view we are to take if we reject the traditional stance, but find it impossible to accept the alternative view of a totally ideologically blinkered George Eliot. In formulating his answer, Lodge calls upon the ideas of Mikhail Bakhtin, a Russian critic from the 1920s whose work has had a tremendous influence on novel criticism since its translation into English in the 1970s. For Bakhtin, 'the novel can be defined as a diversity of social speech types ... and a diversity of individual voices'.[21] That is to say, rather than there being one voice present in a text, a novel is 'polyphonic'. This, as Lodge notes, has a considerable effect upon novels.

> Different types of discourse can be represented in fiction, of course, as the direct speech of characters, without serious disturbance to the authority of the narrator, as in the novels of Fielding or Scott. But once these discourses enter into the narrative discourse itself, in various forms of reported speech, the interpretative control of the author's voice is inevitably weakened to some degree.[22]

The importance of this idea is that it enables us to move beyond the alternative positions described so far in this Introduction. Rather than seeing the narrative voice in *Middlemarch* as poised, controlled or dominant, it allows us to see how it might be regarded as provisional and uncertain, and to see how the novel itself might not amount to a larger unity. There are, it can be argued, always unresolvable differences, oppositions in novels that cannot be sub-jected to dialectical mediation. Bakhtin's views are now part of the mainstream of contemporary novel criticism and are widely diffused in discussions of many novelists.[23] Lodge's use of Bakhtin enables him to counter MacCabe's comments on the dominating voice of George Eliot's narrator and to show the ways in which the narrative voice, far from being clear and simple, is 'obscure or at least very complicated'.[24] Such a lack of total control in a novel might appear to be a weakness rather than a strength, but, as Lodge explains, 'it is precisely because the narrator's discourse is never entirely unambiguous, predictable, and in total interpretive control of the other discourses in *Middlemarch* that the novel survives, to be read and re-read, without ever being finally closed or exhausted'.[25]

This sense of the uncertainty, even the contradictoriness, of *Middlemarch* is also at the heart of J. Hillis Miller's influential discussions of the novel. Miller presented his ideas in two essays, 'Narrative and History'[26] and the essay reprinted here after Lodge's, 'Optic and Semiotic in *Middlemarch*'. Both are outstanding exam-ples of deconstructive criticism. Deconstruction makes the assump-tion that all texts are disunified and contradictory, and are tacitly involved in contesting their own meaning. Whereas traditional criticism stresses the coherence of *Middlemarch*, in deconstruction there is an extreme move towards stressing the incoherence of all texts. Instead, therefore, of seeing George Eliot as offering a total-ising vision, Miller argues that *Middlemarch* endlessly undermines any positive position in the novel, and, far from affirming unity, does the opposite. To establish his case, he shows that while the text does employ metaphors, such as the web and the stream, which suggest connectedness, it also uses a number of optical metaphors, which undermine this possibility, for such metaphors remind us of the difficulty of all perception. The conclusion this leads to is that there is an irreconcilable gap in the novel's language and thinking.

Both of Miller's essays are characteristically brilliant, forcing us to notice previously neglected features of the novel, and to think again about the work as a whole. Deconstruction, particularly as exem-plified in the work of Miller and other American critics, has, however, attracted a considerable amount of anger. The major objection to the deconstructive position is that it does nothing except delight in contradiction and incoherence in a text, and, indeed, deconstructive criticism can easily become an ahistorical quest for confusion, imposing the twentieth century's lack of certainty on texts from the past.[27] At the same time, Miller's work has also provided a stimulating starting-point for further criticism of the novel. One of the most impressive responses to the challenge presented by J. Hillis Miller's view of *Middlemarch* is to be found in D. A. Miller's book *Narrative and its Discontents*. The essay that appears in this anthology is an excerpt from a long chapter about *Middlemarch*. D. A. Miller accepts that the novel can be seen as open and contradictory, indeed that it can be described as 'self-deconstructive', but he argues that we also gain a sense of a novel which is coherent and moral: 'Like one of those optical drawings that won't resolve once for all into five cubes or six, a vase or two human profiles, *Middlemarch* seems to be traditional and to be beyond its limit, to subvert and to reconfirm the value of its traditional status'.[28] What matters most about *Middlemarch* for D. A. Miller is this 'double valency'[29] of the text.

In some ways the essays by J. Hillis Miller and D. A. Miller set the agenda for recent discussions of George Eliot, making us aware of an open, unstable, contradictory text, but also a text that simultaneously adopts a moral position and moves towards closure as well as openness. It is this doubleness that other critics have explored, though in very different ways.

V

An important direction in which recent criticism has moved is towards a renewed interest in history. Deconstruction (at least in the manner in which it has developed as a critical approach to literary texts) seems to free the text from history, liberating the critic to produce an almost limitless variety of readings. Seeing the text in history, working with a sense of how the text functioned in the society in which it was produced, sets a limit to this. It is interesting to note that this new direction had already been anticipated by Mikhail Bakhtin. At first glance, his critical approach, with its stress on the instability of texts, might seem to lead towards the deconstructionists' delight in incoherence, but Bakhtin's thinking runs counter to the formalist/structuralist tradition in criticism. He is centrally concerned with the social dimension of the language of a text: how language is involved in social relationships which are part of broader political, economic and ideological systems.

In essence, Bakhtin is interested in the kinds of debate that are going on in a novel, the ways in which it articulates and presents the unresolved tensions of its ideology. Such concerns are also at the heart of recent historicist criticism. The best way to grasp these matters is to consider the difference between traditional historical criticism and the kind of work which has appeared in recent years. A traditional approach, as in U. C. Knoepflmacher's book mentioned earlier, usually identifies the main strands of thought and belief in a period and indicates the way in which the author develops a position in his or her work. The emphasis tends to fall upon the coherence of the view and position presented in the text. Recent historicist criticism, by contrast, assumes that the tensions and divisions in a period are fundamental to the political and social structure and stresses the unresolved contradictions of texts. One way of putting this is to say that New Historicism is an approach that accepts much of what poststructuralism and deconstruction have suggested about the open and provisional nature of a text, but that it also attempts to see how such an unstable work can be representative of, and function in, the period in which it was written. Of particular importance here is the influence of the work of the historian Michel Foucault, with its radical criticism of traditional notions of unity and coherence.[30]

A good example of a historicist approach is Suzanne Graver's *George Eliot and Community*, an extract from which follows D. A. Miller's essay in this anthology. Part of Graver's project involves a re-reading of the Victorian period, in which she shows that concepts of community, kinship and social organicism were less straightforward than is sometimes assumed, and that in the social thinking of the period (including George Eliot's novels), the craving for unity was accompanied by an apprehension of multiplicity. The strength of George Eliot's fiction is felt to lie in this tension:

> By capturing polarities that point to antagonistic values, while evoking through the effort to overcome them a vision of wholeness, she created a body of fiction most compelling when it reveals a double consciousness, moving toward fusion while uncovering conflict as each side implicates the other both affirmatively and negatively. As a result, her most successful reconciliations are those tenuous and makeshift ones that render fragile the very principle of fellowship she struggled to affirm.[31]

There are ways in which this might seem to be just a compromise between the traditional view of George Eliot as an author with something important to say and the deconstructionists' celebration of the instability of *Middlemarch*, but there is more to it than this, for Graver is alive both to the complexity of the writing and to the complexity of the cultural function that the text is attempting to serve. To talk of compromise is to suggest a kind of mid-point, but Graver's sense of the fragile or tenuous nature of *Middlemarch* is a world away from traditional praise for George Eliot's balance and control.

At the same time, Graver does see *Middlemarch* intervening in a serious manner in the Victorian period. Similar perspectives inform Sally Shuttleworth's *George Eliot and Nineteenth-Century Science*, an extract from which follows Graver's essay in this collection. Like Graver, Shuttleworth stresses the underestimated complexity of the Victorian period, how it is all too often assumed that Victorian science represented a unified body of knowledge, whereas it was a diffuse and internally divided collection of disciplines. Shuttleworth concentrates on the field of organic theory and points out the appeal of an organicist philosophy to George Eliot, with its promise of showing the interdependence of the whole and the part. *Middlemarch* itself, however, as Shuttleworth argues, reveals an awareness of the gap between any moral ideal and social reality. Once again, then, as in Graver, the stress falls on the unstable nature of George Eliot's text, and the way in which it functions in its period, articulating central debates about the nature of Victorian society.

VI

The order in which the essays appear in this volume, and the order in which they are referred to in this Introduction, might suggest that there has been a steady line of development in discussions of *Middlemarch*. It is as if critics moved from unqualified praise for George Eliot's wisdom to attacks on her narrowness of vision, and then to an appreciation of the complex, open nature of her work. But criticism does not move along in a steady path like this. A great deal of criticism is generated by an irritated dissatisfaction with existing views. Good criticism often meets with a hostile response, because it provocatively challenges established assumptions. The essays in this volume by Terry Eagleton and J. Hillis Miller, in particular, caused a stir because of their radical redefinitions of the character of George Eliot's art, and the position revealed in her work. Other essays, such as those by Suzanne Graver and Sally Shuttleworth, are less openly challenging, but are just as original in forcing us to revise our views about the context in which George Eliot was working and how *Middlemarch* relates to that context. The history of recent criticism of *Middlemarch* is not, therefore, a smooth and continuous story, but is marked by discontinuities, challenges and fresh directions. This is what makes so many of the essays in this volume so exciting, that they are written with an awareness of breaking new ground and heading off in unexpected directions.

New criticism challenges ideas which have become fixed and accepted. What complicates matters, however, is that the critic is not just discovering new things about the text and the period in which it was written. When J. Hillis Miller, for example, discovers a whole range of contradictions in *Middlemarch* he is revealing areas of complication in the text, but the emphases of his criticism are determined by the framework of values and social and political ideas that he exists in at the time of writing his essay. In other words, as well as examining the beliefs and values that are revealed in the text the critic is articulating a contemporary framework of beliefs and values – even if, in the past twenty years, these seem more unstable and to alter more rapidly than at any time in the past. This problematises the position of the reader/critic, as every response will, in a sense, be a blinkered response, but it can also be argued that it is this very limitation that makes criticism a worthwhile activity, as the critic is always involved in discussing, if only implicitly, how our own political and social reality relates to the world presented in the text. Such issues, in particular the way in which changes of attitude in our own society affect how we look at the past, are clearly seen in feminist readings of *Middlemarch*, and the shifting assessments of George Eliot's feminism.

Feminism, as we might expect, is an issue in which traditional critics showed little interest. Critics returned time and time again to how George Eliot's main characters have to compromise with society, but there was seldom any discussion of the fact that such a compromise could have a specifically female dimension. Even Barbara Hardy, the best traditional critic of George Eliot, plays down George Eliot's feminism:

> her books make their feminist protest in a very muted way. *Middle-march* assimilated the earlier project of *Miss Brooke*, and one of the consequences of the assimilation is the way in which Lydgate's tragedy qualifies our response to Dorothea's. Any suggestion of a feminist

moral is controlled and extended by the complex plot, which puts Dorothea in her place as an example less of a feminine problem than of the frustrations of the human condition.[32]

This appears dismissive of a feminist level to the text, but what now seems interesting about this comment (it was written in 1959) is the lingering sense of something unresolved in George Eliot's work, that there is a muted protest working against the more obvious imperatives of the novel. (Indeed, George Eliot's feminism is an issue that Barbara Hardy returns to, for example in a 1976 essay, '*Middlemarch*: Public and Private Worlds', where she writes of George Eliot's 'sharply feminist consciousness'.[33])

When overtly feminist criticism on George Eliot began to appear in the 1970s the initial response to *Middlemarch* tended to be hostile. This was partly due to the nature of feminist criticism at the time, which was then most concerned with looking at recurrent cultural figures of women in literature, and with celebrating positive presentations of women. *Middlemarch* seemed to fail on both of these tests. Some critics focused on how George Eliot makes the women in the novels the preservers of communal values, and, in pointing to George Eliot's use of a traditional cultural figure of the woman, they emphasised the conservative, socially ameliorative traits in her work. The same is true of those critics who concentrated on the fact that George Eliot's heroines are always defeated, that they always accept renunciation. (A contrast can be drawn between her heroines and George Eliot herself who, through her writing, transcended the limitations the age placed on her as a woman.) Such hostile views are ably discussed in Zelda Austen's 'Why Feminist Critics are Angry with George Eliot'.[34] The hostility is not unlike that of Marxist critics such as Eagleton and Williams, who also criticise George Eliot for working within, and acepting, the ideology of her age.

When feminist criticism moves beyond finding fault with George Eliot's portrayal of women, it often focuses on how the presentation of women characters challenges the text's moves towards coherence. This is true of the first of the feminist essays included here, by Kathleen Blake. Blake recognises George Eliot's central issues as women's issues, and sees that there is a sympathetic understanding of the difficulties of a woman's lot in the novel as it reveals how hard it is for women characters who have no active role in society. This is a powerful feminist reading of *Middlemarch* which, as with a great deal of contemporary criticism, is interested in the way in which uncomfortable issues in George Eliot's fiction have to co-exist with her interest in social concord. Where Blake differs from many feminist critics, however, is that she takes a rather traditional view of the kind of authority and overall control that George Eliot exercises in the novel. In order to see the fuller implications of Blake's essay, and to grasp her critical position, we need, though, to understand some of the broader principles that inform feminist discussions of *Middlemarch*. The first point to make is the one I have already raised, that original criticism challenges received views. Feminist criticism, however, is often particularly striking because it offers such a comprehensive exposure of conventional values. The feminist critic can point to the fact that the structure of society is patriarchal, that it is organised in such a way as to offer men all kinds of possibilities in life whereas, traditionally, women were denied fulfilment even through work. Moreover, this pattern of organisation is not just found in the daily domestic life of society, for patriarchal values inform every aspect of life and thought, including the plots and language of literary texts. For example, a basic story in our culture is that of the expulsion of Adam and Eve from the Garden of Eden; it is Eve who is at fault, Eve who is characterised as unsteady and unreliable. From that point of origin, therefore, with only two people in the world, man is thought of as rational, woman as irrational.

One of the best accounts of the patriarchal basis of all our thinking is offered by the French writer Hélène Cixous. She suggests that the man/woman opposition is at the heart of language, but it is an opposition in which the man is seen as superior, the woman as inferior; the man is active, the woman passive.[35] The challenge for women readers (possibly for all readers), and for women writers (possibly for all writers), is to question this mode of organisation which seems not only at the heart of society but also to inform the very nature of language itself.

The first wave of modern feminist criticism, as I have already suggested, saw George Eliot as seeming to submit too readily to the patriarchal imperatives of society. Later feminist criticism, however, has moved towards a sense of something much more positive in George Eliot's fiction. Part of this, particularly influenced by Elaine Showalter's book *A Literature of Their Own: British Women Novelists from Brontë to Lessing*,[36] is the concept of a women's tradition in literature, of women sharing a voice and a view which challenges the values of the dominant male culture. The emphasis of a great deal of subsequent feminist criticism has been on just such a questioning element in *Middlemarch*, although there is usually also a recognition that this co-exists with George Eliot's strong attraction to social conformity. Critics who, from a variety of feminist perspectives, explore such issues include Sandra Gilbert and Susan Gubar in *The Madwoman in the Attic*,[37] Judith Lowder Newton in the chapter on *The Mill on the Floss* in *Women, Power and Subversion: Social Strategies in British Fiction, 1778–1860*,[38] and Mary Jacobus in her chapter on *The Mill on the Floss* in *Reading Woman: Essays in Feminist Criticism*.[39] Feminist criticism varies in its approaches – and in its level of difficulty, the work of Gilbert and Gubar, for example, is fairly easy to read and understand, whereas Jacobus, who is interested in questions of psychoanalysis and theory, is much harder to absorb – but feminist criticism is always political criticism, interested in effecting a real change in society. In addition, at some point in feminist criticism the topic becomes far broader than just women. As Judith Lowder Newton writes: 'to see women we must see men ... to see gender we must also see heterosexism, race and class, that to examine the face of ideologies we must examine the social relations which they insure.'[40]

A book which rises to the challenge of looking at such a broad range of issues is Gillian Beer's *George Eliot*, an extract from which provides the last essay in this collection. It is one of the most sophisticated and illuminating critical books one could hope to read (something which is also true of her *Darwin's Plots: Evolutionary Narrative in Darwin, George Eliot and Nineteenth-Century Fiction*,[41] which contains a substantial and important section on George Eliot). Beer writes with a full familiarity with recent narrative and cultural theory, and her book is at once an assured and thought-provoking feminist reading of George Eliot and an outstanding New Historicist reading of *Middlemarch*, making us reconsider the force of George Eliot's importance in the Victorian period. Beer is particularly good on how the formal qualities of George Eliot's novels embody their social themes:

> the key bond is that between the sexes, with its immense power to yoke unlike people and to bind them in desire, or into flesh in generation. This contradiction – difference and connection – sustains the tension of her work. ... She values interdependence even above independence: and she gives it that high valuation because of (as well as in spite of) its difficulty ... by whatever route we approach her writing, we shall find always, a feeling for interconnection and yet a strong awareness of how difficult it is to keep different experiences simultaneously within meaning.[42]

What Beer is looking at, from a fresh angle, is the central issue of the unresolved ideological tensions at the heart of the text. She is looking at the kind of control George Eliot exercises in the novel, the extent to which George Eliot speaks for social conformity, and yet at the same time maintains a sense of conflict alongside her desire for fusion.

There are two related strengths to criticism such as Beer's. On the one hand, and this is true of all good criticism, it makes us look at the text in a new and challenging way. This, it is worth mentioning, is very different from coming up with eccentric or ingenious ideas about a book. Good criticism does not strain to say something new just for the sake of saying something new. On the contrary, it re-engages with central questions about power and relationships in the society presented in the work, and also looks at the kind of power the author is exercising in shaping the text. Good criticism, time and time again, discovers a new kind of urgency and relevance in works from the past. But to be credible, such re-readings have to be based upon close reading of the text – the words on the page must actually support the view the critic develops – and there has to be a historical credibility to the fresh reading – an analysis of the tensions in evidence in *Middlemarch* must correspond to tensions that existed in the Victorian era. Beer's criticism has this kind of critical and historical authority, as indeed does most good criticism. But feminist criticism also has an added quality, which is often only implicit in a great deal of criticism, for feminist criticism forces us to consider our own relationship to a text, the ways in which we are members of a society and bring our own political and social values into play in our response; the reader is forced to look not just at the text but also at her/his assumptions about the text. And this in turn underlines the point that there is no single, correct reading of a text, that if there has been a cultural consensus about how a book should be viewed, that it is possible to step outside that consensus and read the book from the margins, or in a variety of dissenting and disconcerting ways.

Indeed, that is what the critics in this collection do, and why all the essays remain relevant and still worth reading. The latest movement in criticism does not supersede or invalidate earlier criticism, for there is no correct view of the text to be worked towards. Even the most traditional piece of criticism remains vital and interesting, for it reveals the critic writing from a position we might not share but which can serve as the basis of a persuasive reading of a novel. Every worthwhile piece of criticism will permanently offer fresh perspectives on a text and help other readers see the text in a new way. And this is particularly true in the case of such a monumental work as *Middlemarch*, where the sheer scale and range of the book should make clear to us that we can never settle for a simple and stable view, that we need constantly to re-engage with the text and consider again how it relates to us as twentieth-century readers.

NOTES

1. Patrick Swinden (ed.), *George Eliot: 'Middlemarch'* (London, 1972).

2. Barbara Hardy, *The Novels of George Eliot* (London, 1959), p. 233.

3. U. C. Knoepflmacher, *Religious Humanism and the Victorian Novel* (Princeton, 1965).

4. Bernard J. Paris, *Experiments in Life: George Eliot's Quest for Values* (Detroit, 1965).

5. W. J. Harvey, *The Art of George Eliot* (London, 1961).

6. Barbara Hardy, *The Novels of George Eliot* (London, 1959).

7. Ibid., p. 143.

8. Arnold Kettle, *An Introduction to the English Novel*, vol. 1 (London, 1951), pp. 188–210.

9. See p. 33 below.

10. See p. 35 below.

11. Raymond Williams, *The Country and the City* (London, 1973), p. 101.

12. Colin MacCabe, *James Joyce and the Revolution of the Word* (London, 1979).

13. Ibid., p. 15.

14. Ibid.

15. Catherine Belsey, *Critical Practice* (London, 1980).

16. Ibid., p. 51.

17. Geoffrey N. Leech and Michael H. Short, *Style in Fiction* (London, 1981).

18. Roger Fowler, *Linguistics and the Novel* (London, 1977) and *Literature as Social Discourse* (London, 1981).

19. See p. 46 below.

20. See p. 45 below.

21. M. M. Bakhtin, *The Dialogic Imagination* (Austin, 1981), pp. 262–3.

22. See p. 53 below.

23. The most sustained Bakhtin-based reading of George Eliot is in Peter K. Garrett's *The Victorian Multiplot Novel: Studies in Dialogical Form* (New York, 1980).

24. See p. 56 below.

25. See p. 61 below.

26. J. Hillis Miller, 'Narrative and History', *English Literary History*, 41 (1974), 455–73.

27. The most fully presented case against deconstruction, and also the most sophisticated and least angry, is Frank Lentricchia's *After the New Criticism* (London, 1980).

28. See p. 85 below.

29. See p. 85 below.

30. See, for example, Foucault's *Language, Counter-Memory, Practice* (Oxford, 1977).

31. Suzanne Graver, *George Eliot and Community* (Berkeley, 1984), p. 148.

32. Barbara Hardy, *The Novels of George Eliot* (London, 1959), p. 52.

33. Barbara Hardy, '*Middlemarch*: Public and Private Worlds', *English*, 25 (1976), 5–26.

34. Zelda Austen, 'Why Feminist Critics are Angry with George Eliot', *College English*, 37 (1976), 549–61.

35. See the essays by Hélène Cixous, 'Sorties' and 'The Laugh of the Medusa', in *New French Feminisms: An Anthology*, ed. Elaine Marks and Isabelle de Courtivron (Brighton, 1981), pp. 90–8 and 245–64.

36. Elaine Showalter, *A Literature of Their Own: British Women Novelists from Brontë to Lessing* (Princeton, 1977).

37. Sandra Gilbert and Susan Gubar, *The Madwoman in the Attic* (New Haven, 1979), pp. 443–535.

38. Judith Lowder Newton, *Women, Power and Subversion: Social Strategies in British Fiction, 1778–1860* (London, 1981), pp. 125–57.

39. Mary Jacobus, *Reading Woman: Essays in Feminist Criticism* (London, 1986), pp. 62–79.

40. Judith Lowder Newton, *Women, Power and Subversion: Social Strategies in British Fiction, 1778–1860* (London, 1981), p. xx.

41. Gillian Beer, *Darwin's Plots: Evolutionary Narrative in Darwin, George Eliot and Nineteenth-Century Fiction* (London, 1983).

42. Gillian Beer, *George Eliot* (Brighton, 1986), pp. 14–15.

1

'Middlemarch': Art, Ideas, Aesthetics

KERRY McSWEENEY

By 1842 George Eliot had rejected Christian belief so emphatically that even though it deeply hurt her father she refused to attend church. The turning-point had been her reading during the previous year of Charles Hennell's *Inquiry Concerning the Origin of Christianity* (1838), which offered a historical, psychological and literary explanation of the supposed supernatural and miraculous events recounted in scripture. The effect of Hennell's arguments on George Eliot was comparable to the effect that the *Leben Jesu* of the great German scholar David Friedrich Strauss (who admired Hennell's work and arranged for its translation into German) was to have on many British readers when an English translation was published in 1846. The translator was Mary Ann Evans [George Eliot], who eight years later turned into English another key work of German religious thought, Ludwig Feuerbach's *Wesen des Christenthums*. In it, Feuerbach passionately argued that all of the enormous positive value of traditional Christianity could be recovered for the modern age once it was recognised that what earlier ages had regarded 'as objective, is now recognized as subjective; that is, what was formerly contemplated and worshipped as God is now perceived to be something *human* ... The divine being is nothing else than the human being, or rather the human nature purified, freed from the limits of the individual man [and] contemplated and revered as another, a distinct being. All the attributes of divine nature are, therefore, attributes of human nature.'[1]

Feuerbach's subjective, humanised Christianity powerfully appealed to Eliot because it offered a way of healing the split between her intellect, which could no longer accept the existence of a supernatural god, and her deepest emotions, which were inextricably linked with the religious culture of her early life. Furthermore, it widened the channels of sympathy and fellow-feeling between the agnostic intellectual and ordinary humanity. 'I begin to feel for other people's wants and sorrows', Eliot wrote in 1853, 'a little more than I used to do. Heaven help us! said the old religions – the new one, from its very lack of that faith, will teach us all the more to help one another.'[2] Far from being anti-religious, Eliot (as she explained in a letter of 1859) had come to have no antagonism

> towards any faith in which human sorrow and human longing for purity have expressed themselves; on the contrary, I have a sympathy with it that predominates over all argumentative tendencies. I have not returned to dogmatic Christianity – to the acceptance of any set of doctrines as a creed, and a superhuman revelation of the Unseen – but I see in it the highest expression of the religious sentiment that has yet found its place in the history of mankind, and I have the profoundest interest in the inward life of sincere Christians in all ages.[3]

For George Eliot, then, the replacement for traditional Christianity was to be a religion of humanity. Like all her books, *Middlemarch* has as its 'main bearing a conclusion . . . without which I could not have cared to write any representation of human life – namely, that the fellowship between man and man which has been the principle of development, social and moral, is not dependent on conceptions of what is not man: and that the idea of God, so far as it has been a high spiritual influence, is the ideal of a goodness entirely human (i.e., an exaltation of the human).'[4] In *Middlemarch*, Eliot presents a non-theological and non-metaphysical body of beliefs that she believes capable of providing a basis for non-egotistic values and other-regarding actions, and of performing for gifted members of the modern social organism the same ennobling function that traditional religious ideals had performed for St Theresa of Avila, who lived in a society still in its theological phase. These beliefs form the doctrinal core of *Middlemarch*; since they are directly articulated by the narrator, as well as reflected in character and action, it is not difficult to extrapolate them from the text.

The fundamental epistemological tenet in *Middlemarch* is the relativity of truth to point of view, and the subjectivity, partiality and fallibility of human perception. It is frequently expounded and exemplified: 'Signs are small measurable things, but interpretations are illimitable' (ch. 3); 'Probabilities are as various as the faces to be seen at will in fretwork or paperhangings: every form is there, from Jupiter to Judy, if you only look with creative inclination' (ch. 32); changing the lens in a microscope will lead to a different interpretation of exactly the same observed phenomenon (ch. 6); 'In watching effects, if only of an electric battery, it is often necessary to change our place and examine a particular mixture' from more than one perspective (ch. 40); 'who can represent himself just as he is, even in his own reflections?' (ch. 70). Sir James Chettam naturally interprets a change in Dorothea's complexion 'in the way most gratifying to himself' (ch. 3); when Dorothea looks into Casaubon's mind, she sees 'reflected there in vague labyrinthine extension every quality she herself brought' (ch. 3); her sister Celia has a 'marvellous quickness in observing a certain order of signs generally preparing her to expect such outward events as she had an interest in' (ch. 5); and Fred Vincy 'fancied that he saw to the bottom of his uncle Featherstone's soul, though in reality half of what he saw there was no more than the reflex of his own inclinations' (ch. 12). In short, we all belong to 'the fellowship of illusion' (ch. 34).

Egotism is the moral correlative of the subjectivity of all perception. A 'pier-glass or extensive surface of polished steel [may be] multitudinously and randomly scratched in all directions; but place now against it a lighted candle as a centre of illumination, and lo! the scratches will seem to arrange themselves in a fine series of concentric circles around that little sun'. This is a 'parable', as the narrator explains at the beginning of chapter 27: 'the scratches are events, and the candle is the egoism of any person now absent'. The comparison is ingenious and elegant, but calls attention to the universality of egotism less tellingly than does the narrator's raw and abrupt exclamation at the end of chapter 21: 'We are all of us born in moral stupidity, taking the world as an udder to feed our supreme selves.' This inherited stupidity has the same importance in Eliot's religion of humanity as does the doctrine of original sin in traditional Christian belief. The antidote to this primal taint is strong feeling, particularly fellow-feeling, the only certain stimulus to non-egotistical action. As early as 1843, Eliot had realised what other Victorian writers – Tennyson in *In Memoriam* is one example – were also discovering: 'Speculative truth begins to appear but a shadow of individual minds, agreement between intellects seems unattainable, and we turn to the *truth of feeling* as the only universal bond of union.'[5]

This quality is often referred to in *Middlemarch*: Dorothea's ardent feelings are repeatedly called attention to; Caleb Garth is a person who knows his duty because of 'a clear feeling inside me' (ch. 56); the narrator's final comment on Bulstrode's appalling inhumanity is that 'there is no general doctrine which is not capable of eating out our morality if unchecked by the deep-seated habit of direct fellow-feeling with individual fellow-men' (ch. 61). (This is a more abstract and generalised restatement of the principle that the title character of *Adam Bede* enunciates in simpler and more pragmatic terms in his novel's seventeenth chapter: 'It isn't notions sets people doing the right thing – it's feelings.') And, finally, the narrator remarks of Casaubon that his wounded egotism and withdrawal from life 'is only to be overcome by a sense of fellowship deep enough to make all efforts at isolation seem mean and petty instead of exalting' (ch. 42). It is not that any person's egotism can be fully eradicated, any more than subjectivity can be removed from human perception. If elimination of egotism were the goal, then Farebrother, Caleb Garth and Mary Garth would be the moral exemplars of *Middlemarch*. It is, rather, the case that an individual's egotism should be modified by the awareness of 'an equivalent centre of self' (ch. 21) in others and of the 'involuntary, palpitating life' (ch. 80) of ordinary humanity.

For George Eliot, then, ardent feeling and a sense of human fellowship are the humanistic equivalents of, and replacement for, the Christian conception of grace. But if 'our good depends on the quality and breadth of our emotion', as the narrator of *Middlemarch* insists in chapter 47, how does a person come to possess this saving capacity? Depending on how it is put, this question can be a difficult, even embarrassing, one to ask of *Middlemarch*, for in some cases the answer would seem to be that either you have it or you don't. Take the cases of Ladislaw and Lydgate, who by the climax of the novel have both arrived at a 'perilous margin' (ch. 79) in their life-journeys, but whose lots turn out to be quite different. Ladislaw finds private and public fulfilment, while Lydgate, 'pitifully' carrying the 'burthen' (ch. 81) of his appalling wife, ends as a failure in both his private and professional life. A contemporary reviewer was among the first to find it difficult to see the appropriateness of these contrasting fates:

> [Ladislaw] does what he likes, whether right or wrong, to the end of the story; he makes no sacrifices; even his devotion to Dorothea does

not preserve him from an unworthy flirtation with his friend Lydgate's wife. He is happy by luck, not desert . . . while poor Lydgate – ten times the better man – suffers not only in happiness, but in his noblest ambitions, and sinks to the lower level of a good practice and a good income because he marries and is faithful to the vain selfish creature whom Ladislaw merely flirts with.[6]

In terms of Eliot's humanistic religion, the reason for their different lots would seem to be that intense feeling and emotional depth are naturally present in Ladislaw (though they need Dorothea's nurture in order to flourish) and naturally absent in Lydgate, the outward sign of which is his socially nurtured 'spots of commonness' (ch. 15). But, if neither is responsible for the presence or absence in himself of these saving qualities, how can it be morally appropriate that one is rewarded and the other punished? The answer is that their lots are not morally appropriate; but they are necessary to the exposition of Eliot's doctrine which, like any general doctrine, is 'capable of eating out our morality'.

This difficult question and its subversive implications can be sidestepped if one follows Eliot's own practice in *Middlemarch* and focuses attention not on the origin of the secular grace of intense feeling but on the beneficent effect that one human being who possesses it can have on the egotism of another. As the narrator puts it in one of the novel's most florid passages: 'There are natures in which, if they love us, we are conscious of having a sort of baptism and consecration: they bind us over to rectitude and purity by their pure belief about us; and our sins become the worst kind of sacrilege which tears down the invisible altar of trust' (ch. 77). This central tenet of George Eliot's faith, which might in less sentimental terms be called the humanistic economy of salvation, is not only asserted by the narrator. It is also shown in operation in the climactic sections of *Middlemarch* when it becomes an important part of the resolution of the novel's principal plots. The turning-point in Fred Vincy's love for Mary, for instance, comes when Farebrother lays down his own possible happiness for another's and warns Fred that he is once again slipping into a way of living that may cost him Mary's love. This fine act – Farebrother himself, despite his habitual self depreciation, calls it 'a very good imitation of heroism' – has a powerful effect on Fred, producing 'a sort of regenerating shudder through the frame' and making him 'feel ready to begin a new life' (ch. 66). Dorothea has a similar effect on Lydgate when she comes to his assistance in his hour of greatest need. He feels 'something very new and strange' entering his life and tells Dorothea that 'you have made a great difference in my courage by believing in me'. The narrator underlines the doctrinal point: 'The presence of a noble nature, generous in its wishes, ardent in its charity, changes the lights for us: we begin to see things again in their larger, quieter masses, and to believe that we too can be seen and judged in the wholeness of our character' (ch. 76). This same 'saving influence of a noble nature, the divine efficacy of rescue that may lie in a self subduing act of fellowship' (ch. 82), is also seen in operation in Dorothea's meeting with Rosamond in chapter 81, a crucial scene in which the two central female characters in the novel talk together for the first time. Indeed, so powerful is Dorothea's outward-flowing fellow-feeling that it moves Rosamond, the novel's most complete egotist, to the performance of her first unselfish act when she tells Dorothea what had actually transpired during her interrupted conversation with Ladislaw and thereby makes possible the final coming together of Dorothea and Will. Rosamond is said to be 'taken hold of by an emotion stronger than her own', to be urged by 'a mysterious necessity', and to deliver 'her soul under impulses which she had not known before'. Rosamond's unselfish act has been called a moral surprise; but it is better placed in a religious rather than an ethical perspective. The 'mysterious necessity' is the amazing grace of intense fellow-feeling, and Rosamond's act is a secular version of the Christian *etiam peccata* paradox: even the most self-centred character in *Middlemarch* is shown to be capable of contributing to the humanistic economy of salvation. It is these acts that ultimately provide Eliot's secular religion of humanity with a certain eschatological dimension. They contribute to what in the last paragraph of *Middlemarch* is called 'the growing good of the world' that makes the noble spirits who have gone before parts of the mystical body of evolving humanity, and, if their deeds have made them widely known, members of what in her Positivist hymn Eliot calls

> the choir invisible
> Of those immortal dead who live again
> In minds made better by their presence.

No wonder that Emily Dickinson could say of *Middlemarch* that 'the mysteries of human nature surpass the "mysteries of redemption"'.

In the 1866 letter in which Eliot speaks of 'aesthetic teaching' she also speaks of her continuing effort to make 'certain ideas thoroughly incarnate, as if they had revealed themselves to me first in the flesh and not in the spirit'. She insists that if aesthetic teaching 'ceases to be purely aesthetic – if it lapses anywhere from the picture to the diagram – it becomes the most offensive of all teaching'. The presentation of ideas has to 'lay hold on the emotions as human experience'; the aim of the work of art devoted to aesthetic teaching is not to showcase ideas, however attractively, but to '"flash" conviction on the world by means of aroused sympathy'.[7] Ardent emotion and strong feeling could not simply be described or drama-tised; they had to be communicated to the reader – otherwise the teaching was pointless. As Dorothea tells Celia in explaining her refusal to describe how her union with Ladislaw came about: 'you would have to feel with me, else you would never know' (ch. 84).

George Eliot did not restrict her thinking about aesthetic teaching to her correspondence; it is also reflected in the text of *Middlemarch* to a degree sufficient to make the reflexive concern with its own intentions and meanings a subsidiary theme of the novel. These concerns find expression in three different ways: in comments about art and aesthetics made by certain characters; in the reflexive comments of the intrusive omniscient narrator; and in places where something in the text may be taken to refer at another level to the creative process or aesthetic goals of the author.

[At this point McSweeney discusses the development of Dorothea Brooke's aesthetic sense, in particular the improvement of her aesthetic understanding during her meetings with Will Ladislaw in Rome. This raises questions about the relation of art to common humanity. McSweeney then turns to discussing the narrator ...]

One of the first things one notices about the narrator is her concern with the transmission and control of meanings: 'signs are small measurable things', she observes early on, 'but interpretations are illimitable' (ch. 3); and two chapters later the reader is warned that 'the text, whether of prophet or of poet, expands for whatever we can put into it'. Both of these remarks are instances of the novel's pervasive epistemological concern with the relativity of truth to point of view. But they also have a particular application to what the author is trying to achieve in *Middlemarch*. The novel's major characters are concerned to find a significance in their lives and actions, though quotidian reality often seems to deny the possibility of any resonant action or radiant meaning.[8] Her reflexive comments suggest that the narrator is in the similar position of trying to find meaning and a *bona fide* significance in the mundane reality of her subject-matter without imposing arbitrary interpretations or symbolic meanings. To do so successfully would heal the breach between art and life 'outside the walls'. Living in the nineteenth century, Dorothea cannot lead a heroic life as could St Theresa of Avila in the sixteenth century. But the narrator of *Middlemarch*, who also lives in the nineteenth century, may be able to avoid the lot of Dorothea through the heroic act of writing a major work of literature that would adapt to a modern prose idiom and a realistic subject-matter the two traditionally highest literary genres, epic and tragedy. This attempt is the subject of most of the narrator's comments on the work she is presenting.

The possibility of writing an epic work in the nineteenth century – a subject of consuming interest to most of the major creative artists of the Romantic and Victorian periods – is raised at the very beginning of *Middlemarch*. In the sixteenth century, St Theresa's 'passionate, ideal nature' demanded, and found, 'an epic life'. But 'many Theresas' born into the modern world have found 'no life wherein there was a constant unfolding of far-resonant action'; their 'spiritual grandeur [was] ill-matched with the meanness of opportunity' (prelude). The point is again underlined in the finale: 'A new Theresa will hardly have the opportunity of reforming a conventual life, any more than a new Antigone will spend her heroic piety in daring all for the sake of a brother's burial: the medium in which their ardent deeds took shape is for ever gone.' Since the necessary subject-matter is lacking, *Middlemarch* cannot be an epic work in the traditional sense. For Dorothea Brooke, the central female character, there proves no way to 'lead a grand life here – now – in England' (ch. 3). There is, however, a modern equivalent to epic action that the narrator calls 'the home epic'; she explains in the finale that its 'great beginning' is marriage, which leads to 'the gradual conquest or irremediable loss of that complete union which makes the advancing years a climax, and age the harvest of sweet memories in common'. This definition is incomplete, however, for it makes no mention of what might be called the home-epic prelude of attraction and desire that figures prominently in the novel's story of several young lives. When Rosamond meets Lydgate in chapter 12, the attraction is mutual and she is perfectly correct in thinking that 'the great epoch of her life' is beginning.

As a literary subject, the home epic has the advantage of freshness.

Even though marriage has been 'the bourne of so many narratives' (finale), Lydgate is never more victimised by his spots of commonness than when he thinks that 'the complexities of love and marriage' are subjects on which he has been 'amply informed by literature, and that traditional wisdom which is handed down in the genial conversation of men' (ch. 16). The literature from which Lydgate has picked up his information has presumably included poetry and romance, but for the subject of modern love and marriage the appropriate literary vehicle is realistic prose fiction – or so the narrator seems to imply in a cryptic aside in chapter 37 concerning Will Ladislaw's impatience to see Dorothea alone: 'However slight the terrestrial intercourse between Dante and Beatrice or Petrarch and Laura, time changes the proportion of things, and in later days it is preferable to have fewer sonnets and more conversation.' Furthermore, the home epic requires no epic machinery or supernatural causation: 'the cloud of good or bad angels' that fill the air in chapter 37 is simply a simile for Dorothea Brooke's memories of the 'spiritual struggles [and] spiritual falls' of her inner life that have been brought on by her marriage to Casaubon. Such struggles have an intensity, a profundity and a perilousness that make marriage and its prelude a uniquely testing human experience: 'Marriage is so unlike anything else,' says Dorothea. 'There is something even awful in the nearness it brings' (ch. 81). Mr Brooke puts it more bluntly: Marriage 'is a noose' (ch. 4). The narrator speaks more dispassionately when she observes that its conditions 'demand self-suppression and tolerance' (ch. 75). That is to say, they demand a movement away from egotistic self-absorption and towards fellow-feeling. As such, marriage is for the author of *Middlemarch* what the university was for her older contemporary Newman – a great but ordinary means to a great but ordinary end; the end in this case being the mitigation of the moral stupidity into which we are all born.

Just as there is a modern form of epic, so the narrator argues that there is also a viable modern form of tragedy.

[McSweeney discusses how some Victorian critics felt that tragedy and the realistic novel were incompatible. As against these critics, he quotes the views of G. H. Lewes who felt that tragedy could be produced from the petty materials of everyday life.]

Eliot certainly agreed that the essence of modern tragedy lay not in the exceptional nature of the action or the idealisation of its participants but in its very commonness, even sordidness. One justification for her belief was Wordsworthian: 'a common tale / An ordinary sorrow of man's life' (as its narrator describes the story of Margaret in the first book of *The Excursion*) had an affective power which could touch the quick of fellow-feeling. A second justification was provided not by Wordsworth but by science, not by the emotions but by the intellect. As the narrator of *The Mill on the Floss* explains in that novel's thirtieth chapter: 'does not science tell us that its highest striving is after the ascertainment of a unity which shall bind the smallest things with the greatest? In natural science, I have understood, there is nothing petty to the mind that has a large vision of relations, and to which every single object suggests a vast sum of conditions. It is surely the same with the observation of human life.' In this perspective, Eliot's humanistic economy of salvation and her aesthetic theory become one. Just as modern science gives to each aspect of the visible world, however common, a function and a dignity similar to that with which they were formerly endowed by the Christian cosmology, so, too, in the historical advance of mankind every human struggle, however prosaic, acquires a significance that makes no longer tenable the traditional aesthetic distinctions between high and low subject-matter and the prescription that tragedy must involve exalted persons.

In *Middlemarch*, it is Lydgate, the scientist who aspires to discover a unity binding the smallest things with the highest, who is the protagonist of the modern tragedy. The narrator is at pains to have the reader recognise this. In order to do so, he must learn to overcome aesthetic spots of commonness similar to Lydgate's social ones that might cause him to find 'beneath his consideration' details like the cost of keeping two horses and of supplying a dinner table without stint, the price paid for life insurance, and the high rent for house and garden (ch. 58). Since the 'element of tragedy which lies in the very fact of frequency, has not yet wrought itself into the coarse emotion of mankind', as the narrator puts it at one point (ch. 20), she is at pains in several places in the novel to help the reader to recognise the tragic dimension in Lydgate's ordinary history. A 'commoner', and therefore more realistic, 'history of perdition than any single momentous bargain' is the 'pleasureless yielding to the small solicitations of circumstance' (ch. 79). Other protagonists

have made an amazing figure in literature by general discontent with the universe as a trap of dullness into which their great souls have fallen by mistake; but the sense of a stupendous self and an insignificant world may have its consolations. Lydgate's discontent was much harder to bear: it was the sense that there was a grand existence in thought and effective action lying around him, while his self was being narrowed into the miserable isolation of egoistic fears, and vulgar anxieties for events that might allay such fears. His troubles will perhaps appear miserably sordid, and beneath the attention of lofty persons who can know nothing of debt except on a magnificent scale. Doubtless they were sordid; and for the majority, who are not lofty, there is no escape from sordidness but by being free from money-craving, with all its base hopes and temptations, its watching for death, its hinted requests, its horse-dealer's desire to make bad work pass for good, its seeking for function which ought to be another's, its compulsion often to long for Luck in the shape of a wide calamity.

(ch. 64)

These reflections of the narrator do not perhaps go very much beyond the familiar lofty-ordinary, Rhine-Rhône contrasts made by the narrators of Eliot's early novels. But in the most important of the passages in which the narrator reflects on the nature of Lydgate's history a more distinctive note is struck. The passage occurs in chapter 15 when we are first given an inside view of Lydgate:

Is it due to excess of poetry or of stupidity that we are never weary of describing what King James called a woman's 'makdom and her fairnesse', never weary of listening to the twanging of the old Troubadour strings, and are comparatively uninterested in that other kind of 'makdom and fairnesse' which must be wooed with industrious thought and patient renunciation of small desires? In the story of this passion, too, the development varies: sometimes it is the glorious marriage, sometimes frustration and final parting. And not seldom the catastrophe is bound up with the other passion, sung by the Troubadours. For in the multitude of middle-aged men who go about their vocations in a daily course determined for them much in the same way as the tie of their cravats, there is always a good number who once meant to shape their own deeds and alter the world a little. The story of their coming to be shapen after the average and fit to be packed by the gross, is hardly ever told even in their consciousness; for perhaps their ardour in generous unpaid toil cooled as imperceptibly as the ardour of other youthful loves, till one day their earlier self walked like a ghost in its old home and made the new furniture ghastly. Nothing in the world more subtle than the process of their gradual change.

Lydgate's great passion and its gradual frustration is not like the ennobling but unrequited love sung of by the troubadours during the

Middle Ages. Like St Theresa of Avila's epic life or Faustian bargains with the devil, this kind of literary subject-matter belongs to an earlier stage of historical evolution. Lydgate's story belongs to the modern age and can only be properly told by using techniques that are closely similar to the ones Lydgate brings to his own scientific investigations and that will enable the artist to bring into focus the subtle process of gradual change. The appropriate instrument for this revelation is not a telescope scanning the tempting 'range of relevencies called the universe' but a microscope concentrated on 'this particular web'.

The similarity between Lydgate's scientific method of investigation and the creative method of the author of *Middlemarch* is memorably expressed in the splendid description in chapter 16 of the arduous invention that enamours the young doctor, which is at the same time a celebration of the imaginative power of his creator:

> Fever had obscure conditions, and gave him that delightful labour of the imagination which is not mere arbitrariness, but the exercise of disciplined power – combining and constructing with the clearest eye for probabilities and the fullest obedience to knowledge; and then, in yet more energetic alliance with impartial Nature, standing aloof to invent tests by which to try its own work.
>
> Many men have been praised as vividly imaginative on the strength of their profuseness in indifferent drawing or cheap narration: – reports of very poor talk going on in distant orbs; or portraits of Lucifer coming down on his bad errands as a large ugly man with bat's wings and spurts of phosphorescence; or exaggerations of wantonness that seem to reflect life in a diseased dream. But these kinds of inspiration Lydgate regarded as rather vulgar and vinous compared with the imagination that reveals subtle actions inaccessible by any sort of lens, but tracked in that outer darkness through long pathways of necessary sequence by the inward light which is the last refinement of Energy, capable of bathing even the ethereal atoms in its ideally illuminated space. He for his part had tossed away all cheap inventions where ignorance finds itself able and at ease: he was enamoured of that arduous invention which is the very eye of research, provisionally framing its object and correcting it to more and more exactness of relation; he wanted to pierce the obscurity of those minute processes which prepare human misery and joy, those invisible thoroughfares which are the first lurking-places of anguish, mania, and crime, that delicate poise and transition which determine the growth of happy or unhappy consciousness.

The reference to the tawdry and exaggerated effects of inferior artists, rather than to the work of inferior medical researchers, signals that this account is as much about the narrator of *Middle-march* as about Lydgate; so does the removal of the normal distance that is kept between the narrator and her protagonist. Indeed, the ambition to discover the sources of human misery and joy and of the growth of happy or unhappy consciousness is not – as it has sometimes been taken to be – an indication of Lydgate's superbia and his flawed knowledge of human beings. It is, rather, the one expression in all of *Middlemarch* of the confident ambition that, together with the passion and excitement that the passage also communicates, must have sustained George Eliot during the com-position of her great novel of provincial life. But the passage also exemplifies the same quality of 'patient diligence' that fifteen years before in 'Silly Novels by Lady Novelists' Eliot had identified as one of the 'moral qualities that contribute to literary excellence'. It is this combination of high ambition and patient diligence that makes for the disciplined power with which in *Middlemarch* George Eliot penetrates beneath the surface of her subject-matter – not in order to implant symbolic meanings that will inflate it to lofty dimensions but in order to reveal the 'minute processes' that are the source of tragic misery to some and of home-epic happiness for others.

From Kerry McSweeney, '*Middlemarch*' (London, 1984), pp. 24–30, 32–4, 35–9.

NOTES

[This opening essay is part of a chapter from Kerry McSweeney's book on *Middlemarch*, which provides a comprehensive and very useful guide to the novel. In the extract printed here McSweeney discusses George Eliot's loss of faith, and the kind of humanised Christianity she wished to construct in its place. This leads him on to George Eliot's awareness that her art might become too diagrammatically moral, a danger that, he argues, is countered in part by her use of the narrator in *Middlemarch*, who is especially successful in making us aware of the complexity of the issues in the novel. It is worth drawing attention to the way in which McSweeney, like all the critics in this anthology, combines attention to the context in which George Eliot was writing, and a sense of the challenge she was setting herself as a novelist, with equally close attention to the texture of the novel. All quotations from *Middlemarch* in this essay are from the Riverside edition, ed. G. S. Haight (Boston, 1956). Ed.]

1. Quoted in Basil Willey, *Nineteenth-Century Studies: Coleridge to Matthew Arnold* (London, 1949), p. 242.

2. G. S. Haight (ed.), *The George Eliot Letters*, vol. 2 (New Haven and London, 1954–5), p. 82.

3. Ibid., vol. 3, p. 231.

4. Ibid., vol. 6, p. 98.

5. G. S. Haight, *The George Eliot Letters*, vol. 1 (New Haven and London, 1954–5), p. 162.

6. D. R. Carroll (ed.), *George Eliot: The Critical Heritage* (London, 1971), pp. 318–19.

7. G. S. Haight (ed.), *The George Eliot Letters*, vol. 4 (New Haven and London, 1954–5), pp. 300–1. Eliot made the same point to another correspondent twelve years later: 'My function is that of the *aesthetic*, not the doctrinal teacher – the rousing of the nobler emotions, which make mankind desire the social right, not the prescribing of special measures, concerning which the aesthetic mind, however strongly moved by social sympathy, is often not the best judge. It is one thing to feel keenly for one's fellow-beings; another to say, "This step, and this alone, will be the best to take for the removal of particular calamities."' (Ibid., vol. 7, p. 44.)

8. See D. A. Miller, *Narrative and its Discontents: Problems of Closure in the Traditional Novel* (Princeton, 1981), pp. 130–5.

2

George Eliot: Ideology and Literary Form

TERRY EAGLETON

The ideological matrix of George Eliot's fiction is set by the increasingly corporate character of Victorian capitalism and its political apparatus. Eliot's work attempts to resolve a structural conflict between two forms of mid-Victorian ideology: between a progressively muted Romantic individualism, concerned with the untrammelled evolution of the 'free spirit', and certain 'higher', corporate ideological modes. These higher modes (essentially, Feuerbachian humanism and scientific rationalism) seek to identify the immutable social laws to which Romantic individualism, if it is to avoid both ethical anarchy and social disruption, must conform. In principle, it is possible for Romantic individualism to do so without betraying its own values. For if it is true on the one hand that scientific rationalism, in judiciously curbing the disruptive tendencies of Benthamite egoism, also obstructs Romantic self-expression, it is also true that it reveals certain historically progressive laws with which the developing individual may imaginatively unite. Moreover, the Religion of Humanity imbues scientific law with Romantic humanist spirit, discovering that law inscribed in the very passions and pieties of men. Unlike the obsessively abstract, systemic symbology of Comtism, it can offer itself as a totalising doctrine without detriment to the 'personal' – to a lived relation with immediate experience. The Religion of Humanity protects Romantic values against an aggressive rationalism; but by rooting those values in the human collective, it defends them equally against an unbridled individualism. By virtue of this ideological conjuncture, the Romantic individualist may submit to the social totality without sacrifice to personal self-fulfilment.

In principle, that is; in practice, a potentially tragic collision between 'corporate' and 'individualist' ideologies is consistently defused and repressed by the forms of Eliot's fiction. As the daughter of a farm-agent, the social locus of corporate value for Eliot is rural society; it is here, most obviously in *Adam Bede* and *Silas Marner*, that the cluster of traditionalist practices and 'organic' affiliations imputed to the English provincial countryside is 'selected' by the national ideology as paradigmatic, at a point where that ideology demands precisely such images of social incorporation. Rural society in *Adam Bede*, as John Goode has commented,[1] is chosen as a literary subject not for its cloistered idiosyncratic charm but as a simplifying model of the whole social formation – a formation whose determining laws may be focused there in purer, more diagrammatic form. The function of the framing, externalising forms of Eliot's rural novels – pastoral, myth, moral fable – is to allow for such 'transparency', but in doing so to recast the historical contradictions at the heart of Eliot's fiction into ideologically resolvable terms.

It is not, naturally, that the organicist modes of Eliot's novels are the 'expression' of her authorial ideology. As a literary producer, George Eliot delineates a 'space' constituted by the insertion of 'pastoral', religious and Romantic ideological sub-ensembles into an ideological formation dominated by liberalism, scientific rationalism and empiricism. This conjuncture is overdetermined in her case by elements of sexual ideology, which both reinforce the drive to individual emancipation and ratify the 'feminine' values (compassion, tolerance, passive resignation) called upon to forestall it. There is no question of reducing the metropolitan rationalist intellectual George Eliot to the 'subject' of a provincial, petty-bourgeois 'class-ideology'. The phrase 'George Eliot' signifies nothing more than the insertion of certain specific ideological determinations – Evangelical Christianity, rural organicism, incipient feminism, petty-bourgeois moralism – into a hegemonic ideological formation which is partly supported, partly embarrassed by their presence. This contradictory unity of ideological structures provides the productive matrix of her fiction; yet the ideology of her texts is not, of course, reducible to it. For Eliot's literary production must be situated, not only at the level of 'general' ideology, but also at the relatively autonomous level of the mutation of literary forms. For each of her texts displays a complex amalgam of fictional devices appropriate to distinct generic modes: 'pastoral', historical realism, fable, mythopoeic and didactic discourse, even (with *Daniel Deronda*) elements of utopian fantasy. None of these discourses can be placed in any simple expressive relation to ideological forms; on the contrary, it is the mutual articulation of these discourses within the text which *produces* those ideological forms as literary signification. Two examples of this process will have to suffice. The biographical mode of *The Mill on the Floss* encompasses at least two distinct forms of literary discourse: a kind of descriptive 'pastoral' (the Dodsons, Maggie's early life at the mill), and the complex psychological drama of Maggie's subjective development. It is the interplay of these mutually conflictual modes which produces the ideological contention between 'tradition' and 'progress' inscribed in the figures of Tom and Maggie Tulliver. But it is a contention which the novel's 'pastoral' devices simultaneously resolve. For just as the text's synthetic closure simplifies Tom to a type of eternal childhood, so the image of the river – symbol of moral drifting and wayward desire – naturalises and thus deforms the values of liberal individualism, figuring them as a mindless yielding to natural appetite rather than as positive growth. An opposition between 'natural' and 'cultural' discourses is transformed into a polarity between two modes of 'natural' signification: Nature as positive (pastoral), and Nature as negative (appetitive). Again, it is not difficult to see how in *Middlemarch* the realist form itself determines a certain 'ideology of the text'. In the earlier 'pastoral' novels, Eliot's realism is partly signified by her apologetic engagement with socially obscure destinies; yet that engagement does not necessarily extend to a fully 'internal' mode of characterisation. Once it does so, however, the novel-form is instantly decentred: since every destiny is significant, each is consequently relativised. Realism, as Eliot conceives of it, involves the tactful unravelling of interlaced processes, the equable distribution of authorial sympathies, the holding of competing values in precarious equipoise. The 'general' ideological correlative of this textual ideology is, naturally, liberal reformism; no other ideological effect could conceivably be produced by such an assemblage of fictional devices.

That Eliot's fiction recasts historical contradictions into ideologically resolvable form is evident enough in the case of *Adam Bede*. Adam himself, with his Carlylean gospel of work and stiff-necked moralism, is an 'organic' type – a petty-bourgeois pragmatist who 'had no theories about setting the world to rights', and who thus functions as a reliable agent of the ruling class. Yet these 'organic' values are forbidden by the novel's form from entering into significant deadlock with any 'authentic' liberal individualism. Such individualism figures in the text only in the debased and trivialised form of a hedonistic egoism (the anarchic sexual appetite of Arthur Donnithorne and Hetty Sorrel), which the stable structures of rural society can expel or absorb without notable self-disruption. Hetty has unwittingly ruptured the class-collaboration between squire and artisan, turning Adam against Arthur; but once she is, so to speak, deported from the novel, that organic allegiance can be gradually reaffirmed. Moreover, the morally intransigent Adam has been humanised by his trials to the point where he is now spiritually prepared to wed the 'higher' working-class girl, Dinah Morris, whose Evangelical fervour for duteous self-sacrifice matches his own doggedly anti-intellectual conformism. Adam is thus allowed to advance into more richly individualised consciousness (he ends up owning a timber-yard) without damage to his mythological status as organic type, an admirable amalgam of naturalised culture and cultivated nature.

In choosing rural petty-bourgeois life as a 'paradigmatic' region, Eliot betrays towards it an ambiguous attitude which reveals, in turn, her problematic relationship to her readership. She extends the conventions of literary realism to a sensitive treatment of socially obscure figures; but while she insists on the latent significance of the apparently peripheral lives she presents, she also apologises, with a blend of genial patronage and tentative irony, for choosing such an unenlightened enclave as the subject-matter of serious fiction. That hesitancy of tone focuses an ideological conflict. It exposes the contradiction between a rationalist critique of rural philistinism (one coupled with a Romantic individualist striving beyond those stifling limits), and a deep-seated imperative to celebrate the value of such bigoted, inert traditionalism, as the humble yet nourishing soil which feeds the flower of higher individual achievement. *Adam Bede* tries for a partial solution of this dilemma by romantically idealising the common life in the figures of Adam and Dinah, fusing the intense with the ordinary.

[Eagleton at this point discusses *The Mill on the Floss* and *Felix Holt*, and the manner in which both novels manipulate literary devices in order to create a synthesis. After drawing parallels between Adam Bede and Felix Holt, he turns to *Middlemarch*.]

The Bede-Holt character in *Middlemarch* is Caleb Garth, stock type of rural organicism, but decidedly muted and marginal within the novel's structure. As such figures decline in ideological impact, value shifts to an alternative oppositional standpoint: in the case of *Middlemarch*, to the cosmopolitan artist Will Ladislaw. If the traditionalist craftsman forms a pocket of spiritual resistance within bourgeois society, the cosmopolitan artist inhabits such a dissentient space outside it. He is, however, no complete compensation for the out-moded organicist type: if Ladislaw has the edge over Garth in liberal culture it is because he lacks his social rootedness. It is only with Daniel Deronda, who combines synoptic vision with settled allegiance, that this ideological dilemma can be finally dissolved.

This is not to say, however, that Garth's values do not finally triumph in *Middlemarch*. They do, but in the 'higher' mode of a wide-eyed liberal disillusionment which, with the collapse of more ambitious commitments, is compelled to find solace in the humble reformist tasks nearest to hand. The irony of *Middlemarch* is that it is a triumph of aesthetic totalisation deeply suspicious of ideological totalities. Each of the novel's four central characters represents such an historically typical totalisation: Casaubon idealism, Lydgate scientific rationalism, Bulstrode Evangelical Christianity, Dorothea Brooke Romantic self-achievement through a unifying principle of action. Each of these totalities crumbles, ensnared in the quotidian; and that ensnarement can be read in two ways. It is in part a salutary empiricist check to the tyranny of theoreticism; but it also signifies the bleak victory of an entrenched provincial consciousness over rationalist or Romantic drives to transcend it. That stalemate, the novel's title suggests, springs from a transitional phase of rural society at the time of the first Reform Bill; yet there is no doubt that the novel's judiciously muted disillusion, its 'end-of-ideologies' ambience, belongs to its post-second Reform Bill present. The problem which *Middlemarch* objectively poses, and fails to resolve, is how ideology is to be conceptually elaborate yet emotionally affective – how it is to nurture 'irrational' personal pieties while cohering them into a structure which surpasses mere empiricism and Romantic spontaneity. What is needed, according to Ladislaw, is 'a soul in which knowledge passes instantaneously into feeling, and feeling flashes back as a new organ of knowledge' – a question to which we have seen Matthew Arnold address himself. Confronted with the aggressive modes of working-class consciousness caricatured in *Felix Holt*, the cautious empiricism of the bourgeois liberal tradition must be reaffirmed; yet that empiricism is in itself an ideologically inadequate response to the historical moment of post-Reform Bill England, with its demand for a more intensively incorporating ideology.

This dilemma is figured in *Middlemarch* in one of its key images: that of the *web* as image of the social formation. The web is a *derivative* organic image, a mid-point between the animal imagery of *Adam Bede* and some more developed theoretical concept of *structure*. The complexity of the web, its subtle interlacing of relatively autonomous strands, its predatory overtones, the possibilities of local complication it permits, accommodate forms of conflict excluded by the more thoroughgoing organicist imagery of *Adam Bede*. But at the same time the web's symmetry, its 'spatial' de-historicising of the social process, its exclusion of levels of contradiction, preserve the essential unity of the organic mode. The web's complex fragility impels a prudent political conservatism: the more delicately inter-laced its strands, the more the disruptive consequences of action can multiply, and so the more circumspect one must be in launching ambitiously totalising projects. Yet conversely, if action at any point in the web will vibrate through its filaments to affect the whole formation, a semi-mystical relationship to the totality is nevertheless preserved. Here, as in the novel's closing trope of the river, which in diffusing its force to tributaries intensifies its total impact, natural imagery is exploited to signify how a fulfilling relation to the social totality can be achieved, not by ideological abstraction, but by pragmatic, apparently peripheral work. And if *Middlemarch*'s natural metaphors perform this function, so does its aesthetic imagery. As Ladislaw remarks to Dorothea: 'It is no use to try and take care of all the world; that is being taken care of when you feel delight – in art or in anything else.' The problem of totality within the novel is effectively displaced to the question of aesthetic form itself, which gives structure to its materials without violating their empirical richness. The novel, in other words, formally answers the problem it thematically poses. Only the novelist can be the centred subject of her own decentred fiction, the privileged consciousness which at once supervenes on the whole as its source, and enters into empathetic relation with each part.

Middlemarch, one might say, is an historical novel in form with little substantive historical content. The Reform Bill, the railways, cholera, machine-breaking: these 'real' historical forces do no more than impinge on the novel's margins. The mediation between the text and the 'real' history to which it alludes is notably dense; and the effect of this is to transplant the novel from the 'historical' to the 'ethical'. *Middlemarch* works in terms of egoism and sympathy, 'head' and 'heart', self-fulfilment and self-surrender; and this predominance of the ethical at once points to an historical impasse and provides the means of ideologically overcoming it. History in the novel is officially in a state of transition; yet to read the text is to conclude that 'suspension' is the more appropriate term. What is officially offered as an ambivalent, intermediate era leading eventually to the 'growing good of the world' is in fact more of an historical vacuum; the benighted, traditionalist-minded Middlemarch seems little more responsive to historical development than does the Hayslope of *Adam Bede*. There is, then, a discrepancy between what the novel claims and what it shows: in aesthetically 'producing' the melioristic ideology intimated by its title, it betrays a considerably less sanguine view of historical progress. It reveals, in fact, an image of the early eighteen-thirties which belongs to the jaundiced viewpoint of where they actually led to – the early eighteen-seventies, where Will Ladislaw's pioneering reformist zeal 'has been much checked'. *Middlemarch* projects back onto the past its sense of contemporary stalemate; and since the upshot of this is a radical distrust of 'real' history, that history is effectively displaced into ethical, and so 'timeless', terms. Yet such displacement thereby provides Eliot with an ideological solution: for what cannot be resolved in 'historical' terms can be accommodated by a moralising of the issues at stake. This, indeed, is a mystification inherent in the very forms of realist fiction, which by casting objective social relations into interpersonal terms, constantly hold open the possibility of reducing the one to the other.[2] In *Middlemarch*, such an ethical reduction of history is achieved in the 'solution' of self-sacrifice, to which, in their various ways, Dorothea, Lydgate and (in a sense) Bulstrode struggle through. The suffering abnegation of the ego offers itself as the answer to the riddle of history.

Yet such a solution is ideologically insufficient, as Will Ladislaw's presence in the novel would suggest. For Ladislaw, while consenting to the course of social evolution, also retains an individualist verve which challenges such mature resignation. As a politically reforming artist, he suggests that empirical labour and Romantic self-affirmation need not be incompatible; in Mr Brooke's words, he is 'a sort of Burke with a leaven of Shelley'. The novel's difficulty in 'realising' him springs from its incapacity to see how this desirable ideological conjuncture, yoking prudent gradualism to visionary

Romanticism, can be achieved in the historical conditions it describes. At this point, therefore, a different kind of history becomes necessary. What cannot be effectively achieved in Ladislaw can be re-attempted on more propitious terms in that later amalgam of Romantic prophet and reformist politician, Daniel Deronda.

What is demanded, in fact, is a 'totalising' vision which binds the individual to the laws of a social formation, preserves the 'personal' pieties violated by such visions in *Romola* and *Middlemarch*, and romantically liberates the self. The answer to this problem is *Daniel Deronda*. In that novel, Eliot finds a magical solution to her ideological dilemma in Deronda's Jewishness, which provides him with a fulfilling romantic identity while incorporating him into the complex totality of a corporate historical culture. Deronda's early liberalism is fruitlessly hellenistic, a decentred spreading of sympathies which erodes his capacity for principled action: 'a too reflective and diffuse sympathy was in danger of paralysing in him that indignation against wrong and selectness of fellowship which are the conditions of moral force'. Hebraism provides the essential corrective – a faith which involves 'the blending of a complete personal love in one current with a larger duty' through an obedient 'submission of the soul to the Highest'. Such submission, however, leaves the 'personal' values of liberalism intact: Deronda's vision is of 'a mind consciously, energetically moving with the larger march of human destinies, but not the less full of conscience and tender heart for the footsteps that tread near and need a leaning-place (*sic*)'.

The problem, in other words, can be 'solved' only by the invention of a *displaced* totality outside the sterile detotalisation of post-Reform Bill England – a totality which is then, as it were, instantly exported, as Deronda leaves to discover his destiny in the Middle East. The difficulty then is to bring this factitious totality into regenerative relation with bourgeois England – a difficulty 'solved' by Deronda's redemptive influence on the broken, dispirited victim of that society, Gwendolen Harleth. But in attempting this solution the novel splits into self-contradiction – splits, indeed, down the middle. For Daniel can only fulfil his destiny by withdrawing from Gwendolen to the Middle East, abandoning her to a nebulous Arnoldian trust in some ideal goodness. The formal dislocations of *Daniel Deronda* are the product of its attempt to overcome the ideological contradictions from which it emerges; it is in the silence between its 'Gwendolen' and 'Daniel' episodes that the truth of those contradictions speaks most eloquently.

Middlemarch's relative obliquity to 'real' history is in part a consequence of Eliot's belief (compounded of positivism and idealism) in the power of ideas to shape social existence. Yet what the novel manifests is precisely the fatal disjunction between the notion and fact, rendering the one emptily utopian and the other banally empirical. If Deronda's visions are to assume historical flesh, the possibility of such contradiction must be eradicated. The novel therefore presses Eliot's trust in the determining force of ideas to a mystical extreme: dreams, desires, shadowy impulses are now grasped as proleptic symbols of what is actually to be. Such dreams effectively conspire in creating the future: Daniel muses that Mordecai's nature may be one of those in which 'a wise estimate of consequences is fused in the fire of the passionate belief which determines the consequences it believes in'. History becomes the phenomenal expression of spiritual forces at work within it; and there can thus be no essential contradiction between what the imagination seizes as true and what historically transpires. The novel, in other words, is driven to the desperate recourse of adopting a mystical epistemology to resolve its problems, and so is effectively forced beyond the bounds of realism. The whole implausible structure of coincidence and hidden kinship which props up the narrative suggests a significant transmutation of the realism of *Middlemarch*, where such devices are sparingly used.

In this sense, *Daniel Deronda* marks one major terminus of nineteenth-century realism – a realism now buckling under ideological pressures it is unable to withstand. But it is not merely a question of the 'aesthetic' being rudely invaded by the 'ideological'. For *Daniel Deronda* also signifies a crisis-point in the relatively autonomous evolution of realist forms – a point at which the problematic *fictionality* of those stolidly self-confident forms is becoming incorporated as a level of signification within the text itself. The novel's notable preoccupation with art is in one sense a displaced desire for the organicist ideal: art liberates the individual subject but exacts submission to an impersonal order, incarnates an ideal excellence but demands much humble labour, elicits an ascetic Hebraism but calls forth a devotion akin to sexual love. Yet it also signifies the text's constant oblique meditation on its own fictive status – on that circular movement whereby 'real' events within the fiction are themselves in some sense 'fictions' which prefigure a 'reality' of illusory proportions. That there could be no Mordecai outside the limits of fictional discourse (as there could indeed be a Bulstrode) is the true index of the novel's ideological dilemma – a dilemma which is nothing less than the crisis of realist signification itself. *Daniel Deronda* is itself a proleptic sign of a desired social reality; but since that social reality is a fictional construct, unable to project itself beyond the bounds of aesthetic discourse, the text can in the end only signify itself. What it discloses, in that process of self-signification, is an absence which must necessarily evade its aesthetic constructions – the suppressed blankness of the abandoned Gwendolen Harleth, sign of the 'real' ideological paucity to which the novel is a mythological riposte.

Eliot's fiction, then, represents an attempt to integrate liberal ideology, in both its Romantic and empiricist forms, with certain pre-industrial, idealist or positivist organic models. It is an enterprise determined in the last instance by the increasingly corporate character of nineteenth-century capitalism during the period of her literary production. Yet this is not to argue for a simple homology between literary and historical systems, or for a reductively diachronic reading of Eliot's *oeuvre*. It is not a question of Eliot's work evolving from pre-industrial 'pastoral' to fully-fledged realism in response to some linear development of bourgeois ideology. On the contrary, it is a question of grasping at once the ideological synchronies and formal discontinuities of her texts – of theorising the set of disjunctures whereby distinct literary discourses produce a corporatist ideology which is present from the outset. The *differences* of Eliot's fiction are the effect of a continual repermutation of the literary forms into which it is inserted – a repermutation which in each of her texts 'privileges' a particular, dominant discourse which 'places' and deforms the others. Within this synchronic practice a significant development can be discerned: one from an essentially *metaphorical* closure of ideological conflict (social history as analogous to natural evolution) towards an essentially *metonymic* resolution of such issues ('personal' values, visions and relations as the solution to social ills).[3] The naturalising, moralising and mythifying devices of the novels effect such closures, but in the act of doing so lay bare the imprint of the ideological struggles which beset the texts. It is in the irregular transmutation of one fictional code into another, the series of formal displacements whereby turbulent issues are marginalised yet remain querulously present, that Eliot's organic closures betray their *constructing* functions. What threatens to subvert them is not a suppressed 'outside', but the absences and dislocations they internally produce.

As Victorian capitalism moves into its imperialist stage, the true historical basis of the 'idyllic' rural organicism of *Adam Bede* becomes progressively exposed. *Impressions of Theophrastus Such* (1879) places its plea for 'corporate existence' in the context of nationalist rhetoric and a warning of the dangers involved in undergoing 'a premature fusion with immigrants of alien blood'. 'The pride which identifies us with a great historic body', Eliot writes, 'is a humanising, elevating habit of mind, inspiring sacrifices of individual comfort, gain, or other selfish ambition, for the sake of that ideal whole; and no man swayed by such a sentiment can become completely abject.' The corporate society which in *Daniel Deronda* remained a goal to be realised, and so an idealist critique of contemporary England, has now become an effusive celebration of the *status quo*. The voice of liberal humanism has become the voice of jingoist reaction.

From Terry Eagleton, *Criticism and Ideology* (London, 1976), pp. 110–15, 118–25.

NOTES

[Terry Eagleton's essay, extracted from his book *Criticism and Ideology*, starts, as does the previous essay in this anthology, by setting George Eliot in a Victorian context. But, whereas Kerry McSweeney emphasises George Eliot's personal crisis of faith, Eagleton stresses the broader conflicts in Victorian society. It is immediately apparent, therefore, that Eagleton is interested in the political dimensions of George Eliot's fiction. Consequently, where McSweeney praises the power and effectiveness of the mediating voice of the narrator, Eagleton takes the view that the narrator cannot legitimately reconcile the contradictions at the heart of the novel between the needs of the individual and the needs of society. His analysis describes the ways in which George Eliot contrives to recast such historical contradictions into ideologically resolvable form. This is achieved by 'a moralising of the issues at stake', by casting everything, ultimately, in personal and ethical terms. Eagleton's attitude to George Eliot might, on the surface, seem dismissive, but his essay offers a forceful sense of the tensions at work in Victorian society (and in George Eliot's novel), and in addition offers a persuasive view of how George Eliot controls her material and attempts to come to terms with problems. The essays that follow in this anthology all consciously or unconsciously acknowledge this kind of limiting judgement on the dominance exerted by the author, but most argue that the controlling voice is more uncertain than is suggested by Eagleton. Ed.]

1. In *Critical Essays on George Eliot*, ed. Barbara Hardy (London, 1970), p. 20.

2. A point made by Francis Mulhern in 'Ideology and Literary Form – a comment', *New Left Review*, 91 (May/June 1975).

3. For this general distinction in fiction, see Francis Mulhern (article cited above).

3

'Middlemarch' and the Idea of the Classic Realist Text

DAVID LODGE

Middlemarch has achieved a unique status as both paradigm and paragon in discussion of the novel as a literary form. If a teacher or critic wishes to cite a representative example of the nineteenth-century English novel at its best, the chances are that it will be *Middlemarch*. Indeed it is scarcely an exaggeration to say that, for many critics, *Middlemarch* is the *only* truly representative, truly great Victorian novel – all other candidates, including the rest of George Eliot's fiction, being either too idiosyncratic or too flawed. Barbara Hardy was surely right when she said in her introduction to *Middlemarch: critical approaches to the novel* (1967) that 'if a poll were held for the greatest English novel there would probably be more votes for *Middlemarch* than for any other work';[1] while one of her contributors, Hilda Hulme, quoted a judgement that 'every novel would be *Middlemarch* if it could'.[2]

That symposium edited by Barbara Hardy probably registered the highwater mark of *Middlemarch*'s modern reputation. More recently criticism has begun to express a more reserved admiration for George Eliot's masterpiece, echoing and amplifying Henry James's suave judgement on reviewing *Middlemarch*: 'It sets a limit, we think, to the development of the old-fashioned English novel.'[3] George Eliot's realism is now regarded not as a kind of timeless truthfulness to human experience (as implied by the tribute, every novel would be *Middlemarch* if it could), but as an historically conditioned, ideologically motivated construction of 'the real'. J.

Hillis Miller, for instance, while acknowledging that *Middlemarch* is 'perhaps the masterwork of Victorian realism',[4] is concerned to expose the rhetorical devices by which George Eliot achieves her 'totalising' effect, and to reveal, beneath her apparently serene mastery of her fictional world, a gnawing epistemological doubt. A still more radical critique of George Eliot's realism, especially as displayed in *Middlemarch*, is to be found in Colin MacCabe's *James Joyce and the Revolution of the Word* (1979). This important and original study of Joyce incorporates an influential theory of the 'classic realist text', which George Eliot is taken to exemplify, but which seems to me to misrepresent her writing in ways worth detailed examination.

At the time of writing this book, MacCabe was clearly influenced by the poststructuralist phase of criticism in France in the late sixties and early seventies, when the purely formal, semiological analysis of literary texts and genres, with which structuralist criticism was originally concerned, was polemicised by the infusion of Roland Barthes's literary historicism, Jacques Lacan's reading of Freud, Louis Althusser's reading of Marx, and Jacques Derrida's deconstruction of the metaphysical basis of Western philosophy.[5] In this school of thought, the purely methodological separation made by Saussure between the signifier and the signified in the sign is given ontological status and importance. There is never a perfect fit between language and the world. It is impossible absolutely to say what we mean or mean what we say, since the subject who completes an utterance is no longer exactly the same as the subject who originated it, and the language used by the subject has its own materiality capable of signifying beyond the subject's intention or control. The subject (what George Eliot would have called the individual man or woman) is not a concrete, substantial identity situated outside language, but is produced and continually modified by the entry into language. It is the ideas of language as a kind of 'material' and of consciousness and social relations as a kind of 'production' which perhaps enable proponents of this school of thought to reconcile their rather bleakly anti-humanist semiology with their commitment to revolutionary politics. Certainly they seem closer in spirit to Nietzsche than to Marx, and at times to come perilously near a kind of epistemological abyss of infinitely recessive interpretations of interpretations, rendering all human intellectual effort essentially futile. The underlying message seems to be that, however bleak and frightening this view of man and consciousness may be, it is true; and to deny it can only have the ill effects of all repression – whether in society, the psyche, or literature.

Colin MacCabe claims that Joyce's importance resides in the fact that he puts his readers to school in precisely this way, though his critics have misunderstood the lesson and obstinately persist in trying to explain (or 'recuperate') his works, making them conform to a notion of stable 'meaning' such as it was precisely his intention to undermine. In his mature work, Joyce was concerned 'not with representing experience through language, but with experiencing language through a destruction of representation'.[6] To throw into relief Joyce's liberation of language, and destruction of representation, MacCabe contrasts his fiction with 'the classic realist text', as represented by *Middlemarch*, 'which purports to represent experience through language'.

The 'classic realist text' is a term that derives from the criticism of Roland Barthes, especially *S/Z* (1970), and MacCabe is certainly indebted to Barthes in some ways. But his definition of the classic realist text is simpler, and I think less subtle, than Barthes'. According to MacCabe, a novel is a tissue of discourses – the discourses of the characters, as rendered in their speech, and the discourse of the narrator; and it is characteristic of the classic realist text that in it the narrative discourse acts as a 'metalanguage',[7] controlling, interpreting, and judging the other discourses, and thus putting the reader in a position of dominance over the characters and their stories. Joyce, in contrast, refuses to privilege one discourse over another in his writing, or to privilege the reader's position *vis-à-vis* the text. Even in his early work, such as the stories of *Dubliners*, superficially consistent with the techniques of classic realism, the narrator's discourse proves ambiguous and enigmatic on close examination; while in, for instance, the Cyclops episode of *Ulysses*, a characteristic specimen of his mature work, the conflicting discourses of the anonymous patron of Barney Kiernan's pub who narrates the main action, the Citizen, Bloom, and all the other characters in the bar, are interrupted not by the metalanguage of a reliable authorial narrator but by passages of parodic inflation and hyperbole (sanctioned purely aesthetically by the 'gigantism' theme of the episode) – a counter-text, MacCabe calls it, which 'far from setting up a position of judgement for the reader, merely proliferates the languages available'.[8] Thus the reader of *Ulysses* is never allowed to sink into the comfortable assurance of an interpretation guaranteed by the narrator, but must himself produce the meaning of the text by opening himself fully to the play of its diverse and contradictory discourses.

One symptom of Joyce's rejection of the conventions of reading and representation employed in the classic realist text, which Mac-Cabe seizes on with understandable enthusiasm, is Joyce's refusal, from his earliest days as a writer, to employ what he called 'perverted commas' in rendering direct speech – using an introductory dash instead. It is the typographical marking off of direct speech from narrative by quotation marks that enforces the authority of the narrator's metalanguage, in MacCabe's view. 'The narrative prose is the metalanguage that can state all the truths in the object-language(s) (the marks held in inverted commas) and can also explain the relation of the object-language to the world.'[9]

Let us acknowledge that there is a real difference between the art of George Eliot and the art of James Joyce which MacCabe helps to define. Let us note also that MacCabe himself admits that classic realism is never absolute, and that within George Eliot's novels 'there are always images which counter the flat and univocal process which is the showing forth of the real'.[10] Nevertheless it seems to me that the distortion of George Eliot's practice implied by MacCabe's model of the classic realist text is sufficiently great to be worth contesting, and that this might be a way of extending our under-standing of classic realism generally, and of George Eliot's art in particular.

What MacCabe calls a metalanguage (a term borrowed from linguistics and philosophy) will be better known to students of George Eliot as the convention of the omniscient and intrusive narrator, which has a venerable history as a subject of contention in criticism of her work. In the period of her relative eclipse, in the 1920s, 30s and 40s, when the Jamesian aesthetic of 'showing' rather than 'telling' was dominant in novel criticism, this feature of her work counted heavily against her. In the 1950s and 1960s several critics such as Wayne Booth, W. J. Harvey, and Barbara Hardy instituted a successful defence of the convention and George Eliot's exploitation of it, thus complementing on the aesthetic plane the reinstatement of George Eliot as a great novelist which F. R. Leavis had achieved on the ethical plane.

As Gérard Genette has observed, in his excellent study *Narrative Discourse*, the James–Lubbock distinction between 'showing' and 'telling', and the corresponding pair of terms, 'scene' and 'summary' derive from the distinction drawn between mimesis and diegesis in the third book of Plato's *Republic*; and MacCabe's discussion of the matter seems particularly close to Plato's (though it reverses Plato's preferences) because of the importance he gives to the marking off of speech from narration in the classic realist text. Plato illustrates the distinction between mimesis and diegesis by reference to the opening scene of the *Iliad* in which Chryses appeals to the Achaeans to let him ransom his daughter.

> You know that as far as the lines
>
> > *He prayed the Achaeans all,*
> > *But chiefly the two rulers of the people,*
> > *Both sons of Atreus*
>
> the poet himself speaks, he never tries to turn our thoughts from himself or to suggest that anyone else is speaking; but after this he speaks as if he was himself Chryses, and tries his best to make us think that the priest, an old man, is speaking and not Homer.[11]

Mimesis, then, is narrating by imitating another's speech. Diegesis is narrating in one's own voice. To make his distinction clearer, Plato, through his mouthpiece Socrates, rewrites the scene from Homer in unbroken diegesis, in which Chryses' actual words are summarised in indirect form, *oratio obliqua*, and assimilated to the linguistic register of the narrator, Homer himself. A typology of literary modes (later to evolve into a typology of literary genres)[12] thus emerges: pure diegesis, as exemplified by dithyramb (a kind of hymn), in which the poet speaks exclusively in his own voice; pure mimesis, as exemplified by tragedy and comedy, in which the poet speaks exclusively in imitated voices; and the mixed form of the epic, which combines both modes. Needless to say, Plato greatly distrusted the most mimetic kind of writing, since it is ethically undiscriminating; and he will admit into the Republic only the most austere kind of writing – the purely diegetic, or that which combines diegesis with a little mimesis, but of good personages only.

Plato's discussion is more relevant to the comparison of George Eliot and James Joyce than might at first appear. Realism as a literary quality, or effect, of verisimilitude, is something we think of as very close to, if not quite synonymous with, the classical notion of mimesis or imitation, and we often describe the novel casually as a 'mimetic' literary form. In fact, of course, only drama is a strictly mimetic form, in which only words are imitated *in* words, and what is non-verbal – spectacle, gesture, etc. – is imitated non-verbally. Anything that is not dialogue in a novel, if only *he said* and *she said*, is diegesis, the report of a narrator, 'the poet himself' however impersonal. The only way of getting round this rule is to put the narrating entirely into the hands (or mouths) of a character or characters, as in the pseudo-autobiographical novel or the epistolary novel: then the narrative becomes mimetic of diegesis. But as Genette concludes, 'the truth is that mimesis in words can only be mimesis of words. Other than that, all we have and can have is degrees of diegeses.'[13]

There is no *necessary* connection between mimesis and realism: some novels that consist largely of dialogue (Ronald Firbank, Henry Green, Ivy Compton-Burnett) are highly artificial; and some of the most realistic (i.e. convincing, lifelike, compelling) passages in *Middlemarch* are diegetic (for example the account of Lydgate's unpremeditated declaration to Rosamond in chapter 31). But it is true that mimesis is inherently better adapted to realistic effect than diegesis, simply because it uses words to imitate words. The classic realist novel of the nineteenth century maintained a fairly even balance between mimesis and diegesis, showing and telling, scene and summary, and it did so at the expense of some degree of realistic illusion, in the interests of ethical control of the story and the reader's response.

The eighteenth-century novel began with the discovery of new mimetic possibilities in prose fiction − the pseudo-confessions of Defoe, the pseudo-correspondences of Richardson. But these achievements, remarkable as they were, tended to confirm Plato's fears about the morally debilitating effects of skilful mimesis of imperfect personages without diegetic guidance from the author. However highminded the intentions of Defoe (which is doubtful) or of Richardson (which is not), there is no way in which the reader can be prevented from delighting in and even identifying with the vitality, energy and resourcefulness of Moll Flanders or Lovelace, even in their wicked actions. Fielding, his mind trained in a classical school, restored the diegetic element in his 'comic-epic poem in prose' − though paradoxically in the interests of a more liberal morality than Richardson's or Defoe's. And it was Fielding's narrative method (though not his morality) which provided the model for the nineteenth-century novelists from Scott to George Eliot. In the classic Victorian novel, not only is there a great deal of narrative in proportion to speech, summary in proportion to scene, but the writers exploit the diegetic possibilities of the mixed form to speak very much 'in their own voice' − not merely reporting events, but delivering judgements, opinions, and evaluations about the story and about life in general. Even when characters act as narrators (e.g. in

Jane Eyre, Great Expectations) they behave more like novelists, shaping and improving their own stories, than do the naïve memoir-writers of Defoe, or the pressured correspondents of Richardson.

With the advent of the modern novel, the pendulum swings back towards mimesis, in more subtle and sophisticated forms. Flaubert begins the process: in *Madame Bovary* the narrator is omnipresent, but it is impossible to discover what he thinks about the story he is telling. In James, the narrator is either a created character of doubtful reliability (e.g. the governess in *The Turn of the Screw*) or an authorial narrator who deliberately restricts himself to the limited perspective of a character (such as Lambert Strether in *The Ambassadors*) entangled in circumstances he does not fully understand. In Joyce, the author is progressively 'refined out of existence, indifferent, paring his fingernails'. The impersonal, but reliable and tonally consistent narrator of the early episodes of *Ulysses*, who tells us, for instance, that 'Stately, plump Buck Mulligan came from the stairhead, bearing a bowl of lather on which a mirror and a razor lay crossed,' or that 'Mr Leopold Bloom ate with relish the inner organs of beasts and fowls,' gradually disappears under a welter of different discourses, parodies and pastiches of journalese, officialese, obsolete literary styles, pub talk, women's magazine language, scientific description, and is finally displaced by the supreme example of mimesis in English narrative literature, the interior monologue of Molly Bloom.

I think there is some advantage to be gained from substituting the Platonic distinction between mimesis and diegesis for MacCabe's distinction between language and metalanguage. Instead of seeing a total break of continuity between the classic realist text and the modern text, we see rather a swing of the pendulum from one end of a continuum of possibilities to the other, a pendulum that has been swinging throughout literary history. Mimesis and diegesis, like metaphor and metonymy, are fundamental, and, on a certain level, all-inclusive categories of representation, and a typology of texts can be established by assessing the dominance of one over the other. We are also better placed to see that: (1) the distinction between mimesis and diegesis in George Eliot is by no means as clear-cut as MacCabe implies; and (2) the diegetic element is much more problematic than he allows.

When Plato refers to the epic as a mixed form, he means that it combines, or alternates between, mimesis and diegesis, the voice of the poet and the voices of the characters he imitates in dialogue. But the classic realist novel 'mixes' the two discourses in a more fundamental sense: it fuses them together, often indistinguishably and inextricably, through the device of free indirect speech by means of which the narrator, without absenting himself entirely from the text, communicates the narrative to us coloured by the thoughts and feelings of a character. The reference to this character in the third person pronoun, and the use of the past tense, or 'epic preterite', still imply the existence of the author as the source of the narrative; but by deleting the tags which affirm that existence, such as *he said, she wondered, she thought to herself*, etc., and by using the kind of diction appropriate to the character rather than to the authorial narrator, the latter can allow the sensibility of the character to dominate the discourse, and correspondingly subdue his own voice, his own opinions and evaluations. It was Jane Austen who first perfected the use of free indirect speech in English fiction, and thus showed succeeding novelists, including George Eliot, how the novel might combine Fielding's firm diegetic control with Richardson's subtle mimesis of character. The device is an extremely flexible one, which allows the narrator to move very freely and fluently between the poles of mimesis and diegesis within a single paragraph, or even a single sentence; and its effect is always to make the reader's task of interpretation more active and problematic. If we are looking for a single formal feature which characterises the realist novel of the nineteenth century, it is surely not the domination of the characters' discourses by the narrator's discourse (something in fact more characteristic of earlier narrative literature) but the extensive use of free indirect speech, which obscures and complicates the distinction between the two types of discourse.

The work of the Russian literary theorists Mikhail Bakhtin and Valentin Volosinov, which goes back to the nineteen-twenties, but has only recently been translated into English, is very relevant here. They (or he – for they may be one and the same person) have suggested that it is precisely the dissolution of the boundaries between reported speech and reporting context (i.e. the author's speech) that characterises the novel as discourse and distinguishes it from earlier types of narrative prose and from lyric verse. Bakhtin characterised novel discourse as 'polyphonic' or 'polyglottal', and maintained that, 'One of the essential peculiarities of prose fiction is the possibility it allows of using different types of discourse, with their distinct expressiveness intact, on the plane of a single work, without reduction to a single common denominator.'[14] Different types of discourse can be represented in fiction, of course, as the direct speech of characters, without serious disturbance to the authority of the narrator, as in the novels of Fielding or Scott. But once these discourses enter into the narrative discourse itself, in various forms of reported speech, or thought, the interpretative control of the author's voice is inevitably weakened to some degree, and the reader's work increased.

Derek Oldfield, in an essay entitled 'The Character of Dorothea', contributed to that symposium on *Middlemarch* edited by Barbara Hardy to which I have already referred, pointed out how George Eliot's narrative method is complicated by this alternation of narrator's and characters' voices, compelling the reader to, in his words, 'zig-zag' his way through the discourse, rather than following a straight, well-marked path.[15] One of the examples he gives describes Dorothea's naïve ideas about marriage at the beginning of the story. I shall cite the same passage, hoping to add a few points to his excellent commentary:

> She was open, ardent, and not in the least self-admiring; indeed, it was pretty to see how her imagintion adorned her sister Celia with attractions altogether superior to her own, and if any gentleman appeared to come to the Grange from some other motive than that of seeing Mr Brooke, she concluded that he must be in love with Celia; Sir James Chettam, for example, whom she constantly considered from Celia's point of view, inwardly debating whether it would be good for Celia to accept him. That he should be regarded as a suitor to herself would have seemed to her a ridiculous irrelevance. Dorothea, with all her eagerness to know the truths of life, retained very childlike ideas about marriage.[16]

So far, this is diegetic: the narrator describes Dorothea's character authoritatively, in words that Dorothea could not use about herself without contradiction. (She cannot say or think about herself that she is not self-admiring, for that would be to admire herself. Nor can she acknowledge that her ideas about marriage are childlike without ceasing to hold them.) It is the justification of the diegetic method that it can give us such information, lucidly, concisely, and judiciously. In the rest of the passage, however, the narrator's discourse becomes permeated with Dorothea's discourse, but without wholly succumbing to it.

> She felt sure that she would have accepted the judicious Hooker, if she had been born in time to save him from that wretched mistake he

made in matrimony: or John Milton when his blindness had come on;
or any of the other great men whose odd habits it would have been
glorious piety to endure; but an amiable handsome baronet, who said
'Exactly' to her remarks even when she expressed uncertainty—how
could he affect her as a lover? The really delightful marriage must be
that where your husband was a sort of father, and could teach you
even Hebrew, if you wished it.[17]

As Oldfield observes, the tag, 'she felt' is an ambiguous signal to the
reader, since it can introduce either objective report or subjective
reflection. Such colloquial phrases in the sequel as 'that wretched
mistake' and 'when his blindness had come on', seem to be the words
in which Dorothea herself would have articulated these ideas, though
the equally colloquial 'odd habits' does not. Why does it not?
Because, in unexpected collocation with 'great men' it seems too
literary an irony for Dorothea, and so we ascribe it to the narrator.
But that is not to imply that Dorothea is incapable of irony. '[W]ho
said "Exactly" to her remarks even when she expressed uncertainty'
– do we not infer that Sir James's illogicality has been noted by
Dorothea herself in just that crisp, dismissive way? Then what about
the immediately succeeding phrase, '—how could he affect her as a
lover?' This is a really interesting challenge to analysis. If the
immediately preceding phrase is attributed to Dorothea, as I suggest,
then it would be natural to ascribe this one to her also; and the
immediately following sentence is certainly Dorothea's own thought,
communicated in free indirect speech: 'The really delightful marriage
must be that where your husband was a sort of father, and could
teach you even Hebrew, if you wished it.' But a problem of contradiction arises if we attribute the rhetorical question to Dorothea.
For if Dorothea can formulate the question, 'How can Sir James
affect me as a lover?' her alleged unconsciousness of her own
attractions to visiting gentlemen is compromised. Is the question,
then, put by the narrator, appealing directly to the reader, over
Dorothea's head, to acknowledge the plausibility of her behaviour,
meaning: 'You do see, gentle reader, why it never crossed Dorothea's
mind that Sir James Chettam was a possible match for her.' There is
such an implication, but the reason given – that Sir James says
'Exactly' when Dorothea expresses uncertainty – seems too trivial
for the narrator to draw the conclusion, 'How could he affect her as
a lover?' We can perhaps naturalise the utterance by interpreting it as
Dorothea's likely response to a hypothetical question – 'Do you
think you could fall in love with Sir James Chettam?' But the fact is

that mimesis and diegesis are fused together inextricably here, and for a good purpose. For there is a sense in which Dorothea knows what the narrator knows – namely, that Sir James is sexually attracted to her – but is repressing the thought, on account of her determination to marry an intellectual father-figure. When Celia finally compels Dorothea to face the fact that not only Sir James, but even the servants, assume that he is courting Dorothea, the narrator tells us that she was 'not less angry because details asleep in her memory were now awakened to confirm the unwelcome revelation'. One of those details was surely that very habit of Sir James's of saying 'Exactly' when she expressed uncertainty – a sign, surely, of his admiration, deference, and anxiety to please.

I am not claiming a Flaubertian *impassibilité* for the narrator of *Middlemarch*. The first part of the passage under discussion establishes very clearly the ethical terms in which Dorothea is to be judged: selflessness on the one hand, self-deception on the other. But as the writing proceeds to flesh out this diegetic assessment more mimetically, the reader is progressively more taxed to negotiate the nuances of irony and to resolve the ambiguities of deixis. Exactly how far Dorothea misconceives the nature of the great intellectual figures of the past; whether she is right or wrong in her assessment of Sir James Chettam's intelligence; whether she emerges from the whole passage with more credit than discredit, are questions which the reader must finally decide for himself. I think it will be granted that there are many other such passages in *Middlemarch*.

It is not, however, only because mimesis often contaminates diegesis in this way that MacCabe's account of the narrator's voice in George Eliot's fiction seems inaccurate.

> The metalanguage within such a text refuses to acknowledge its own status as writing. The text outside the area of inverted commas claims to be the product of no articulation, it claims to be unwritten. This unwritten text can then attempt to staunch the haemorrhage of interpretations threatened by the material of language. Whereas other discourses within the text are considered as materials which are open to reinterpretation, the narrative discourse functions simply as a window on reality. This relationship between discourses can be taken as the defining feature of the classic realist text.[18]

The assertion that the narrator's discourse claims to be 'unwritten' may be puzzling unless one traces it back to Derrida's argument that Western culture has always privileged the spoken word over the written, because the spoken word appears to guarantee the 'metaphysics of presence' on which our philosophical tradition is predicated. Speech implies the presence of a speaker, and by inference of an authentic, autonomous self who is the arbiter of his own meanings and able to pass them intact to another. But Derrida argues that this is a fallacy and an illusion. It is the absence of the addresser from the message which allows the materiality of language to generate its own semantic possibilities among which the addressee may romp at will. Writing, in which such absence is obvious, is thus a more reliable model of how language works than speech; and writing which claims truthfulness by trying to disguise itself as speech, as the discourse of a man speaking to men, is in bad faith, or at least deluded.

Now it is true that the narrator's discourse in George Eliot's fiction is modelled on the I-thou speech situation, and certain that she would have endorsed Wordsworth's description of the writer as a man speaking to men. But in obvious ways, whether consciously or unconsciously, she reminds us that her narration is in fact written. This is particularly true of the more ostentatiously diegetic passages, when she suspends the story to deliver herself of opinions, generalisations, judgements. To call these passages transparent windows on reality seems quite inappropriate. They are in fact often quite obscure, or at least very complicated, and have to be scrutinised several times before we can confidently construe their meaning – a process that is peculiar to reading, and cannot be applied to the spoken word. Consider, for example, this comment on Mr Farebrother, shortly after Lydgate has voted against him in the selection of the hospital chaplaincy.

> But Mr Farebrother met him with the same friendliness as before. The character of the publican and sinner is not always practically incompatible with that of the modern Pharisee, for the majority of us scarcely see more distinctly the faultiness of our own conduct than the faultiness of our own arguments, or the dullness of our own joke. But the Vicar of St Botolph's had certainly escaped the slightest tincture of the Pharisee, and by dint of admitting to himself that he was too much as other men were, he had become remarkably unlike them in this— that he could excuse others for thinking slightly of him, and could judge impartially of their conduct even when it told against him.[19]

I would defy anyone to take in the exact sense of this passage through the ear alone. There are too many distinctions being juggled, and too many swerves and loops in the movement of the argument:

first, we encounter the idea (stated in a double negative, and thus made more difficult to assimilate) that the modern publican and sinner may be combined with the modern Pharisee in the same person, unlike their Biblical prototypes. Is Mr Farebrother, who has just been mentioned, such a person, we may wonder, as we begin to negotiate this passage? This would be inconsistent with the previous presentation of his character, but we have to wait for some time to be reassured that this is *not* what the narrator means. Before we come to that point, we have to wrestle with another distinction – between faults of manners (arguments and jokes) and faults of morals (conduct) – a distinction which doesn't correspond exactly to the one between publicans and sinners and Pharisees. The exculpation of Farebrother is highly parodoxical: by admitting that he is too much like other men, he becomes remarkably unlike them: which is to say, that by admitting he is a publican and a sinner, he avoids being a Pharisee as well. So why has the narrator introduced the concept of Pharisee at all? It seems to be floating free, and we puzzle our way through the paragraph, waiting to see to whom it applies. We may be disconcerted to realise that it is applied, explicitly, only to 'the majority of us' ourselves. Perhaps it is also applied implicitly to Lydgate, whose conduct over the election, as he himself is well aware, was not entirely disinterested. On reflection we may decide that the negative comparison between Farebrother and Pharisee is justified by the fact that the Pharisees were a Jewish religious sect and that Phariseeism is an occupational failing of men of religion, but this explanation scarcely leaps off the page.

Mr Farebrother seems to emerge from these complex comparisons with credit. But only a few lines later, after a speech from Mr Farebrother in direct (i.e. mimetic) form –

> 'The world has been too strong for *me*, I know,' he said one day to Lydgate. 'But then I am not a mighty man—I shall never be a man of renown. The choice of Hercules is a pretty fable; but Prodicus makes it easy work for the hero, as if the first resolves were enough. Another story says that he came to hold the distaff, and at last wore the Nessus shirt. I suppose one good resolve might keep a man right if everybody else's resolve helped him.'[20]

– we encounter this diegetic comment:

> The Vicar's talk was not always inspiriting: he had escaped being a Pharisee, but he had not escaped that low estimate of possibilities which we rather hastily arrive at as an inference from our own failure.[21]

This seems to check any inclination on the reader's part to overestimate Mr Farebrother's moral stature; and if, in reading the preceding diegetic passage, we mentally defend ourselves against the accusation of Phariseeism by identifying ourselves with Farebrother's candid admission of his faults, we now find ourselves implicated with him in another kind of failing – complacency about one's faults. But if we make *another* adjustment, and take this as a cue to condemn Farebrother, we may be surprised and disconcerted once more, to find ourselves identified with Lydgate – for the passage immediately continues, and ends (as does the whole chapter) with this sentence: 'Lydgate felt that there was a pitiable lack of will in Farebrother.' Since Lydgate has just been portrayed as subordinating his own will to expediency in the matter of the chaplaincy election, he is hardly in a position to throw stones at this particular moral glasshouse, and the sequel will show even greater 'infirmity of will' on his part in the matter of Rosamond.[22] To sum up, the authorial commentary, so far from telling the reader what to think, or putting him in a position of dominance in relation to the discourse of the characters, constantly forces him to think for himself, and constantly implicates him in the moral judgements being formulated.

I like to call this kind of literary effect, the 'Fish effect', because the American critic Stanley Fish has made the study of it so much his own in a series of books and articles – primarily on seventeenth-century poetry and prose, but more lately with a wider range of reference.[23] Basically, his argument is that as we read, lineally, word by word, word group by word group, we form hypotheses and expectations about the meaning that is going to be delivered at the end of the sentence, or paragraph, or text; but, as Fish shows by skilful analyses of particular passages – action-replays of reading in slow motion – very often our expectations are disconfirmed, a different and perhaps entirely opposite meaning from that which we expected is formulated, yet without entirely abolishing the mistakenly projected meaning. In his early work Fish suggested that this effect was contrived by writers who had didactic, usually religious, designs upon their readers, using it to defamiliarise familiar truths; thus Milton reminds us that we are fallen creatures not merely by the fable of *Paradise Lost* but by constantly tripping us up with his syntax. More recently, Fish has argued that the effect is inherent in all discourse, but especially literary discourse, because the meaning of an utterance is determined entirely by its context and the interpretative assumptions that are brought to it – which, in the case of literary utterances, are never simple or fixed. I think both arguments are valid, and both apply to George Eliot's diegetic style, although such deviousness might, superficially, seem incompatible with her chosen stance as narrator: the privileged historian of the moral lives of characters who, it suits her purpose to pretend, are real people in real situations. The opening paragraph of Chapter 15 is *à propos*:

> A great historian, as he insisted on calling himself, who had the happiness to be dead a hundred and twenty years ago, and so to take his place among the colossi whose huge legs our living pettiness is observed to walk under, glories in his copious remarks and digressions as the least imitable part of his work, and especially in those initial chapters to the successive books of his history, where he seems to bring his arm-chair to the proscenium and chat with us in all the lusty ease of his fine English. But Fielding lived when the days were longer (for time, like money, is measured by our needs), when summer afternoons were spacious, and the clock ticked slowly in the winter evenings. We belated historians must not linger after his example; and if we did so, it is probable that our chat would be thin and eager, as if delivered from a camp-stool in a parrot-house. I at least have so much to do in unravelling certain human lots, and seeing how they were woven and interwoven, that all the light I can command must be concentrated on this particular web, and not dispersed over the tempting range of relevancies called the universe.[24]

Colin MacCabe's comment on this paragraph is that 'Although at first sight, George Eliot would appear to be questioning her form, the force of the passage is to leave us convinced that we have finally abandoned form to be treated to the simple unravelling of the real.'[25] But this seems a very stubborn refusal to credit George Eliot with ironic selfconsciousness. It is patently obvious by Chapter 15 that the narrator of *Middlemarch* *is* ranging over the tempting range of relevancies called the universe, especially through her famous scientific analogies. And by comparing her own writing to Fielding's, she is implicitly placing it in a tradition of literary fiction, even if this admission is neatly disguised by invoking Fielding's description of himself as a historian. The Fish effect is immediately apparent in the opening of this passage: 'A great historian, as he insisted on calling himself. . . .' We don't know, yet, of course, who this historian is, and it is quite a time before we discover this identity, and that he is not a historian at all, but a novelist. '[A]s he insisted on calling himself . . .' might give us a clue that he wasn't a proper historian, but it might equally well be construed as meaning he was a proper historian who insisted on calling himself great. '[W]ho had the happiness to be dead a hundred and twenty years ago ...' 'Dead' is surely a surprising word in the context. 'Who had the happiness to be alive' would be the more predictable formula, expressing that nostalgia for the good old days which George Eliot so often invokes in her fiction, though in fact seldom quite straightforwardly. The paradox is resolved when we read, 'and so to take his place among the colossi whose huge legs our living pettiness is observed to walk under. . . .' Fielding was lucky to have died a hundred and twenty years ago, then, in the sense that he thus became a literary classic – though if he is dead it is hard to see how this brings him any happiness, and the reverence accorded to a classic seems somewhat undercut by the allusion to Shakespeare's Cassius. The narrator, at any rate, takes no responsibility for the analogy. 'Whose huge legs our living pettiness is observed to walk under. . . .' Observed by whom? By the makers of such extravagant analogies? '[G]lories in his copious remarks and digressions as the least imitable part of his work.' Was Fielding right in thinking them inimitable, or has George Eliot improved upon them? Of course, she disowns any attempt to compete with him, but then the whole passage is a digression disowning the intention to digress.

Several critics have recently pointed out the presence of paradox and contradiction in George Eliot's superficially smooth, unproblematic narrative style. J. Hillis Miller, for instance, in his article 'Optic and Semiotic in *Middlemarch*', identifies three groups of totalising metaphors or families of metaphors, and comments, 'Each group of metaphors is related to the others, fulfilling them, but at the same time contradicting them, cancelling them out, or undermining their validity.'[26] Thus, for instance, the recurring image of the lives of the characters as a flowing web, an unrolling fabric, objectively there, to which the narrator brings a truthtelling light, is contaminated by other images of the subjectivity of interpretation, the inevitable distortions of perspective. The famous analogy of the candle-flame which confers pattern on the random scratches of the pier-glass, as Miller points out (and Leslie Stephen pointed out before him) applies as well to the narrator's perspective as to that of any character's. Stephen Marcus, in an interesting, if quirky article entitled, 'Human Nature, Social Orders and Nineteenth-Century Systems of Explanation: starting in with George Eliot' interprets her fondness for setting her novels back in the historical past (a feature of the classic Victorian novel in general) as a defence mechanism designed to control themes that she was both fascinated by and yet feared: sexual passion, class conflict and epistemological scepticism. He notes in her treatment of the past, as early as 'Amos Barton', the first piece of fiction she wrote, the Fish effect, moments when the irony of the narrator's discourse, with which the reader has been feeling a comfortable complicity, suddenly rebounds upon him:

> It is the reader himself who now suddenly discovers that he is being gently but firmly prodded in the ribs, although it is not altogether clear why he should all at once find himself on the wrong end of the stick. . . . The effect, however, is momentarily to loosen the reader's grip on the sequence of statements through which he has just worked his way and to cause him to look back, if only for a fraction of an instant, to see if he can ascertain the logical and syntactical course which led him to this uncertainly dislocated and suspended position.[27]

Very recently, Graham Martin, responding directly to Colin Mac-Cabe's book, has argued that 'we learn as much about *The Mill on the Floss* by looking at discontinuities between the authorial meta-language and the narrated fiction, as by remarking on their fusion'.[28] All these critics tend to regard the fractures they discern in the smooth surface of George Eliot's narrative method as signs or symptoms of the tremendous stresses and strains she experienced in trying to deal truthfully and yet positively with an increasingly alienated and alienating social reality. But it is not necessary to see them as aesthetic flaws. On the contrary, it is precisely because the narrator's discourse is never entirely unambiguous, predictable, and in total interpretative control of the other discourses in *Middlemarch* that the novel survives, to be read and re-read, without ever being finally closed or exhausted. And this, paradoxically, follows inevitably from the post-Saussurian theories about language and discourse to which Colin MacCabe, and other critics of the same persuasion, subscribe. If it is true that language is a system of differences with no positive terms, that the subject is inevitably split in discourse between the 'I' who speaks and the 'I' who is spoken of, that the relationship between words and things is not natural but cultural, not given but produced, then George Eliot could not write fiction that was a 'transparent window on reality' even if she wanted to. The question, therefore, is whether in trying – or pretending – to do so, she was betrayed into false consciousness and bad art. It has been my purpose to suggest that she was well aware of the indeterminacy that lurks

in all efforts at human communication, and frequently reminded her
readers of this fact in the very act of apparently denying it through
the use of an intrusive 'omniscient' authorial voice.

From *The Nineteenth Century Novel: Critical Essays and Documents*, ed. Arnold Kettle (London, 1981), pp. 218–38. Slightly
revised by the author, 1989.

NOTES

[David Lodge's essay on *Middlemarch* is included in this anthology for two
reasons. The first is that the opening pages provide a very clear account of
the cross-currents at work in contemporary criticism. Lodge identifies the
traditional stance of British criticism, and then deals with the kinds of
reservations about George Eliot's art that appear in some Marxist and poststructuralist criticism. The objections of such critics seem to centre on
George Eliot's use of an omniscient and intrusive narrator. Lodge endeavours to show that the manner of the narration in the novel is a good deal
more complex than has often been assumed. This is the second reason why
Lodge's essay is reprinted here: in tackling this issue, Lodge presents us with
a new, and striking, sense of the nature of George Eliot's achievement – she
is neither a poised and all-knowing commentator on human affairs (as much
traditional criticism suggests) nor narrowly moral (as some Marxist and
poststructuralist criticism suggests). Ed.]

1. Barbara Hardy (ed.), *Middlemarch: Critical Approaches to the Novel*
   (London, 1967), p. 3.

2. Ibid., pp. 94–5.

3. Henry James, *The House of Fiction*, ed. Leon Edel (London, 1962),
   p. 267.

4. J. Hillis Miller, 'Optic and Semiotic in *Middlemarch*', in *The Worlds of
   Victorian Fiction*, ed. Jerome Buckley (Harvard, 1975), p. 127. [Re-
   printed in this volume – see p. 65. Ed.]

5. Readers seeking further light on these matters might consult the
   following sources, listed in an order corresponding roughly to a
   progressive shift of focus from structuralism to poststructuralism:
   Robert Scholes, *Structuralism in Literature* (London, 1977); Jonathan
   Culler, *Structuralist Poetics* (London, 1975); *Structuralism and Since*,
   ed. John Sturrock (Oxford, 1980); and Catherine Belsey, *Critical
   Practice* (London, 1980). The last of these is closest to MacCabe's
   position, the theoretical bases of which are also expounded in his own
   book.

6. Colin MacCabe, *James Joyce and the Revolution of the Word* (London, 1979), p. 4.

7. 'Metalanguage: a language or system of symbols used to discuss another language or system', Collins *New English Dictionary*.

8. Colin MacCabe, *James Joyce and the Revolution of the Word* (London, 1979), p. 100.

9. Ibid., p. 14.

10. Ibid., p. 27.

11. *Great Dialogues of Plato*, trans. W. H. Rouse (New York, 1956), p. 190.

12. Gérard Genette has traced this process from Plato to Aristotle to the present day in his monograph, *Introduction à l'architexte* (Paris, 1979), arguing that in developing Plato's distinction between three modes of poetic utterance into a theory of three basic genres (lyric, drama, epic), later poeticians not only misrepresented the classical authors, but created a great deal of confusion in poetics. For a short account in English of this work, see James Kearns, 'Gérard Genette: a Different Genre', *The Literary Review*, no. 33 (Jan. 1981), 21–3.

13. Gérard Genette, *Narrative Discourse*, trans. Jane E. Lewin (Oxford, 1980), p. 164.

14. Mikhail Bakhtin, 'Discourse Typology in Prose', an extract from *Problems in Dostoevsky's Poetics* (Leningrad, 1929), in *Readings in Russian Poetics*, ed. Ladislav Matejka and Krystyna Pomorska (Ann Arbor, 1978), p. 193. This anthology also contains an extract, entitled 'Reported Speech', from Volosinov's *Marxism and the Philosophy of Language* (Leningrad, 1930). For a survey of Bakhtin's work, and a discussion of the vexed question of his relationship to Volosinov, see Ann Shulman, 'Between Marxism and Formalism: the stylistics of Mikhail Bakhtin', *Comparative Criticism: A Yearbook*, vol. 2, ed. E. S. Shaffer (Cambridge, 1980), pp. 221–34.

15. Barbara Hardy (ed.), *Middlemarch: Critical Approaches to the Novel* (London, 1967), pp. 67–9.

16. George Eliot, *Middlemarch* (Penguin edition, Harmondsworth, 1965), p. 32.

17. Ibid.

18. Colin MacCabe, *James Joyce and the Revolution of the Word* (London, 1979), p. 15.

19. George Eliot, *Middlemarch* (Penguin edition, Harmondsworth, 1965), p. 217.

20. Ibid., p. 217.

21. Ibid., pp. 217–18.

22. Farebrother's allusions to the various versions of the Hercules myth are indeed full of proleptic irony in application to Lydgate, whose 'resolve' to make a contribution to medical science will be sacrificed to Rosamond's feminine and domestic desires (equivalent to 'holding the distaff'), and who will eventually wear the Nessus shirt of failure and disillusionment in his professional and emotional life.

23. See particularly *Surprised by Sin, The Reader in 'Paradise Lost'* (London and New York, 1967); *Self-Consuming Artefacts: The Experience of Seventeenth-Century Literature* (Berkeley and Los Angeles, 1972); and *Is There a Text in this Class? The Authority of Interpretive Communities* (Cambridge, 1980).

24. George Eliot, *Middlemarch* (Penguin edition, Harmondsworth, 1965), p. 170.

25. Colin MacCabe, *James Joyce and the Revolution of the Word* (London, 1979), p. 19.

26. J. Hillis Miller, 'Optic and Semiotic in *Middlemarch*', in *The Worlds of Victorian Fiction*, ed. Jerome Buckley (Harvard, 1975), p. 128. [Reprinted in this volume – see p. 65. Ed.]

27. Steven Marcus, 'Human Nature, Social Orders, and Nineteenth-Century Systems of Explanation: Starting in with George Eliot', *Salmagundi*, 26 (1975), 21.

28. Graham Martin, '*The Mill on the Floss* and the Unreliable Narrator', in *George Eliot: Centenary Essays and an Unpublished Fragment*, ed. Anne Smith (London, 1980), p. 38.

4

Optic and Semiotic in 'Middlemarch'

J. HILLIS MILLER

> . . . this power of generalising which gives men so much the superiority
> in mistake over the dumb animals.
>
> George Eliot, *Middlemarch*

George Eliot's apparent aim in *Middlemarch* (1871–72) is to present
a total picture of provincial society in England at the period just
before the first Reform Bill of 1832. She also wants to interpret this
picture totally. She wants both to show what is there and to show
how it works. This enterprise of totalisation, as one might call it, is
shared with an important group of other masterworks of Victorian
fiction, including Thackeray's *Vanity Fair* (1847–48), Dickens'
Bleak House (1852–53), *Little Dorrit* (1855–57), and *Our Mutual
Friend* (1864–65), and Trollope's *The Way We Live Now* (1874–
75). All these novels have many characters and employ multiple
analogous plots. They cast a wide net and aim at inclusiveness, in
part by a method of accumulation. Nevertheless, since the actual
societies in question were unmanageably complex and multitudinous,
some strategy of compression, of economy, had to be devised in each
case. As George Meredith puts it in the 'Prelude' to *The Egoist*, 'the
inward mirror, the embracing and condensing spirit, is required to
give us those interminable mile-post piles of matter . . . in essence, in
chosen samples, digestibly.'[1] The means of condensation used vary
considerably, however, from novelist to novelist.

Dickens, for example, achieves inclusiveness by making the part
explicitly stand for the whole. He emphasises the synecdochic,

representative, emblematic quality of his characters. Mr. Krook, the rag and bottle shopkeeper in *Bleak House*, stands for the lord chancellor, his shop for the Court of Chancery. Chancery, in turn, is a synecdoche for the state of 'wiglomeration' of English society as a whole. In the same novel, Sir Leicester Dedlock is presented as an example of the whole class of aristocrats; Gridley, the Man from Shropshire, is an emblem for all the suitors who are destroyed by the delays of Chancery, and so on. Moreover, the range of examples includes by this method of synecdoche all of England. Characters from the country and from the city, from the lowest level of society to the highest, are presented.

George Eliot is more straightforwardly 'realistic' in her procedure. *Middlemarch* presents a large group of the sort of people one would in fact have been likely to find in a provincial town in the Midlands. Their representative or symbolic quality is not insisted upon. This would be the wrong track to follow, I believe, in a search for her methods of totalisation. Moreover, Eliot does not present examples from the whole range of English society. The relation of Middle-march to English society is rather that of part to whole, or that of a sample to the whole cloth, according to a metaphor I shall be examining later. The relationship is once more synecdochic, but the kind of synecdoche in question is different from the one used by Dickens. In *Bleak House* the member of a class is presented as a 'symbol' of the whole class. In *Middlemarch* a fragment is examined as a 'sample' of the larger whole of which it is a part, though the whole impinges on the part as the 'medium' within which it lives, as national politics affect Middlemarch when there is a general election, or as the coming of the railroad upsets rural traditions. Eliot's strategy of totalisation is to present individual character or event in the context of that wider medium and to affirm universal laws of human behaviour in terms of characters whose specificity and even uniqueness is indicated by the completeness of the psychological portraits of each – Dorothea, Lydgate, Casaubon, Bulstrode, Fred Vincy, Mary Garth, and the rest. This fullness of characterisation and the accompanying circumstantiality of social detail in *Middle-march* have been deservedly admired. They make this novel perhaps the masterwork of Victorian realism.

The subtitle of *Middlemarch* is *A Study of Provincial Life*. This may put the novel under the aegis of a kind of painting, a 'study from life'. The more powerful association of the word, however, is with a scientific 'study'. In *Middlemarch* Eliot is attempting to fulfil for the life of a provincial town that enterprise she had mapped out in her important early essay on the German sociologist of peasant life, Wilhelm Heinrich von Riehl. In that essay, 'The Natural History of German Life' (*Westminster Review*, 1856), she had implicitly proposed the writing of works of fiction which would do for English life what Riehl had done for the German peasant: 'Art is the nearest thing to life: it is a mode of amplifying experience and extending our contact with our fellow-men beyond the bounds of our personal lot. All the more sacred is the task of the artist when he undertakes to paint the life of the People. Falsification here is far more pernicious than in the more artificial aspects of life.'[2] Much of *Middlemarch* is modelled on the sociologist's respect for individual fact George Eliot so praises in this essay. The experience of each character in *Middlemarch* is described in such detail that the reader is encouraged not to forget its differences from the experiences of the other characters.

Nevertheless, the narrator of *Middlemarch* assumes throughout that the behaviour of these unique people manifests certain general and universal laws. These laws may be formulated and are in fact constantly formulated, as when the narrator says: 'We are all of us born in moral stupidity, taking the world as an udder to feed our supreme selves.'[3] The special mode of totalisation in *Middlemarch* is this combination of specificity, on the one hand, and, on the other hand, generalising interpretation on the basis of specificity. Such generalising is proposed as valid not just for all people in the particular middle-class society of Middlemarch, and not just for the English society at a specific moment of its history of which Middlemarch is a part, but for all people in all cultures in all times.

I intend here to explore one mode of this generalising interpretation, the presentation by the narrator of certain all-encompassing metaphors which are proposed as models for Middlemarch society. Such metaphors are put forward as a means of thinking of all the people in Middlemarch in their interrelations through time. Each metaphor is an interpretative net which the reader is invited to cast over the whole society, to use as a paradigm by means of which to think of the whole. I shall argue that there are three such totalising metaphors, or rather families of metaphors. Each group of metaphors is related to the others, fulfilling them, but at the same time contradicting them, cancelling them out, or undermining their validity.

The recurrence of such metaphors throughout *Middlemarch* and their assumed validity affirms one of the most important presuppositions of the novel. The unique life of each of the characters is presented as part of a single system of complex interaction in time and space. No man, for Eliot, lives alone. Each exists in 'the same embroiled medium, the same troublous fitfully-illuminated life' (ch. 30). The nature of this 'medium' and of the interaction of character with character within it is analysed throughout by the narrator. The voice of the narrator, sympathetic certainly, but also clairvoyant in his insight into human folly, is in *Middlemarch*, as in Victorian novels generally, the most immediate presence for the reader and the chief generating force behind the stylistic texture of the novel.

> *text* ... from Medieval Latin *textus*, (Scriptural) text, from Latin, literary composition, 'woven thing,' from the past participle of *texere*, to weave.[4]

Perhaps the most salient totalising metaphor presented as a model for the community of Middlemarch is in fact a family of related metaphors. Each member of this family compares Middlemarch society or some part of it to a spatially or temporally deployed material complex – a labyrinth, or flowing water, or woven cloth. There are two important implications of these metaphors as they are used in the novel. The first is the assumption that a society is in some way like a material field and therefore is open to the same kind of objective scientific investigation as may be applied to such a field, for example, to flowing water. The other is the assumption, reinforced by many passages in the novel, that the structure or texture of small-scale pieces of the whole is the same as the structure or texture of the whole and so may be validly described with the same figures. This is the assumption of the validity of one kind of synecdoche. The part is 'really like' the whole, and an investigation of a sample will lead to valid conclusions about the whole. If Middlemarch society as a whole is like flowing water or like woven cloth, the mental life of each of its inhabitants may also be validly described in the same metaphors. In a similar way, when the reader or the narrator focuses on the relation between two of the characters out of the whole lot, the metaphors will be found to be valid on that scale too. In the other direction, as I have suggested, it is implied that what is true in Middlemarch is also true for English society as a whole, or even for any human life anywhere and at any time. *Middlemarch* is full of such shifts in perspective from close up to far away and back to close up again, according to that law of scientific method which Lydgate admirably formulates: 'there must be a systole and diastole in all inquiry', and 'a man's mind must be continually expanding and shrinking between the whole human horizon and the horizon of an object-glass' (ch. 63). Eliot's assumption is that in the social world, at least, such changes in scale reveal a strict homogeneity between the large-scale and small-scale grain or texture of things. As Will Ladislaw phrases it, 'the little waves make the large ones and are of the same pattern' (ch. 46).

The most persistent of these structural metaphors, as has often been noticed, is the metaphor of the web. One explicit application of the image of a web to the whole range of social relationships in the novel comes in the passage where the narrator distinguishes his[5] enterprise from that of Fielding. Whereas Fielding lived in more spacious times and could allow himself the luxury of the famous 'copious remarks and digressions', 'I at least', says the narrator, 'have so much to do in unravelling certain human lots, and seeing how they were woven and interwoven, that all the light I can command must be concentrated on this particular web, and not dispersed over that tempting range of relevancies called the universe' (ch. 15). The narrator's effort is not merely that of observation. He must, like a good scientist, take apart the specimen being analysed, unravel all its fibres to see how it is put together, how it has been woven and interwoven. That the texture of Middlemarch society as a whole may be accurately represented in a metaphor of woven cloth is taken for granted throughout the novel. It appears in many apparently casual texts as a reinforcement of more elaborate passages inviting the reader to keep the paradigm of the web before his mind. Lydgate, to give one example from early in the novel, finds himself for the first time 'feeling the hampering threadlike pressure of small social conditions, and their frustrating complexity' (ch. 18).

The metaphor of a web, however, is also used repeatedly in *Middlemarch* to describe the texture of smaller-scale entities within the larger social fabric. The lovemaking of Rosamond and Lydgate, for example, is described as the collective weaving of an intersubjective tissue:

> Young love-making—that gossamer web! Even the points it clings to—the things whence its subtle interlacings are swung—are scarcely perceptible; momentary touches of finger-tips, meetings of rays from blue and dark orbs, unfinished phrases, lightest changes of cheek and lip, faintest tremors. The web itself is made of spontaneous beliefs and indefinable joys, yearnings of one life towards another, visions of completeness, indefinite trust. And Lydgate fell to spinning that web

> from his inward self with wonderful rapidity . . . As for Rosamond,
> she was in the water-lily's expanding wonderment at its own fuller life,
> and she too was spinning industriously at the mutual web.
>
> (ch. 36)

Another important use of the metaphor of a web is made in the description of Lydgate's scientific researches. Lydgate's attempt to find the 'primitive tissue' is based on the assumption that the metaphor of woven cloth applies in the organic as well as in the social realm. His use of the figure brings into the open the parallelism between Eliot's aim as a sociologist of provincial life and the aims of contemporary biologists.[6] Lydgate's research is based on the hypothesis that all the organs of the body are differentiations of 'certain primary webs or tissues': 'have not these structures some common basis from which they have all started, as your sarsnet, gauze, net, satin and velvet from the raw cocoon?' (ch. 15). If Lydgate assumes that biological entities may be described as tissues, the narrator of Middlemarch makes the same assumptions about the subjective lives of the characters. Of Lydgate, for example, the narrator says that 'momentary speculations as to all the possible grounds for Mrs. Bulstrode's hints had managed to get woven like slight clinging hairs into the more substantial web of his thoughts' (ch. 31). Much later in the novel, basing the generalisation again on Lydgate's psychology, the narrator asks: 'It is not rather what we expect in men, that they should have numerous strands of experience lying side by side and never compare them with each other?' (ch. 58). This image of mental or intersubjective life as a reticulated pattern like a grid is implicit when a few pages earlier the narrator says of Rosamond and Lydgate that 'between him and her indeed there was that total missing of each other's mental track, which is too evidently possible even between persons who are continually thinking of each other'. The image of mental or social life as travelling along tracks which may or may not intersect with others is also latent in an earlier remark about Ladislaw: 'There are characters which are continually creating collisions and nodes for themselves in dramas which nobody is prepared to act with them' (ch. 19).

To the metaphor of the web, however, must be added the metaphor of the stream. Collective or individual life in Middlemarch is not a fixed pattern like a carpet. The web is always in movement. The pervasive figure for this is that of flowing water. This figure is homogeneous with the figure of the web in that flowing water, for Eliot, is seen as made up of currents, filaments flowing side by side, intermingling and dividing. Flowing water is, so to speak, a temporalised web. Casaubon, for example, is said, in a fine series of phrases, to have possessed 'that proud narrow sensitiveness which has not mass enough to spare for transformation into sympathy, and quivers thread-like in small currents of self-preoccupation or at best of an egoistic scrupulosity' (ch. 29). Lydgate, after he has met Rosamond, 'had no sense that any new current had set into his life' (ch. 16). Of his life as a whole when it is in the midst of being lived (in the middle of its march, as one might say), the narrator asserts that it has 'the complicated probabilities of an arduous purpose, with all the possible thwartings and furtherings of circumstance, all the niceties of inward balance, by which a man swims and makes his point or else is carried headlong', for 'character too is a process and an unfolding' (ch. 15). In another place, the narrator speaks of 'the chief current' of Dorothea's anxiety (ch. 22), and, as opposed to the egotistic scrupulosity of Casaubon's small soul, 'in Dorothea's mind there was a current into which all thought and feeling were apt sooner or later to flow—the reaching forward of the whole consciousness towards the fullest truth, the least partial good' (ch. 20). In the climactic scene of Dorothea's renunciation of her fortune to marry Will, 'the flood of her young passion bear[s] down all the obstructions which had kept her silent' (ch. 83).

One final element must be added to complete the description of Eliot's admirable development of a quasi-scientific model to describe the subjective life of the individual, the relations of two persons within the social 'medium', and the nature of that medium as a whole. This element has already been anticipated in what has been said about the correspondence, in Eliot's view of things, between small- and large-scale structures. This idea, however, is but one aspect of a larger assumption, that is, the notion that any process in any of the three 'scales' is made up of endlessly subdividable 'minutiae'. Anything that we call a 'unit' or a single fact, in social or in mental life, is not single but multiple. A finer lens would always make smaller parts visible. The smaller parts, in turn, are made up of even smaller entities.

One corollary of this vision of things is the rejection of that straightforward idea of single causes which had characterised, for example, *Adam Bede*. In *Middlemarch* Eliot still believes in causality, but in the psychological and social realms the causes are now seen as unimaginably multiple. No fact is in itself single, and no fact is explicable by a single relationship to a single cause. Each fact is a kind of multitudinous node which exists only arbitrarily as a single thing because we happen to have the microscope focused as we do. If the focus were finer, the apparently single fact would subdivide and reveal itself to be made of multiple minutiae. If the focus were coarser the fact would disappear within the larger entity of which it is a part. A single momentary state of mind, for example, exists in relation to all its latent motives, the minutiae of mental life which underlie it, in relation also to its own past and future, and in multiple relation to what is outside it, all the other people to whom the person is socially related. The metaphor of the variable lens of a microscope is in fact used by Eliot to make this point:

> Even with a microscope directed on a water-drop we find ourselves making interpretations which turn out to be rather coarse; for whereas under a weak lens you may seem to see a creature exhibiting an active voracity into which other smaller creatures actively play as if they were so many animated tax-pennies, a stronger lens reveals to you certain tiniest hairlets which make vortices for these victims while the swallower waits passively at his receipt of custom.
>
> (ch. 6)

One might ask, parenthetically, how and why the metaphor of the microscope has been contaminated here by another apparently unrelated metaphor, that of money, taxes, and 'custom'. This interpretation of one metaphor by another metaphor is characteristic of Eliot's use of figure. An attempt to explain fully this linguistic habit must be postponed, but one can say that the displacement of one figure by another is asymmetrically parallel to the displacement of the weak lens by the strong lens of the microscope. In each case, one vision of things is replaced by another. The optical visions are apparently reconcilable, whereas the two metaphors interfere with one another even if they are not wholly contradictory. The text of *Middlemarch*, in any case, goes on to apply the metaphor of the double-lensed microscope to a particular case in the novel: 'In this way, metaphorically speaking, a strong lens applied to Mrs. Cadwallader's match-making will show a play of minute causes producing what may be called thought and speech vortices to bring her the sort of food she needed.'

The phrase 'play of minute causes' is echoed throughout the novel by similar phrases keeping before the reader the idea that the mental and social events being described are extremely complex. This complexity is essential to their mode of existence. The narrator speaks, for example, of 'a slow preparation of effects from one life on another' (ch. 11), or of an ardour which cooled 'imperceptibly', like other youthful loves ('Nothing in the world more subtle than the process of their gradual change!' ch. 15), or of 'the minutiae of mental make in which one of us differs from another' (ch. 15), or of Lydgate's 'testing vision of details and relations' (ch. 16), or of 'the suppressed transitions which unite all contrasts' (ch. 20), or of the 'nice distinctions of rank in Middlemarch' (ch. 23), or of 'the living myriad of hidden suckers whereby the belief and the conduct are wrought into mutual sustainment' (ch. 53), or of a 'fact' which 'was broken into little sequences' (ch. 61), or of the way Bulstrode's 'misdeeds were like the subtle muscular movements which are not taken account of in the consciousness' (ch. 68).

All this family of intertwined metaphors and motifs[7] – the web, the current, the minutely subdivided entity – make up a single comprehensive model or picture of Middlemarch society as being a complex moving medium, tightly interwoven into a single fabric, always in process, endlessly subdividable. This medium can be seen and studied objectively, as if there could be an ideal observer who does not change what he observes and who sees the moving web as it were from all perspectives at once, from close up and far away, with both gross and fine lenses, in a continual systole and diastole of inquiry. The storyteller in *Middlemarch* is in short the ideal observer of Victorian fiction, the 'omniscient' narrator. His aim is to do full representative justice to the complexity of the condition of man in his social medium. There are many admirable passages in *Middlemarch* giving examples of what the narrator sees, each a new application of the model I have been describing. None is perhaps so comprehensive an exploitation of the totalising implications of this family of metaphors as an admirable passage in chapter 11 describing 'old provincial society':

> Old provincial society had its share of this subtle movement: had not only its striking downfalls, its brilliant young professional dandies who ended by living up an entry with a drab and six children for their establishment, but also those less marked vicissitudes which are constantly shifting the boundaries of social intercourse, and begetting new consciousness of interdependence. Some slipped a little downward, some got higher footing: people denied aspirates, gained wealth, and fastidious gentlemen stood for boroughs; some were caught in political currents, some in ecclesiastical, and perhaps found themselves surprisingly grouped in consequence; while a few personages or families that stood with rocky firmness amid all this fluctuation, were slowly presenting new aspects in spite of solidity, and altering with the double change of self and beholder.

> Therefore speak I to them in parables: because they seeing see not; and hearing they hear not, neither do they understand.
>
> (Matthew 13:13)
>
> ... er hat das Auge nicht dafür, das Einmalige zu sehen; die Ähnlichseherei und Gleichmacherei ist das Merkmal schwacher Augen.[8]

'Double change of self and beholder'! I have said that my first family of metaphors in *Middlemarch* does not raise problems of perspective, or that in any case it presupposes the possibility of an ideal observer such as that assumed in much nineteenth-century science, in the days before operationalism, relativity, and the principle of indeterminacy. This is true, but in fact an optical or epistemological metaphor has already introduced itself surreptitiously into many of my examples. The narrator must concentrate 'all the light [he] can command' (ch. 15) on his particular web in order to see clearly how it is woven. Study of the web requires constant changes of the lens in the systole and diastole of inquiry. Any conceivable observer in Middlemarch will be changing himself along with all the other changes and so will change what he sees.

A pervasive figure for the human situation in *Middlemarch* is that of the seer who must try to identify clearly what is present before him. This metaphor contaminates the apparently clear-cut objectivist implications of the metaphor of the flowing web. As more and more examples of it accumulate, it struggles with a kind of imperialistic will to power over the whole to replace that objectivism with a fully developed subjectivism or perspectivisim. The 'omniscience' of the narrator, according to this alternative model for the human condition, can be obtained only because he is able to share the points of view of all the characters, thereby transcending the limited vision of any single person. 'In watching effects', as the narrator says, 'if only of an electric battery, it is often necessary to change our place and examine a particular mixture or group at some distance from the point where the movement we are interested in was set up' (ch. 40). The narrator can move in imagination from one vantage point to another, or from close up to far away. He can be, like the angel Uriel, 'watching the progress of planetary history from the Sun' (ch. 41), and at the same time share in that microscopic vision of invisible process, perceptible only to inward imaginative vision, so splendidly described in a passage about Lydgate's method as a scientist. It is a passage which also describes covertly the claims of Eliot's own fictional imagination. Lydgate, the narrator says, is endowed with the imagination that reveals subtle actions inaccessible by any sort of lens, but tracked in that outer darkness through long pathways of necessary sequence by the inward light which is the last refinement of Energy, capable of bathing even the ethereal atoms in its ideally illuminated space ... he was enamoured of that arduous invention which is the very eye of research, provisionally framing its object and correcting it to more and more exactness of relation; he wanted to pierce the obscurity of those minute processes which prepare human misery and joy ...

(ch. 16)

The metaphor of the complex moving web, the 'embroiled medium', is, one can see, further complicated, or even contradicted, by the metaphor of vision. Each of those nodes in the social web which is a separate human being is endowed with a power to see the whole. This power is defined throughout the novel as essentially distorting. Each man or woman has a 'centre of self, whence the lights and shadows must always fall with a certain difference' (ch. 31). The 'radiance' of Dorothea's 'transfigured girlhood', as the narrator says, 'fell on the first object that came within its level' (ch. 5). Her mistakes, as her sister Celia tells her, are errors in seeing, of which her literal myopia is a metonymy. 'I thought it right to tell you,' says Celia apropos of the fact that Sir James intends to propose to Dorothea, 'because you went on as you always do, never looking just where you are, and treading in the wrong place. You always see what nobody else sees; it is impossible to satisfy you; yet you never see what is quite plain' (ch. 4). Mr. Casaubon, however, is also 'the centre of his own world'. From that point of view he is 'liable to think that others were providentially made for him, and especially to consider them in the light of their fitness for the author of a "Key to all Mythologies"' (ch. 10). Of the inhabitants of Middlemarch generally it can in fact be said that each makes of what he sees something determined by his own idiosyncratic perspective, for 'Probabilities are as various as the faces to be seen at will on fretwork or paperhangings: every form is there, from Jupiter to Judy, if you only look with creative inclination' (ch. 32).

Seeing, then, is for Eliot not a neutral, objective, dispassionate, or passive act. It is the creative projection of light from an egotistic centre motivated by desire and need. This projected radiance orders the field of vision according to the presuppositions of the seer. The act of seeing is the spontaneous affirmation of a will to power over what is seen. This affirmation of order is based on the instinctive desire to believe that the world is providentially structured in a neat pattern of which one is oneself the centre, for 'we are all of us born in moral stupidity, taking the world as an udder to feed our supreme selves'. This interpretation of the act of seeing is most fully presented in the admirable and often discussed 'parable' of the 'pier-glass' at the beginning of chapter 27:

> An eminent philosopher among my friends, who can dignify even your ugly furniture by lifting it into the serene light of science, has shown me this pregnant little fact. Your pier-glass or extensive surface of polished steel made to be rubbed by a housemaid, will be minutely and multitudinously scratched in all directions; but place now against it a lighted candle as a centre of illumination, and lo! the scratches will seem to arrange themselves in a fine series of concentric circles round that little sun. It is demonstrable that the scratches are going everywhere impartially, and it is only your candle which produces the flattering illusion of a concentric arrangement, its light falling with an exclusive optical selection. These things are a parable. The scratches are events, and the candle is the egoism of any person now absent—of Miss Vincy, for example. Rosamond had a Providence of her own who had kindly made her more charming than other girls, and who seemed to have arranged Fred's illness and Mr. Wrench's mistake in order to bring her and Lydgate within effective proximity.[9]

This passage is perhaps more complicated than it at first appears. It begins with an example of what it describes, an example which implicitly takes note of the fact that Eliot's own 'parabolic' method, in this text, as in many other passages in *Middlemarch*, is a seeing of one thing in the 'light' of another. The word 'parable', like the word 'allegory', the word 'metaphor', or indeed all terms for figures of speech, is of course itself based on a figure. It means 'to set aside', from the Greek *para*, beside, and *ballein*, to throw. A parable is set or thrown at some distance from the meaning which controls it and to which it obliquely or parabolically refers, as a parobolic curve is controlled, across a space, by its parallelism to a line on the cone of which it is a section. The line and the cone may have only a virtual or imaginary existence, as in the case of a comet with a parabolic course. The parabola creates that line in the empty air, just as the parables of Jesus remedy a defect of vision, give sight to the blind, and make the invisible visible. In Eliot's parable of the pier glass the 'eminent philosopher' transfigures 'ugly furniture', a pier glass, by 'lifting it into the serene light of science', but also makes an obscure scientific principle visible. In the same way, the candle makes the random scratches on the pier glass appear to be concentric circles, and so Rosamond interprets what happens around her as being governed by her private providence, just as Eliot sees provincial society as like a woven web, or the ego of an individual person in the light of a comparison to a candle. The same projective, subjective, even egotistic act, seeing one thing as set or thrown, parabolically, beside another, is involved in all four cases.

At this point the reader may remember that the narrator, in a passage I earlier took as a 'key' expression[10] of Eliot's use of a model of objective scientific observation, says 'all the light I can command must be concentrated on this particular web'. With a slight change of formulation this could be seen as implying that the subjective source of light not only illuminates what is seen but also, as in the case of the candle held to the pier glass, determines the structure of what is seen. Middlemarch society perhaps appears to be a web only because a certain kind of subjective light is concentrated on it. The passage taken in isolation does not say this, but its near congruence with the passage about the pier glass, a slightly asymmetrical analogy based on the fact that the same metaphorical elements are present in each allows the contradictory meaning to seep into the passage about the web when the two texts are set side by side. Each is seen as a modulation of the other. The same key would not open both, though a 'master key' might.

In spite of the disquieting possibilities generated by resonances between two similar but not quite congruent passages, the narrator in various ways throughout *Middlemarch* is clearly claiming to be able to transcend the limitations of the self-centred ego by seeing things impersonally, objectively, scientifically: 'It is demonstrable that the scratches are going everywhere impartially.' This objective vision, such is the logic of Eliot's parable, shows that what is 'really there' has no order whatsoever, but is merely random scratches without pattern or meaning. The pier glass is 'minutely and multi-tudinously scratched in all directions'. The idea that reality is chaotic, without intrinsic order or form, and the corollary that any order it may appear to have is projected illicitly by some patterning ego, would seem to be contradicted by the series of totalising metaphors I have explored – web, flowing water, and so on – as well as by the generalising, rationalising, order-finding activity of the narrator throughout the book. It would seem hardly plausible, at this point at least, to say that reality for Eliot is a chaotic disorder. It might seem more likely that this is an irrelevant implication of the parable, an implication which has by accident, as it were, slipped in along with implications which are 'intended'. A decision about this must be postponed.

Among the 'intended' implications, however, may be one arising from the fact that a pier glass is a kind of mirror, while the examples of the 'flattering illusion' Eliot would have encountered in Herbert Spencer or in Ruskin lacked this feature. Ruskin, for example, speaks of the path of reflected moonlight seen across the surface of a lake by a spectator on the shore.[11] The pier glass would, after all, reflect what was brought near it, as well as produce its own interfering illusion of concentric circles, and the candle is a displacement or parable for the ego, of Rosamond or whomever. Rosamond would of course see her own image in the mirror, Narcissus-like. This implication of the parable links it with all those other passages, not only in *Middlemarch* but also in *Adam Bede*, for example, or in *Daniel Deronda*, where egotism is symbolised by the admiration of one's image in a mirror, or where the work of representation is expressed in the traditional image of holding a mirror up to reality. A passage in chapter 10, for example, apropos of the low opinion of Mr Casaubon held by his neighbours, says that even 'the greatest man of his age' could not escape 'unfavourable reflections of himself in various small mirrors'. This apparently uses the figure of the mirror in a way contradicting the parable of the pier glass. The mirror is now the ego rather than the external world. In fact, however, what is always in question when the mirror appears is narcissistic self-reflection. This may be thought of as seeing our own reflection in the mirroring world outside because we have projected it there. Or it may be thought of as our distortion of the world outside in our reflecting ego, so that it takes the configurations of our private vision of things. Any two subjectivities, according to this model, will face one another like confronting mirrors. If Casaubon was 'the centre of his own world', had 'an equivalent centre of self, whence the lights and shadows must always fall with a certain difference', the people in whom he seeks the reflection of his own sense of himself are not innocent mirrors, but are themselves instruments of distortion: 'even Milton, looking for his portrait in a spoon, must submit to have the facial angle of a bumpkin' (ch. 10). The projection of one's selfish needs or desires on reality orders that random set of events into a pattern, the image of the mirror would imply. This pattern is in fact a portrait of the ego itself, an objective embodiment of its subjective configurations. The terrible isolation of each person, for Eliot, lies in the way each goes through the world encountering only himself, his own image reflected back to him by the world because he (or she) has put it there in the first place, in the illusory interpretation of the world the person spontaneously makes.

The narrator of *Middlemarch*, it would seem, can escape from this fate only by using perspective to transcend perspective, by moving from the microscopic close-up to the panoramic distant view, and by shifting constantly from the point of view of one character to the point of view of another. Such shifts will give a full multidimensional picture of what is 'really there', as when the narrator, after a prolonged immersion within the subjective experience of Dorothea, asks: '—but why always Dorothea? Was her point of view the only possible one with regard to this marriage? I protest against all our interest, all our efforts at understanding being given to the young skins that look blooming in spite of trouble ... In spite of the blinking eyes and white moles objectionable to Celia, and the want of muscular curve which was morally painful to Sir James, Mr. Casaubon had an intense consciousness within him, and was spiritually a-hungered like the rest of us' (ch. 29).

The word 'interpretation', however, which I used just above, will serve as a clue indicating the presence within the optical metaphors of an element so far not identified as such. This element contaminates and ultimately subverts the optical model in the same way that the optical model contaminates and makes more problematic the images of the web or of the current. All the optical passages in fact contain elements which show that for Eliot seeing is never 'merely' optical. Seeing is never simply a matter of identifying correctly what is seen, seeing that windmills are windmills and not giants, a washpan a washpan and not the helmet of Mambrino, to use the example from *Don Quixote* cited as an epigraph for chapter 2. Seeing is always interpretation, that is, what is seen is always taken as a sign standing for something else, as an emblem, a hieroglyph, a parable.

Superimposed on the models for the human situation of the objective scientist and the subjective perspectivist, interlaced with them, overlapping them in each of their expressions, is a model for the situation of the characters and of the narrator which says all human beings in all situations are like readers of a text. Moreover, if for Eliot all seeing is falsified by the limitations of point of view, it is an even more inevitable law, for her, that we make things what they are by naming them in one way or another, that is, by the incorporation of empirical data into a conventional system of signs. A corollary of this law is the fact that all interpretation of signs is false interpretation. The original naming was an act of interpretation which falsified. The reading of things made into signs is necessarily a further falsification, an interpretation of an interpretation. An important sequence of passages running like Ariadne's thread through the labyrinthine verbal complexity of *Middlemarch* develops a subtle theory of signs and of interpretation. Along with this goes a recognition of the irreducibly figurative or metaphorical nature of all language.

I have elsewhere discussed George Eliot's theory of signs, of interpretation, and of figurative language in *Middlemarch*.[12] Limitations of space would in any case forbid discussion of this third model for the human situation here. It is possible, however, to conclude on the basis of what I have said about two families of metaphors in *Middlemarch* that the models are multiple and incompatible. They are incompatible not in the sense that one is more primitive or naïve and gives way to a more sophisticated paradigm, but in the sense that any passage will reveal itself when examined closely to be the battleground of conflicting metaphors. This incoherent, heterogeneous, 'unreadable', or nonsynthesisable quality of the text of *Middlemarch* jeopardises the narrator's effort of totalisation. It suggests that one gets a different kind of totality depending on what metaphorical model is used. The presence of several incompatible models brings into the open the arbitrary and partial character of each and so ruins the claim of the narrator to have a total, unified, and impartial vision. What is true for the characters of *Middlemarch*, that 'we all of us, grave or light, get our thoughts entangled in metaphors, and act fatally on the strength of them' (ch. 10), must also be true for the narrator. The web of interpretative figures cast by the narrator over the characters of the story becomes a net in which the narrator himself is entangled and trapped, his sovereign vision blinded.

George Eliot's insight into the dismaying dangers of metaphor is expressed already in an admirably witty and perceptive passage in *The Mill on the Floss*, published over a decade before *Middlemarch*, in 1860. Here already she formulates her recognition of the deconstructive powers of figurative language, its undoing of any attempt to make a complete, and completely coherent, picture of human life. This undoing follows from the fact that if we can seldom say what a thing is without saying it is something else, without speaking parabolically, then there is no way to avoid the ever present possibility of altering the meaning by altering the metaphor.

It is astonishing what a different result one gets by changing the metaphor! Once call the brain an intellectual stomach, and one's ingenious conception of the classics and geometry as ploughs and harrows seems to settle nothing. But then it is open to some one else to follow great authorities, and call the mind a sheet of white paper or a mirror, in which case one's knowledge of the digestive process becomes quite irrelevant. It was doubtless an ingenious idea to call the camel the ship of the desert, but it would hardly lead one far in training that useful beast. O Aristotle! if you had had the advantage of being 'the freshest modern' instead of the greatest ancient, would you not have mingled your praise of metaphorical speech, as a sign of high intelligence, with a lamentation that intelligence so rarely shows itself in speech without metaphor—that we can so seldom declare what a thing is, except by saying it is something else?

(Bk 2, ch. 1)[13]

From *The Worlds of Victorian Fiction*, ed. Jerome Buckley (Harvard, 1975), pp. 125–45.

NOTES

[J. Hillis Miller's essay is the finest example of a poststructuralist, or in this instance perhaps we should say deconstructionist, reading of *Middlemarch*. The reader might, however, find it difficult to grasp the difference between a poststructuralist approach and deconstruction. It should clarify matters if we suggest that poststructuralism covers all those approaches that have developed in the wake of, and take account of, the new insights into language that stemmed from structuralism. Broadly speaking, such approaches take a step back and look at how we conventionally organise our world. Deconstruction, at least in the form that it developed in American criticism, is a rather less broadly-based outgrowth of structuralism. It is, at the same time, more totally sceptical, tending to expose all the tactics any writer employs to marshal experience, and working with an idea of the impossibility of language achieving any kind of coherent engagement with the world; in the end, the words are always too unstable, too vague in meaning, throwing up fresh associations. We can see how such an approach can be developed in Miller's essay, where he explores the unreliability and contradictoriness of the metaphors that Eliot employs in order to try to make sense of the world she is creating. The reading of *Middlemarch* that J. Hillis Miller develops is very impressive: there is none of that dismissiveness towards George Eliot's achievement that can characterise some poststructuralist criticism. Reading Miller on George Eliot increases our sense of her sophistication as a novelist rather than making us feel that there is anything naïve or over-dominating about her approach. Yet at the same time reservations about J. Hillis Miller's approach have been voiced frequently: some suggest that what he says about the total uncertainty of a novel – its ultimate inability to know anything – is a critical stance that is highly relevant to postmodernist novels, but is at odds with Victorian fiction. Ed.]

1. George Meredith, *The Works of George Meredith*, vol. 13 (London, 1910), p. 2.

2. *Essays of George Eliot*, ed. Thomas Pinney (New York, 1963), p. 271.

3. George Eliot, *Middlemarch* (Cabinet edition, Edinburgh and London, 1877–80), ch. 21. Further references to this work are given in the text.

4. *American Heritage Dictionary of the English Language*, s.v. 'text'.

5. Her? After all, the fiction of the male narrator is still maintained in *Middlemarch*. To speak of the narrator as a 'he' allows the reader to keep firmly in mind the distinction between the author of the novel, Marian Evans, and the created role of the storyteller, George Eliot.

6. For the relation of Lydgate's researches to the science of Eliot's day, see W. J. Harvey, 'The Intellectual Background of the Novel', in *Middlemarch: Critical Approaches to the Novel*, ed. Barbara Hardy (London, 1967), pp. 25–37.

7. What, exactly, is the nature of the resemblance which binds together the members of this family and makes it seem of one genetic stock? Why, if Eliot's goal is to describe what is 'really there', objectively, must there be more than one model in order to create a total picture?

8. Friedrich Nietzsche, *Die Fröhliche Wissenschaft*, para. 228, in *Werke*, vol. 2, ed. Karl Schlecta (Munich, 1966), pp. 152–13; '... they lack eyes for seeing what is unique. Seeing things as similar and making things the same is the sign of weak eyes.' (*The Gay Science*, trans. Walter Kaufmann [New York, 1974], p. 212.)

9. Although several hypothetical originals, including G. H. Lewes, have been suggested for the 'eminent philosopher', N. H. Feltes argues persuasively that the philosopher was Herbert Spencer and that the image may be traced back from Spencer to a passage in Ruskin. See 'George Eliot's "Pier-Glass"; the Development of a Metaphor', *Modern Philology*, 67 (1969), 69–71.

10. The metaphor of the key, which I have borrowed for the language of the novel to use as language about the novel, contains exactly the ambiguity I am exploring here. A 'key' as in the 'Key to all Mythologies', is both an intrinsic pattern organising from within a large body of apparently heterogeneous material and at the same time something introduced from the outside which 'unlocks' an otherwise hidden pattern. A key is a formula which cracks a code, as when George Eliot in *Daniel Deronda* says, 'all meanings, we know, depend on the key of interpretation' (ch. 6). The meaning of a text is both intrinsic to that text and yet

present in it only when it is projected by a certain extrinsic set of assumptions about the code or 'key'. This shifting from intrinsic to extrinsic definitions of 'key' is present in the various meanings of the word, which include mechanical, architectural, musical, and botanical senses.

11. See N. N. Feltes, 'George Eliot's "Pier-Glass"' (details in note 9 above), p. 69, for a discussion of the passage from Ruskin's letter of February 1844 to the *Artist and Amateur's Magazine*, reprinted in *The Works of John Ruskin*, vol. 3, ed. E. T. Cook and Alexander Wedderburn (London, 1903), pp. 656–7.

12. In 'Narrative and History', *English Literary History*, 41 (1974), 455–73. I have also tried to indicate in this essay the alternative positive theories of history, of individual human life, and of the work of art with which Eliot, in *Middlemarch*, replaces the 'metaphysical' theories, governed by concepts of totality, of origin, of end, and of substantial analogy, which she so persuasively dismantles in the novel.

13. It is worth noting that George Eliot's rueful complaint about the proliferating contradictions of metaphor, which has arisen apropos of Tom Tulliver's difficulties in school, is followed almost immediately by an ostentatious and forceful metaphor, as if Eliot were compelled, in spite of herself, to demonstrate that we cannot say what a thing is except by saying that it is something else: 'At present, in relation to this demand that he should learn Latin declensions and conjugations, Tom was in a state of as blank unimaginativeness concerning the cause and tendency of his sufferings, as if he had been an innocent shrewmouse imprisoned in the split trunk of an ash-tree in order to cure lameness in cattle.'

5

George Eliot: 'The Wisdom of Balancing Claims'

D. A. MILLER

It was characteristic of Henry James's acuteness to see that *Middle-march* 'sets a limit to the development of the old-fashioned English novel'.[1] It was equally characteristic of his tact that he never went on to specify what sort of limit it set, or even on which side of the limit the novel ultimately came down: whether the limit was set by remaining – just barely – within the assumptions of traditional form, or by going beyond them to a point where their validity would seem challenged. James's remark suggests *Middlemarch* as an inevitable reference in our study of traditional form in the nineteenth-century novel. Even the ambiguity of his comment offers a useful preliminary formulation of the doubleness that shapes George Eliot's novel itself.

Middlemarch indeed oscillates in a curious and exemplary way: between a confident re-enactment of traditional form, in the magisterial manner of a *summa*, and an uneasy subversion of its habitually assumed validity, as though under the less magisterial pressure of a doubt. If we insist on the extent to which the novel retreads the itinerary of, say, *Emma*, we find ourselves embarrassed by those aspects of the text that put a question mark before its own traditional form.[2] Yet if we turn about and stress the novel's 'self-deconstructive' dimension, we are hard put to explain why its deconstructive insights – far from issuing in a novelistic form more fully commensurate with them – impede neither the rhetorical power with which traditional form is able to impose itself nor the earnest moral apology that is made for traditional-formal usages.[3] Moreover, if we allow its full ambiguity to the presence of both a traditional ground and a deconstructive abyss beyond its limits, we seem carried into further ambiguity over the possible meaning of their co-functioning. Does the novel intend to subject this traditional ground to a covert erosion, slyly destining it for the abyss below? or does the novel mean to use the abyss in a cautionary way, offering its sublime, vertiginous prospect only to frighten us back from it – back to safer, beaten ground whose value is proportionately enhanced by the danger of having strayed?

Like one of those optical drawings that won't resolve once for all into five cubes or six, a vase or two human profiles, *Middlemarch* seems to be traditional and to be beyond its limit, to subvert and to reconfirm the value of its traditional status. We shall explore the double valency of such a text as what matters most about it: not necessarily in the hope of giving its terms their proper balance (as though this were possible), far less of being able to favour one of them over the other, but with the suspicion that their full contradictory value may best define the novel's peculiar relationship to traditional form.

I have already charted what I think are the two basic requirements of traditional novelistic form: a moment of suspense and instability, and a moment of closure and resolved meaning. The first institutes the narratable disequilibrium, which the second converts back to a state of non-narratable quiescence. We might ask again our fundamental question: with what representations of content and value does *Middlemarch* motivate its constructional categories (non-narratability, narratability, closure)? In answer, however, the novel presents not merely a variety of different determinations, but what are actually different *systems* of determination. How the constructional categories are motivated depends on the level at which the story is being told. Three main levels of motivation easily stand out. The novelistic community (Hegel's world of 'maintaining individuals') views the story according to one scheme of reference and value; the protagonists (that world's 'historical individuals') perceive it according to another; and the narrator (would he be the providential *Geist*?) collaborates with his invented reader to tell it according to still another. The text pluralises the perspective from which traditional form is commonly perceived and delimited, offering not a single, univocal movement from the narratable to closure, but in effect three such movements. One recalls the virtual unanimity that obtained among levels of telling the story at the end of a Jane Austen novel: Emma finally came to share the narrator's view of her errancy, and even Mary Crawford ended up recognising 'the better taste acquired at Mansfield'. In *Middlemarch*, the different ways of perceiving and delimiting the story all conspire to identify what is, in terms of its main actions, *the same story*. Yet if they are narratologically identical, they remain to the end hermeneutically distinct. Each system of delimitation accounts for more or less the same events, but each system derives meaning from different sources and puts its stresses and values in different places.

This pluralism of perspectives that are conterminous but not covalent opens up some interesting possibilities. If one perspective (such as the narrator's) includes a consciousness of others, it may need to subvert or parody them, in order to maintain its difference by an effect of transcendence. Yet if despite its difference it shares a common structure with its rivals, it may be running the risk of self-subversion or self-parody in the very attempt to undercut them. The need to protect against this risk may even give rise to certain deflections or hesitations of aim. The main force of the pluralism in *Middlemarch*, however, is surely to make us aware of perspective itself. What traditional form shows us is no longer exhibited in a spirit of naïve realism, as simply what is there to be seen. Instead it must now be taken as a function of a perceiving system with its own desire, disguises, deletions, and disinterests, *which might have been organised otherwise*. One inroad, then, would be to follow the story of *Middlemarch* according to its three different tellings, its three uncannily synoptic gospels.

NARRATIVE ONE: THE COMMUNITY

'Sane people did what their neighbours did, so that if any lunatics were at large, one might know and avoid them.'[4] Here is the mechanism of social control that allows the community in *Middlemarch* to maintain itself. Here as well is the mechanism of narrative control that allows this community to function, in precise ways, like a traditional novel. The collective scenarios of society constitute the non-narratable equilibrium, and the violations of them (lunacy being only the most extreme form of exorbitancy) represent the narratable difference. This community/novel is apparently constructed to meet the requirements of an important task: to know the narratable in order to avoid it. It would designate a state of story-worthiness only to quarantine it elsewhere: anywhere but in the functioning of what the text ironically calls 'that beneficent harness of routine which enables silly men to live respectably and unhappy men to live calmly' (p. 720). The narratable is a paradoxical, ambivalent phenomenon. Much as the lunatic both affronts and reassures our own sense of mental health, the transgressions of routine both scandalise and ultimately confirm its normativeness.

[At this point, Miller expands his discussion of errant and conformist behaviour, focusing in particular on Dorothea's errant behaviour, which is seen as threatening because she seems to challenge the ideology of social routine. Lydgate also represents a pertinent difference, a perceptible threat, and therefore, not surprisingly, society 'conspires' against him. Miller then considers the characteristics of Bulstrode and Ladislaw.]

It is no accident that the four protagonists in the community (Lydgate, Bulstrode, Dorothea and Ladislaw) are made to leave town at the end of the novel: ritual sacrifices to the recovery of social routine. To be sure, the text gives to each case its own series of mediations, its own balance of choice and necessity, its own moral implications. *Middlemarch* is rightly praised for its ability to complicate the easy analogies that bind different characters together as a single dilemma. Yet even the manifold richness of the text in this respect passes comment on the social processes involved: for if the text's perception is subtle and discriminating, the community's conduct is generally blunt and insensitive. Virtually any kind of history is rejected from its bosom, whether the crimes of Bulstrode, the reforms of Lydgate and Ladislaw, or the imprudent marriages of Dorothea. The community levels their differences by subjecting them to the same fate of social exclusion. The town fathers 'decline to cooperate' with Bulstrode (p. 783); a 'general blackballing' is begun against Lydgate (p. 796); Sir James 'cannot bear to see [Dorothea] again', since Ladislaw 'is not a man we can take into the family' (p. 875, 876). Murder, meliorism and misalliance are made to look like equivalent threats to social well-being. The wholesale rejection of the narratable is excepted only in the case of Mary Garth and Fred Vincy, where the narratable has merely designed the all-but-routine logistical snags of an orthodox social settlement. No wonder that such low-degree, 'Trollopian' narratability is ultimately accommodated within the community: why *not* accommodate it? Even the extreme possibilities of Mary becoming a governess and Fred a genteel clergyman or wastrel mount no substantial challenge to the systematic 'way things are'. If the community seems eager to thwart Lydgate or Dorothea, it shows a surprisingly decent face (in Farebrother, Caleb Garth, Harriet Bulstrode) when it comes to helping this couple get settled. The novel's last scene presents a happy picture of their assimilation, in a sly salute to the only story that ends properly – in Middlemarch proper.

Much has needed to be scanted in this account of the community's telling of *Middlemarch*, but not so much, I hope, that its general correspondences with a certain kind of traditional novel are unclear. Socially given reality has the function of a non-narratable base from which narratable derogations – in the form of ideological threats – can be isolated. Its overriding imperative is self-recovery: to know the narratable in order not just to avoid it, but to void it entirely. Closure is made to seem like a straightforward exorcism rather than the culmination of a dialectical development – like Jane Austen's narrator, the community acknowledges no necessity behind the narratable moment. Unlike in Jane Austen, however, the bonus of such a moment once it is over is fully apparent: in an increased social cohesiveness ('There was hardly ever so much unanimity among them as in the opinion that Lydgate was an arrogant young fellow'); in a reconfirmed normativeness (Lydgate's 'pride must have a fall', Rosamond 'needed a lesson', 'late events . . . were likely to humble those who needed humbling'); and finally, in a renovated pedagogy for reproducing the community thus fortified in a younger generation.

> Sir James never ceased to regard Dorothea's second marriage as a mistake; and indeed this remained the tradition concerning it in Middlemarch, where she was spoken of to a younger generation as a fine girl who married a sickly clergyman, old enough to be her father, and in little more than a year after his death gave up her estate to marry his cousin – young enough to have been his son, with no property; and not well-born. Those who had not seen anything of Dorothea usually observed that she could not have been 'a nice woman', else she would not have married either the one or the other.
>
> (p. 806)

Yet the *Middlemarch* text provides a more complex account of the community telling than the latter is able (or willing) to give of itself. We are never allowed to give its claims the same validity, or take its proceedings with the same artlessness, as the community does.

'*Of course* all the world round Tipton would be out of sympathy with this marriage.' It would only be a slight exaggeration to say that the difference between the community's storytelling and the text's presentation of it turns wholly on the semantic status of that 'of course'. To the community, 'of course' means 'naturally', 'of necessity'; it points to a self-sustaining obviousness in social patterns. In the text, however, the dead metaphor is demonstrably revived into an actual if surreptitious cursiveness – routine, so to speak, would merely be a particularly well traversed route. As I have implicitly been arguing, moreover, to demonstrate that socially given reality is a *busy* quiescence, continually needing to reinvent itself, is already to betray its main assumptions. Once the non-narratable base is shown to be *produced*, to have a *dynamic* of self-maintenance, then a potential affinity with its narratable opposite begins to emerge. Indeed, it starts to seem as though such a non-narratable base existed only by virtue of suppressing and projecting its latent narratability.

Gossip offers a typically blinded form of this busy quiescence. What characterises gossip, after all, is that it never 'minds its own business'. Gossip is always about someone else, always oriented toward a story that both precedes its discourse and stands outside its frame. The opposition between someone else's story and its own discourse works to neutralise its activity, staged as mere observation. What keeps gossip from becoming the subject of a narrative is, precisely, the narrative that is the subject of gossip. One way not to *have* a story is to tell one about somebody who does: narration is a solid protection against the narratable. It is easy to see how the logic of gossip makes it the inevitable practice of a community that would remain unhistorical. Yet subversively, the text will sometimes suggest that gossip is part of the very story it is supposed to be merely telling. For example, the early gossip about Rosamond and Lydgate – relayed by Mrs Pymdale through Mrs Bulstrode to Rosamond and Lydgate themselves – actively helps to produce their marriage; far from simply observing narrative events, such gossip substantially shapes them. Despite the moral reserves that Mrs Bulstrode is ultimately capable of drawing on, she is never troubled by compunction about her interference here – has she even seen its decisiveness? To get the story straight, as she tries to do here, may successfully mask the act of straightening it out. Gossip easily thinks of itself as a more-or-less transparent medium for the stories of others. More interestingly, the text suggests that these stories may only be the most visible dimension of the community's own history, a history it never admits to having.

Middlemarch thus broaches the only scandal that its community shows no eagerness to bring to light: the story of the non-narratable. Most of the time, of course, such a story is not fully or even very overtly told by the novel; rather, its existence is argued for theoretically, in discreet but telling signs of its suppression. It is suggestive, for instance, that some 'strict constructionists' of community norms were formerly normbreakers. Maintaining individuals like the Cadwalladers and the Vincys may currently have no story, but they had one once upon a time. Mrs Cadwallader descended through her marriage. Mrs Vincy rose a little: both have become aggressively *bien-pensant* when it comes to arranging matches for others. The text subtly observes the way in which, late in the novel, the memory of the Cadwalladers' marriage threatens the judgment about to be made on Dorothea's: almost instantly, the disturbing recollection is reduced to orthodoxy (p. 877). It is instructive, too, to notice the potential narratability of social routine itself. The text presents a society of highly detailed differences (between sex roles, social classes, ranks in the medical hierarchy), and places it in a concretely realised historical frame (the Catholic Emancipation and the Reform Act at either end, the railroads coming in the middle). At moments even the community seems vaguely conscious of social contradiction and historical becoming: at Brooke's dinner party, in Dagley's tirade, in the peripheral struggles over national politics. Yet to see the rich narrative possibilities implied by social differentiation and historical time is also to see how reluctant the community is to exploit them. Social differences have been embalmed by everyday repetition, so that a field of potential contradictions capable of generating a history is effectively held at the level of patterns in a picture. An urban bourgeoisie is easily distinguished from a country aristocracy, but one inevitably thinks of a single Middlemarch community: the two social spheres are never shown to resist the general ideological coherence binding them – their actions may be different, but never contradictory. Similarly, the community makes every effort to avoid the history in which the text embeds it: Brooke is forcibly brought back to the fold, and the Reform (whose vicissitudes, in any case, have been carried mainly through the newspapers) is defeated. Like those archaic societies studied by Mircea Eliade, the community substitutes a myth of eternal return for a history of its development.[5]

In short, the text implies a potential narrative field always richer than the community's organisation of it, which is thus made to seem naïvely self-deceptive. Yet this naïveté also seems intrinsically more powerful than the text's strategy for exposing it, mainly because such exposure rarely has practical consequences in novelistic action. Here, for example, is the text's theory of what we *ought* to be finding in this community:

> Old provincial society had its share of this subtle movement: had not only its striking downfalls, its brilliant young professional dandies who ended by living up an entry with a drab and six children for their establishment, but also those less marked vicissitudes which are constantly shifting the boundaries of social intercourse, and begetting new consciousness of interdependence. Some slipped a little downward, some got higher footing; people denied aspirates, gained wealth, and fastidious gentlemen stood for boroughs; some were caught in political currents, some in ecclesiastical, and perhaps found themselves surprisingly grouped in consequence; while a few personages or families that stood with rock firmness amid all this fluctuation, were slowly presenting new aspects in spite of solidity, and altering with the double change of self and beholder. Municipal town and rural parish gradually made fresh threads of connection—gradually, as the old stocking gave way to the savings-bank, and the worship of the solar guinea became extinct, while squires and baronets, and even lords who had once lived blamelessly afar from the civic mind, gathered the faultiness of closer acquaintanceship. Settlers, too, came from distant counties, some with an alarming novelty of skill, others with an offensive advantage in cunning. In fact, much the same sort of movement and mixture went on in old England as we find in older Herodotus.
>
> (pp. 122–3)

The theory is remarkably barren, however, when we look for actual narrative developments that might confirm it. Mrs Cadwallader has slipped downward, Mrs Vincy gained a higher footing, only in a distant past; and Mr Brooke is 'caught in political currents' and 'surprisingly grouped in consequence' only for a time – up to a certain point. Whether with 'an alarming novelty of skill' (Lydgate) or 'an offensive advantage in cunning' (Bulstrode), settlers are consistently never allowed to settle here. Those who dare to shift 'the boundaries of social intercourse' invariably fail, and if they find a 'new consciousness of interdependence', they must go enjoy it elsewhere – in London, like Dorothea and Will. Even the coming of the railroad produces no raised consciousness that we see. The story of the 'movement and mixture' behind a facade of 'rock firmness' exists mainly as a theoretical potential. It is understandable why the community needs to hide this story from itself, but why the text discreetly maintains it *only as a potential* – in discourse

never really supported by narrative action – requires some account-
ing for.

It might be helpful to consider a less discreet, less merely theoretical
demonstration of the bad faith of a non-narratable community:
Zola's *Le Ventre de Paris*. Here too a community wants to suppress
its story-worthiness. Here too only the outsider Florent, a returned
political exile, carries its telling of events. *Le Maigre* in a community
of *les Gras*, he alone is made to assume the burden of narrative,
history, difference – a burden negativity that, typically, gets him
redeported. The collective scapegoating, presided over by his 'respectable' sister-in-law Lisa, would seem to celebrate a community
routine as regular as a healthy digestion. 'Les ventres crevèrent d'une
joie mauvaise.' Yet the 'joy' is 'wicked' not because Florent doesn't
have a story, but because the others do as well. Even the militantly
normative Lisa is involved in narrative actions that have nothing to
do with Florent – like, most notably, her subterranean flirtation with
Marjolin, which ends in his near rape of her and her near murder of
him. Marjolin survives an idiot, and Lisa can bury the episode in
complete silence. 'Elle ne se reprochait rien. Elle avait agi en femme
honnête.'[6] Clearly, however, Florent seems a scapegoat for more
stories than his own. A mechanism of Freudian projection obviously
governs the formation of a non-narratable base and a narratable
difference: the base is nothing more than the difference disguised,
cast out as an opposite. Lisa's telling of *Le Ventre de Paris* may be
efficacious (Florent *is* redeported), but it is also fully a sham, a way
not to tell her own story.

In *Middlemarch*, equivalents of Lisa's 'own story' are missing. The
differences that the community nullifies into a storyless backdrop are
practically voided by the novelist as well. Mrs Cadwallader's 'life
was rurally simple, quite free from secrets either foul, dangerous, or
otherwise important' (p. 83). 'The Vincys had their weaknesses, but
then they lay on the surface: there was never anything bad to be
"found out" concerning them' (p. 799). And if characters like Celia
and Sir James have a story, it is casually dropped in subordinate
clauses ('Celia, who had lately had a baby'), as though snuffed out by
its own predictability (p. 516). Conversely, the community identifies
the very stories that the text, too, wishes to tell (of Dorothea,
Lydgate, Ladislaw, Bulstrode). The text corrects, enriches, even
subsumes the content of the community's narrative-formation, but it
is never quite willing to break with its fundamental form. Certainly,
we shall see, other perspectives are imposed on this narrative-

formation; other, richer meanings are derived from it. Yet these other perspectives and meanings are complicitous with the community's perception, if only in this one crucial sense: 'though of different minds, they concur in action'. Far from opening up an anarchy in the perceptual field, the practice of perspectivism in *Middlemarch* more basically works to avoid it. Indeed, it might be thought of as the most sophisticated reality effect of all. We are familiar with how, in life, various perspectives of an object come to be 'proof' of its reality; how, in novels generally, different views of a character may suggest the depth of a full existence; how, in this novel in particular, weak differences unite to confirm strong ones. Similarly, though other levels of telling significantly overdetermine the community's narrative-formation, they ultimately corroborate the 'reality' to which it gives rise: these stories, these non-stories.

Critics such as Arnold Kettle and Quentin Anderson have identified this complicity as a simple failure of imagination.[7] It seems to me more accurately thought of as an ambivalence of imagination. For the text resists complying with the Middlemarch telling, if only through its subversive insights into the bad faith underlying it. The community's narrative-formation is reduced to its source in the need to protect a fantasised self-image, and on theoretical grounds, the authenticity of every aspect of this formation is put into question. The non-narratable base is merely a 'forgetting', the narrative difference is only a conspicuously partial fraction of what it might have been; and closure is only the tautological extension of these initial sleights of hand: a pretended, effective rather than plausible, ending of difference and history. Yet in so far as these have been insights about novelistic form, the text is reluctant to imagine a novel commensurate with them. Or perhaps better, the text is willing *only* to imagine such a novel, not to realise it. A genuinely open history, a continuity of narratable differences, a full suspension of closure: these are only ghostly possibilities that, as it represents the community's telling, the text glimpses rather than grasps. Like good ghosts, however, they persist in haunting the novelist's house of fiction – as though they knew how spooky an old-fashioned English stately home could be.

From D. A. Miller, *Narrative and its Discontents: Problems of Closure in the Traditional Novel* (Princeton, 1981), pp. 107–11 and 121–9.

NOTES

[D. A. Miller's essay, which is extracted from the first part of a long chapter on George Eliot in his book *Narrative and its Discontents*, develops directly from the previous essay by J. Hillis Miller. He begins by accepting that Hillis Miller's 'self-deconstructive' view of the novel has a great deal of force, but points out that this sense of the novel is difficult to reconcile with the feeling most readers have that they are reading a rhetorically forceful novel. Miller then explores the ambivalence of the novel, how it seems both to subvert and reconfirm. A great deal of recent criticism has focused on this dual aspect of the novel, but it is interesting at this point to see the manner in which Miller develops his argument. His approach might be described as 'narratology': he works from ideas about how narrative functions. He is particularly interested in the tension between suspense and closure in fiction – how there is a 'narratable disequilibrium' and set against this a state of 'non-narratable quiescence' – and how *Middlemarch* as a novel exploits and explores this tension in a complex way. This leads on to an interest in how *Middlemarch* relates to the period in which it was produced. Ed.]

1. Henry James, unsigned review, *Galaxy*, 15 (1873), reprinted in *George Eliot: The Critical Heritage*, ed. David Carroll (London, 1971), p. 359.

2. A perfect instance would be Arnold Kettle, *An Introduction to the English Novel*, vol. 1 (London, 1951). Kettle begins his chapter on *Middlemarch* by claiming that the novel 'is the same kind of novel as *Emma* . . . George Eliot extends the method of Jane Austen, but does not substantially alter it' (p. 160). This perspective governs and simplifies his entire reading of the novel.

3. This seems to me the failing of J. Hillis Miller's two articles, 'Narrative and History' and 'Optic and Semiotic in *Middlemarch*'. Despite it, the articles remain our most sophisticated treatment of the novel's own sophistication, and I shall later, by a long and qualifying detour, want to rejoin some of their conclusions.

4. George Eliot, *Middlemarch* (Penguin edition, Harmondsworth, 1965), p. 31. All quotations from *Middlemarch* are designated in the text by their page number in this edition.

5. Mircea Eliade, *Le Mythe de l'éternel retour: archétypes et répétition* (Paris, 1949).

6. Emile Zola, *Le Ventre de Paris*, in *Les Rougon-Macquart*, vol. 1, ed. Armand Lanoux and Henri Mitterand (Paris, 1963–7), pp. 888 and 796.

7. Arnold Kettle, *An Introduction to the English Novel*, vol. 1 (London, 1951), p. 171; and Quentin Anderson, 'George Eliot in *Middlemarch*', in *The Pelican Guide to English Literature*, vol. 6, ed. Boris Ford (Harmondsworth, 1963–7), pp. 274–93.

6

Organic Fictions: 'Middlemarch'

SUZANNE GRAVER

The novel's mourning of Dorothea's failure to discover and mark out for herself the life to which she aspired resounds through Prelude and Finale — through origins and end. The Prelude takes as a starting point 'the indefiniteness' of woman's nature, opposing to it the 'limits of variation' commonly ascribed to 'the social lot of women'.[1] Dorothea, attempting to break free of those limits, is like the cygnet of the Prelude — a young swan 'reared uneasily among the ducklings in the brown pond' who 'never finds the living stream in fellowship with its own oary-footed kind'. The brown pond is social convention; the cygnet all women who cherish, most of them silently, high aspirations. In the Finale, the stream of her life is described as a river, but it is a river whose strength is broken, spending 'itself in channels which had no great name on the earth.' It is broken metaphorically by Cyrus, a ruler known to be both a liberator and a conqueror. So marriage for Dorothea, whether to a liberator (Ladislaw) or to an oppressor (Casaubon) diverts the strength of 'her full nature' (Finale, p. 613).

Marriage in her world was 'technically styled coverture' to signify 'that husband and wife are treated at Common Law as one person indivisible, the personal and separate existence of the wife being legally considered as absorbed and consolidated in that of her husband, from which it is judicially indistinguishable, and under whose wing, protection, and cover she acts'. The definition, from John J. S. Wharton's *Laws Relating to the Women of England*, makes clear why contract in marriage meant at best not identity but absorption of interests for women. The same point is made by Barbara Bodichon, who writes that the wife's 'existence is entirely absorbed in that of her husband', when she explains marriage as coverture.[2] Similarly, George Eliot describes Dorothea as 'a creature absorbed into the life of another' even after her marriage to Will (Finale, p. 611).

In addition to these parallels in the use of the word *absorbed*, the river image of the Finale echoes a passage Wharton cites to note the origins of the term *coverture*:

> When a small brooke, or little river, incorporated with Rhodanus, Humber, or the Thames, the poore rivulet loseth her name; it is carried and recarried with the new associate; it beareth no sway, it possesseth nothing during coverture. A woman, as soone as she is married, is called *covert*, in Latine, *nupta*, that is, vailed, as it were, clouded and overshadowed, &c.; she hath lost her streame, she is continually *sub potestate viri*.[3]

Sir Henry Maine as well laments the '*Patria Potestas*' given to husbands by English Common Law with no regard to *jus naturale*:

> Modern jurisprudence, forged in the furnace of barbarian conquest, and formed by the fusion of Roman jurisprudence with patriarchal usage, has absorbed, among its rudiments, much more than usual of those rules concerning the position of women which belong peculiarly to an imperfect civilisation.[4]

Summarising Maine's point in her notebook, George Eliot wrote simply: 'The modern position of woman chiefly determined by barbarian elements' ('*Middlemarch*' *Notebooks*, p. 205). In her novel she transforms Maine's entire argument ... into terms that summarise the life of Dorothea (née Brooke):

> Certainly those determining acts of her life were not ideally beautiful. They were the mixed result of young and noble impulse struggling amidst the conditions of an imperfect social state.
>
> (Finale, p. 612)

Given those conditions, the wonder is that Dorothea had any life left to contribute to 'the growing good of the world'. Dorothea is stymied; and among her neighbours and friends 'no one stated exactly what else that was in her power she ought rather to have done'. The form George Eliot gives to the formlessness of Dorothea's life brilliantly uncovers the absence of social structures adequate to individual life; it also challenges the reader to halt the arrest.

Of the three love stories central to the novel, one couple does achieve a gratifying marriage. Content to play a traditional role, Fred and Mary find the existing forms adequate though they had not seemed so at the start. In chapter 52 of Book Five, Fred and Mary are still suffering from the dead hand of Featherstone, and again property rights and a despotic will are the disabling force. But even in Book Five, thanks to Farebrother's self-sacrificing intercession, Featherstone's grasp begins to loosen. By the end of the novel, Mary and Fred finally do marry, creating a 'solid mutual happiness' (Finale, p. 608). Like Mary's parents, the Garths, the younger couple seem a happy throwback. But just as *Middlemarch* disputes the unifying force of any single system, so its critique of each system carries qualifications. In this case the 'limits of variation' include the Freds and Marys, but that they are content with their traditional roles does not mean others can be or should be. The Finale makes this point, too, by way of a few gentle jibes: Mary's *Stories of Great Men* is published by Gripp & Co.; and Letty, her younger sister, is given an entire paragraph to dispute their brother's belief that 'girls were good for less than boys'. More importantly, within the overall structure of Finale and novel alike, the admonitory stories of the Casaubons and the Lydgates carry far greater force of implication than does the benign accommodation Fred and Mary make.

In the last chapter of Book Five, the dead hand of marriage and property rights returns with a vengeance. Raffles for the first time confronts Bulstrode, making known Bulstrode's wholesale betrayal of his first wife. As the epigraph to the chapter suggests, the perversion of the organic is so great as to make sinister and ironic the process 'whereby the belief and the conduct are wrought into mutual sustainment', a union that rests on a 'living myriad of hidden suckers'. Those suckers become continually more diseased as the novel progresses, culminating in Bulstrode's murder of Raffles. While the second Mrs Bulstrode remains loyal, she must endure exile and 'withering' with him (VIII, 85, 602–3). The reader also discovers in chapter 53 what Bulstrode himself does not yet know: his first wife was Ladislaw's grandmother. With this closing revelation, Book Five is the first to interweave all the major plot strands and to relate virtually all the major characters through kinship.

That the book called 'The Dead Hand' reveals these connections suggests how fatal to mutual interest many of them are. Marriage is at their centre, as it is throughout the novel, but a good many social issues and institutions are implicated along the way – class, church, property, and progeny, among others. Most often the criticism of these other social forms is perfectly integrated into the marriage theme. Will's anger, for instance, at 'those barriers of habitual sentiment which are more fatal to the persistence of mutual interest than all the distance between Rome and Britain' is triggered by the 'prejudices about rank and status' that keep him from Dorothea (V, 43, 318); and Mary's attack on men who ' "represent Christianity— as if it were an institution for getting up idiots genteely" ', is motivated by her resistance to Fred's becoming a clergyman (V, 52, 379). Matrimonial government figures as well in the treatment of the two other social issues – medical and political reform – which after marriage are the most important in the fifth book and in the novel. In Lydgate's case, as we have seen, the connection is entirely ironical, effecting a disjunction between inward and outward. At the same time, and again for reasons both public and private, Lydgate's struggle for medical reform works on its own grounds to separate inward from outward.

The major subject of chapters 44 and 45 is the opposition in Middlemarch to Lydgate as medical man set on reforming 'doctrine and practice' (V, 44, 321). Lydgate's arrogance, his position as an outsider, and his alliance with Bulstrode make him an easy target. However, when the doctors of Middlemarch join forces against him, creating out of their aversion a community of interests, the personal factors are revealed to be as much an excuse for their animosity as a cause. As the other medical men recognise only too well, Lydgate's fight for reform is a fight against the ' "*rationale* of the system" '. For them, Lydgate is far more than a rival. He is a challenge to the prevailing system, a man ' "guilty" ' of coming ' "among the members of his profession with innovations which are a libel on their time-honoured procedure" '. His plans for reform – including his medical research, hospital superintendence, and practical criticism (as in his refusal to dispense drugs) – cause his colleagues to charge him with inattention to medical 'etiquette' and 'breaches of medical propriety'. At best, the medical men complain among themselves of an ' "ostentation of reform" ' in Lydgate but ' "no real amelioration" ' (V, 45, 327–30). At worst, they feed by innuendo the ignorance of the townspeople by encouraging them to think of Lydgate as a 'charlatan' engaged in 'reckless innovation for the sake of noise' (p. 332).

From both sides, then, from the professional men and from the laity, Lydgate encounters in Middlemarch not the congenial work-place he had hoped to find but the 'community of vice' alluded to in the epigraph to chapter 45. 'Many different lights' and 'every social shade' are brought to bear upon Lydgate in this chapter, but they nearly all serve to confirm 'the public sentiment, of which the unanimity at Dollop's was an index' (pp. 323–4). That Dollop's, the public house, is located in Slaughter Lane serves nicely to gauge the quality of the public sentiment.

At this point in the novel, Lydgate, taking solace from his identi-fication with Vesalius, is determined to weather the hostility. '"They will not drive me away"', he vows. '"Things can't last as they are: there must be all sorts of reform soon"' (V, 45, 332–3). Things of course don't last as they are, but there is no reform: Lydgate is driven away and things become again as they were. As chapter 45 fore-warns, when Farebrother cautions Lydgate not to get 'tied' to Bulstrode and not to become hampered by money matters, Lydgate's complicity in his own defeat is great. But so is the town's. When Lydgate's ties subsequently cause him to be implicated in Bulstrode's crime, once again the discussion at Dollop's exemplifies a 'type of what was going on in all Middlemarch circles' (*Quarry*, p. 640; VII, 71, 531).[5] Public sentiment leads this time to the town meeting, where discussion of one 'sanitary question' – the threat of cholera – quickly gives way to another, the blight of Bulstrode. Lydgate, the man who would be healer, is thought to be part of the disease. If the town's judgment is to some degree sound, the public sentiment is nonetheless tainted. As Lydgate puts it: '"There is often something poisonous in the air of public rooms"' (VIII, 74, 547). As the entire novel testifies, whenever consensus consists of hostility not sym-pathy, poison is in the air.

'"Most people"', Lydgate complains, '"never consider that a thing is good to be done unless it is done by their own set"' (V, 44 321). Ladislaw, for much the same reason, says: '"If everybody pulled for his own bit against everybody else, the whole question would go to tatters"' (V, 46, 336). The one finds his image of organic wholeness in living tissue, the other in the body politic. Like Lydgate, Ladislaw in Book Five has a certain optimism: '"Things will grow and ripen as if it were a comet year"' (V, 46, 336). The 'things' he has in mind concern the Reform Bill. Because parliamentary legislation is contract writ large, that the question of Reform should be reduced to tatters testifies more directly than do the marital disabilities, or the consensus of hostility suffered by Lydgate, to

George Eliot's sense of the precariousness of revisionary social organicism.

Again, the nature of existing institutions is very much at issue. The pending dissolution of Parliament – evidence of a government pulled apart, not together, by the national struggle for Reform – is mentioned so often in Book Five as to become a leitmotif.[6] At the same time, in chapters 46 and 51, the reconstructive effort is closely examined. As Ladislaw tries to teach Brooke, it is the '"balance of the constitution"', or the balance of power, that needs to be changed. In good organicist fashion, Ladislaw makes his ideal the balancing of different class interests and claims, but the response he receives suggests how difficult or impossible this will be to achieve. His rival, the editor of the *Trumpet*, attacks him for casting '"reflections on solid Englishmen generally"', and for speechifying 'by the hour against institutions "which had existed when he was in his cradle"' (V, 46, 337–9). Partisan newspapers, political parties, geographical situation, social set: all suggest division rather than community of interests.

Chapters 46 and 51 also reveal how Will's ideal itself participates in the haphazard and tentative. He stumbles into his political career from a desire to be in the neighbourhood of Dorothea. The work turns out to fit: 'The easily-stirred rebellion in him helped the glow of public spirit'; but the congruence is accidental (V, 46, 338). His own attitudes, moreover, are far from stable. He is by turns ardent, dreamy, sceptical, practical, cynical; doubtful about whether the 'right side' will win, and repelled by the 'dirty-handed' business on both sides (V, 51, 368).

When Ladislaw engages in political debate with Lydgate in chapter 46, Lydgate charges him with '"crying up a measure as if it were a universal cure, and crying up men who are a part of the very disease that wants curing."' Pointing to decomposition, not wholeness, Lydgate adds: '"You go against rottenness, and there is nothing more thoroughly rotten than making people believe that society can be cured by a political hocus-pocus."' If Lydgate seems to be accusing Ladislaw of the very charlatanism for which he was himself being attacked, the two are nonetheless on good terms, in part because Lydgate is well aware of the parallel obstacles they face. Ladislaw, furthermore, does not entirely disagree with Lydgate's analysis. What he questions are the conclusions: '"But your cure must begin somewhere"', he tells Lydgate, '"Put it that a thousand things which debase a population can never be reformed without this particular reform to begin with."' For Ladislaw, the '"whole question"' dissolves quickly into parts; for Lydgate it leads to 'seeing himself checkmated' because he too, as he knows, has nothing to work with but imperfect parts (V, 46, 341).

The immediate undermining of the 'whole question' of Reform is completed in chapter 51. Brooke's buffoonish performance at the hustings, combined with the 'diabolical procedure' set up by the opposing party, confirms all Lydgate's suspicions and Ladislaw's worst fears (V, 51, 370). That these events are to be taken as no chance matter the epigraph to chapter 51 makes clear:

> Party is Nature too, and you shall see
> By force of Logic how they both agree:
> The Many in the One, the One in Many:
> All is not Some, nor Some the same as Any: ...

Just as the ventriloquist turns Brooke's speech to mockery, so the epigraph takes the language of organicism and turns it to parody. Like Brooke, the 'Many in the One' and the 'One in Many' rise in this novel only in effigy.

Still, 'All is not Some'. The 'some' of the book of 'The Dead Hand' signifies widespread organic dysfunction in individuals and in the institutions regulating their lives ... the community of Middlemarch exhibits stasis or arrest. But George Eliot's study of provincial life also alludes from Middlemarch to the world beyond. In the closing portions of the Finale, municipality, nation, and world to a large extent supplant the local and the provincial. The standard of value changes along with the geography. Community becomes a matter of consciousness more or less independent of time and place.

The resistance of traditional community to change and the need to break free from provincial boundaries – from hereditary custom, habitual practice, and inherited institutions – are suggested all the way through the novel, in part by locating the desire for reform in characters who are outsiders. Those who most disapprove of present conditions are newcomers: Dorothea objects to woman's lot, Lydgate to the medical system, and Ladislaw to social and political institutions. Their final return to the world beyond Middlemarch speaks to the limits of provincial life, but it carries also some new affirmations.

In the case of Will, the closing makes good to some extent what seemed in Book Five to be merely a fantasy. 'Public life' does become 'wider and more national' (V, 51, 372). He happily overturns Brooke's wish and prediction: '"I can't help wishing somebody had a pocket-borough to give you, Ladislaw. You'd never get elected, you know"' (V, 46, 337). But Will would not have been elected had he remained in Middlemarch. As if to make this point, the last chapter closes before the first Reform Bill has been passed. By the time of the Finale, however, two Reform bills have become national law. That Will should be returned to Parliament 'by a constituency who paid his expenses' anticipates future reforms (Finale, p. 611). So, in a larger sense, does Will's life in London. Married to Dorothea, and serving as a 'public man', he comes closer than any other character to fulfilling a telos that is both individual and social.

Will is himself a reformer, moreover, in still another way. He prides himself on the 'sense of belonging to no class' (V, 46, 338). All the characters in the novel who would be reformers are required in some way to break caste, but Will's defection is the most complete. He has, in fact, the marks of being a member of what George Eliot, in her review of Riehl, described as a new Fourth Estate. Composed of 'day-labourers with the quill', it seemed to Riehl a quintessential sign of the decomposition of organic society.[7] In *Middlemarch* George Eliot portrays the decomposition even while she begins to reconstruct the parts.

But the parts are at best incomplete. In the novel, dynamic change is initiated by the estranged and the displaced, and the changes themselves call forth reservations. 'Will became an ardent public man', the Finale tells us, 'working well in those times when reforms were begun with a young hopefulness of immediate good which has been much checked in our days' (p. 610). Legislation, according to revisionary social organicism, is one of the major agencies by which law is brought into harmony with individual needs and society. In *Middlemarch* such harmony is yet to be seen. Will's inadequacies of character – his dilettantism, moments of cruelty, extravagant flights of idealism – speak of a world in which reform and reformer alike are far from perfect or complete. The fragility of George Eliot's affirmation may be seen as well, though probably not by her intention, in the incomplete definition of Will's character. In addition, though Will away from Middlemarch leads a full and fruitful life, for the Bulstrodes expulsion means a life of sad exile, while for Lydgate the diminished life he leads elsewhere comes to much the same result as being swallowed up whole by Middlemarch.

While the Finale's portrait of Will calls attention to national political reform, the farewell to Dorothea celebrates an individual's private contribution to the growing good of the world. Given the structure of values George Eliot brings to the idea of moral evolution, Will's concrete accomplishments can but take second place to Dorothea's 'incalculably diffusive' effect. As represented in the novel, the principle of political reform constitutes only a single 'channel'; Dorothea's 'good', innumerable 'channels' (V, 51, 373; Finale, p. 613). But the price she pays is high – nothing less than the breaking and spending of her nature. Testifying not to organic wholeness, but to the incompleteness of women's lives, qualification and affirmation exist in the Finale, as in Dorothea's telos, side by side.

This incompleteness creates in Dorothea, as it did in Maggie, and in their creator, an emphasis of want. In *Middlemarch*, it takes its most passionate form in Dorothea's visionary yearning for community. 'The sense of connection with a manifold pregnant existence had to be kept up painfully as an inward vision, instead of coming from without in claims that would have shaped her energies', we are told at the moment that Dorothea, just returned from her honeymoon with Casaubon, realises her marriage has brought not liberation from the 'gentlewoman's world' but further and more 'stifling oppression' (III, 28, 202). In the closing book, Dorothea again rescues herself from intense despair, caused this time by her misapprehension of Will's relation to Rosamond, and does so once more by way of inward vision. A glimpse of distant figures – 'a man with a bundle on his back and a woman carrying her baby' – is transformed by her consciousness into an image of 'the largeness of the world and the manifold wakings of men to labour and endurance'. The transformation represents a great moment of awakening for herself as well:

> She was a part of that involuntary, palpitating life, and could neither look out on it from her luxurious shelter as a mere spectator, nor hide her eyes in selfish complaining.
>
> (VIII, 80, 578)

This awakening leads to the 'self-subduing act of fellowship' that brings her into communion with Rosamond and Lydgate, leading in turn to the restoration of her faith in Will.

The controlled nature of the affirmation, however, reveals that George Eliot does not yield in *Middlemarch*, as she had in *The Mill*, to her own emphasis on want. But neither, as a result, is she able to affirm organic wholeness through community. Dorothea never finds the comprehensive outward shaping energy she seeks; the 'loving heart-beats' of the Prelude's 'foundress of nothing' continue to tremble 'after an unattained goodness'. Her sense of 'manifold pregnant existence' is accompanied by the feeling that 'all existence seemed to beat with a lower pulse than her own' (III, 28, 202). Only by an abnormally rapid or violent beating of her own heart is she able to bring the outer pulse into any kind of congruence with the inner. The very language of the affirmation – 'she was a part of that involuntary *palpitating* life' – incorporates organic dysfunction.

From Suzanne Graver, *George Eliot and Community: A Study in Social Theory and Fictional Form* (Berkeley and Los Angeles, 1984), pp. 215–24.

NOTES

[Suzanne Graver, in *George Eliot and Community: A Study in Social Theory and Fictional Form*, explores the concept of community in Victorian England, with a particular emphasis on the competing claims of communal interests and individualism (an issue which, as we have seen, is always central in discussions of George Eliot). She rejects the approach taken by J. Hillis Miller, a reading which, she argues, 'supposes the undermining of all truths . . .'. She agrees with him that 'the novel radically questions the idea of organic unity in society', but, unlike Miller, she also argues that '*Middlemarch* is aesthetically an organic whole, and that it is unified precisely because it self-consciously questions the idea of organic community. Whatever affirmations take place remain tentative, partial, or incomplete.' Graver, then, is a critic who looks at the novel in its historical context, seeing the way in which it articulates the dilemmas of its age. In this extract from her book, Graver focuses on the life Dorothea ends up living as the wife of Will Ladislaw, emphasising how the novel combines a movement towards fusion with the uncovering of yet further conflict. All references – they are given by book, chapter, and page numbers – are to the Riverside edition, edited by G. S. Haight (Boston, 1956). Ed.]

1. John Stuart Mill speaks in *The Subjection of Women* (1869) of the 'extraordinary susceptibility of human nature to external influences, and the extreme variableness of those of its manifestations which are supposed to be most universal and uniform' (in *Essays on Sex Equality: John Stuart Mill and Harriet Taylor Mill*, ed. Alice S. Rossi [Chicago, 1970], p. 149). Just as Eliot's passage seems to echo Mill, so does it also (as Gillian Beer notes in 'Beyond Determinism: George Eliot and Virginia Woolf', in *Women Writing and Writing About Women*, ed. Mary Jacobus [London and New York, 1979], pp. 80–99) hold out a challenge to Darwin.

2. J. J. S. Wharton, *An Exposition of the Laws Relating to the Women of England* (London, 1853), pp. 311–12; Barbara Leigh Smith Bodichon, *A Brief Summary in Plain Language of the Most Important Laws Concerning Women* (London, 1854), p. 6. [On George Eliot's respect for the work of Bodichon and Wharton, see chapter 4 of Graver's book. Ed.]

3. J. J. S. Wharton, *An Exposition of the Laws Relating to the Women of England* (London, 1853), p. 312, n. (a). The passage is from a seventeenth-century legal text, *The Lawes Resolutions of Womens Rights: Or, The Lawes Provision for Women. A Methodicall Collection of such Statutes and Customes, with the Cases, Opinions, Arguments and points of Learning in the Law, as doe properly concerne Women* (London, 1632), pp. 124–5. I am indebted to Thomas E. Foster, LL.B., for locating the source from which Wharton quotes.

4. Henry Maine, *Ancient Law: Its Connection with the Early History of Society and its Relation to Modern Ideas* (first published 1861, New York, 1906), p. 151.

5. A. T. Kitchel, *George Eliot's Quarry for Middlemarch* (Berkeley and Los Angeles, 1950), p. 640.

6. See openings of chapters 46, 50, and 51 in *Middlemarch*, and closings of chapters 47 and 49.

7. See *Essays of George Eliot*, ed. Thomas Pinney (New York, 1963), pp. 294–5.

7

'Middlemarch': An Experiment in Time

SALLY SHUTTLEWORTH

The problems George Eliot encountered in unifying *Felix Holt* seemed to renew her determination to explore fully the social issues of organicism. The themes that, in her earlier novels, had become evident only during the course of the narrative are deliberately asserted in the Prelude to *Middlemarch*. Dorothea's story is that of 'spiritual grandeur ill-matched with the meanness of opportunity'; her goal, the 'rapturous consciousness of life beyond self'.[1] Dorothea exemplifies perfectly the organic ideal: she strives for a form of personal fulfilment which would transcend egoism and integrate individual desire with social demands. The thematic clarity of the novel's introduction does not herald, however, a simplistic social vision. *Middlemarch* possesses neither the political crudeness of *Felix Holt* nor the correlated naïve idealisation of 'woman's lot'. It offers no simple endorsement of theories of organic social harmony. Rather, like the earlier novels *The Mill on the Floss* and *Romola* that also took a woman as their main protagonist, it explores the complexities and contradictions within organicist social theory.

The Prelude poses the question of how originality can survive within an environment whose essence, as the title suggests, is its middlingness. The question is not, however, an innocent one. The form in which the problem is expressed also defines the terms of its ideal resolution. These 'later-born Theresas', the narrator observes, 'were helped by no coherent social faith and order which could perform the function of knowledge for the ardently willing soul'

(Prelude, I, 2). The passage is not simply a lament for a departed era; it simultaneously defines the values that will structure the narrative and the model of social and individual development to which George Eliot adheres. Both are drawn from an organicist perspective. The perfect state will be one in which there is no disjunction between inner consciousness and the external social medium. In *Middlemarch*, however, George Eliot applies the ideal of organic union between the individual and society to a situation that exposes its poverty. Her uncertainty about this ideal had led in *Felix Holt* to a split within the novel: a radical division between the hopeless negativity of Mrs Transome's life, and the optimistic idealisation of Felix. In *Middlemarch* it leads, not to internal division, but to a greater complexity in social vision, narrative technique and structure. Faced with apparent irreconcilable contradictions within the traditional organic social model, George Eliot turned to contemporary theories in biological science and social philosophy for the principles that would structure her narrative.

Middlemarch is a work of experimental science: an examination of the 'history of man' under the 'varying experiments of Time' (Prelude, I, 1).[2] In *Adam Bede*, the scientific methodology of natural history had sustained the novel's static vision of social order. George Eliot brings to *Middlemarch*, however, a more questioning social vision; the Middlemarch of the Prelude is neither a static nor a harmoniously integrated society. The role of natural historian, passively transcribing a given order, will no longer suffice. George Eliot turns instead to the more dynamic methodology of experimental biology, a stance which receives paradigmatic expression in the novel in the research of Lydgate.[3] *Middlemarch* is the first novel in which science is treated as an explicit theme, and in the long discussions of Lydgate's methods and beliefs one can discern George Eliot's reflections on her own assumptions and procedures.[4]

Speaking as an experimental scientist, Lydgate summarily dismisses Farebrother's practice of natural history. He was, he declares, 'early bitten with an interest in structure' (ch. 17, I, 262). This interest in structure is expressed in his belief that living bodies 'are not associations of organs which can be understood by studying them first apart, and then as it were federally' (ch. 15, I, 223–4). Though offered only as a biological observation, Lydgate's statement in fact holds the key to George Eliot's social theory and narrative practice in *Middlemarch*. The natural historian looks at society as a collection of individuals that can be viewed first separately, and then federally, but the experimental scientist challenges this conception of individual autonomy. The characters in *Middlemarch* cannot be abstracted out from the life-processes of the town. As George Eliot tries to suggest through the complex narrative organisation of her novel, each part of Middlemarch life is related to every other part; individual identity is not only influenced by the larger organism, it is actively defined by it.

On a more fundamental level, Lydgate's theory of organic inter-dependence also affects George Eliot's conception of realism. The natural historian's function is to label and classify the individual components of a fixed reality; conceptions of dynamic interdepend-ence, however, undermine that possibility. As the experimental physiologist Claude Bernard argued, to try to discover physiological properties by isolating organs would be like trying to determine the difference between comedy and tragedy by seeing which has more 'a's and 'b's:

> En effet, les lettres ne sont rien par elles-mêmes, elles ne signifient quelque chose que par leur groupement sous telle ou telle forme qui donne un mot de telle ou telle signification. Le mot lui-même est un élément composé qui prend une signification spéciale par son mode de groupement dans la phrase, et la phrase, à son tour, doit concourir avec d'autres à l'expression complète de l'idée totale du sujet. Dans les matières organiques, il y a des éléments simples, communs, qui ne prenent une signification spéciale que par leur mode de groupement.[5]

The linguistic analogy is peculiarly apt. Ideas of organic interdepend-ence challenge equally empiricism in science and naïve realism in art. There can be no one-to-one correspondence between sign and signified, since meaning, like organic life, is a product of a total system. G. H. Lewes extends Bernard's analogy to illustrate why the new science must move beyond the empiricism of natural history to the realm of ideal construction: 'It is through the manifold ideal constructions of the Possible that we learn to appreciate the Actual. Facts are mere letters which have their meaning only in the words they form; and these words again have their meaning, not in them-selves alone but in their positions in the sentence.'[6] The function of the scientist is no longer simply to transcribe the 'real'. Following the theory of organic interdependence, observations only possess meaning when placed in an ideally constructed framework. George Eliot's narrative practice in *Middlemarch* accords with these princi-ples. She no longer adheres to the naïve realism of *Adam Bede* with its apologetic image of the defective mirror, but actively accepts the creative role of author. Dexterously interweaving many strands of material, she uses the resources of both myth and symbol to create the 'ideal experiment' of her novel. The image of the historian untangling the pre-existent web is complemented by that of the creative scientist; and the realism of the Garths' presentation is balanced by the mythological resonances of the story of Dorothea, Causaubon, and Will. George Eliot's method and theory of art in fact look forward to the later *Daniel Deronda* in which the visionary Mordecai's prophetic role is directly compared to that of an experimental scientist.

For Bernard, the experimental scientist was 'a real foreman of creation'; in creating the conditions of his experiments, he actively engineered the appearance of phenomena.[7] His methodology, moreover, was firmly based, as Lewes also believed, on the processes of ideal construction and imaginative pre-vision[8] for, as Bernard observes, 'Ideas, given form by facts, embody science'.[9] Bernard held adamantly to the conviction that 'We must give free rein to our imagination; the idea is the essence of all reasoning and all invention'.[10] This conception of scientific method, which underpins George Eliot's 'experiment in time', is articulated in the novel by Lydgate who adheres, somewhat in advance of his time, to a belief in the scientific imagination. Lydgate disdains the form of imagination present in cheap narration which he regards as

> rather vulgar and vinous compared with the imagination that reveals subtle actions inaccessible by any sort of lens, but tracked in that outer darkness through long pathways of necessary sequence by the inward light which is the last refinement of Energy, capable of bathing even the ethereal atoms in its ideally illuminated space.
>
> (ch. 16, I, 249)

Like his creator, Lydgate conceives science not simply as a process of observation and classification, but rather as the pursuit of ideas and hypotheses. The object of science is not to record the already known, but to reveal hidden connections, through the creation of an 'ideally illuminated space' – Lewes' 'manifold ideal constructions of the Possible' that help to reveal the Actual.

In creating the experimental conditions through which to explore the possible outcome of the life of a 'later-born Theresa' placed in the uncongenial social medium of Middlemarch, George Eliot follows Lydgate's scientific methodology. Her labour of imagination is not 'mere arbitrariness, but the exercise of disciplined power'. She combines and constructs all the multitudinous elements of Middlemarch life 'with the clearest eye for probabilities and the fullest obedience to knowledge' (ch. 16, I, 249). The purpose behind her labour also corresponds to that of scientific practice, for the aim of science, Lewes suggests, is to link together, through imaginative construction, the fragments of the phenomenal world so as to reveal an underlying order. While 'Perception gives the naked fact of Sense, isolated, unconnected, merely juxtaposed with other facts, and without far-reaching significance', science reveals connections and confers significance: 'The facts of Feeling which sensation differentiates, Theory integrates.'[11] George Eliot tries, through the structural organisation of her work, to reveal underlying organic unity beneath apparent surface disorder. The pursuit of significant order constitutes, indeed, both the major theme and methodology of the novel, for George Eliot's characters share her goal. Thus Lydgate searches for the one primitive tissue, and Casaubon for the 'Key to all Mythologies'. Dorothea, in similar fashion, yearns for 'a binding theory which would bring her own life and doctrine into strict connection with that amazing past' (ch. 10, I, 128). On a more humorous level, Mr Brooke seeks, in his usual rambling way, for a means of ordering his documents other than by the arbitrary system of A to Z. Author and characters alike quest for an organising principle or theory which would bind together disparate parts and reveal unity beneath apparent chaos.

In their search, the characters often fall into the stance of natural historians, holding, mistakenly, that meaning actually inheres in external form. Thus Lydgate believes that Rosamond's physical appearance expresses her virtue 'with a force of demonstration that excluded the need for other evidence' (ch. 16, I, 248) while Dorothea is similarly misled by Casaubon: 'Everything I see in him', she responds rather haughtily to Celia, 'corresponds to his pamphlet on Biblical Cosmology' (ch. 2, I, 27). Casaubon is similarly guilty of treating the world as a system of signs to be decoded. His Key is to make 'the vast field of mythical constructions ... intelligible, nay, luminous with the reflected light of correspondences' (ch. 3, I, 33). He wishes to reveal the underlying order of history through the external correspondences of myths, though, as the narrator observes, this approach had been discredited in both mythological studies, and the related science of philology: Mr Casaubon's theory 'floated among flexible conjectures no more solid than those etymologies which seemed strong because of likeness in sound until it was shown that likeness in sound made them impossible' (ch. 48, II, 312). External correspondences can be actively misleading. Thus Lewes, in *Sea-side Studies*, confirmed Bernard's warning against 'attempting to deduce a function from mere inspection of the organ' for the external resemblance of organs cannot be taken as evidence of their similar functions.[12] The same principle of organic interdependence applies to physiological life, language, social relations, or historical development. One must look beyond the details of external form to the underlying dynamic process, for, as in Bernard's linguistic analogy, each part only derives meaning from its position within the whole.

The structure of *Middlemarch* reflects this principle of interdependence. The unity of the novel is not based, as in that earlier study of provincial life, Mrs Gaskell's *Cranford*, on spatial continuity or community of life style.[13] The life portrayed is both geographically and socially dispersed, moving from Tipton to Frick, from the gentry to labourers, and from the measured cadences of Casaubon's speech to the trenchant assertions of Mrs Dollop. Unlike the earlier *Felix Holt* or Dickens' *Bleak House*, the plot does not revolve around the gradual revelation of hidden connections between socially disparate groups, or a cumbersome legal machinery. Indeed the sole links that emerge from the past – those of Bulstrode, Raffles, and Will – seem rather to disturb than affirm our sense of the unity of Middlemarch life. Though the Bulstrode and Casaubon plots are connected by Will, in his capacity as twice disinherited heir, George Eliot actively eschews, in general, the technique of linking all her characters through relations of direct personal contact. No links, for example, are drawn between Dorothea and Farebrother or Caleb until after Casaubon's death, while the sole direct connection between Dorothea and Featherstone occurs with Dorothea's distant glance at Featherstone's funeral. The structure of *Middlemarch* conforms to Lewes' definition of organic life: 'The part exists only as part of a whole; the whole exists only as a whole of its parts.'[14]

The unity of *Middlemarch* is based, primarily, not on relations of direct effect, but on the shared community of language. In constructing her 'Study of Provincial Life' George Eliot adhered to the same social interpretation of organicist premises as Lewes. Her representation of Middlemarch life accords with the theory of the social medium Lewes was concurrently defining in *The Foundations of a Creed*. Lewes differentiates his approach from that of psychologists; his was the first survey, he believed, to take fully into account the role of the social medium in determining individual psychology. Thus, 'The psychologist, accustomed to consider the Mind as something apart from the Organism, individual and collective, is peculiarly liable to this error of overlooking the fact that all mental manifestations are simply the resultants of the conditions external and internal.'[15] These external conditions are not simply the material or economic conditions of society but 'the collective accumulations of centuries, condensed in knowledge, beliefs, prejudices, institutions, and tendencies', and transmitted primarily through language.[16] The individual and social life of Middlemarch conforms to this model. Though characters are linked in material relations of dependency, the primary connecting bond is the shared linguistic medium. Through language characters articulate both their individual and communal identity: gossip, or the exchange of opinion, functions as the fundamental linking force. The structure of the individual chapters reflects this principle. Chapters move either linearly, connecting various strands of plot through an extended chain of characters' opinions about each other, or laterally, from a larger social issue to its effects upon the thoughts and reflections of a single life.[17]

A linear structure is manifest, for example, in chapter 71 which traces the revelation, through gossip, of Bulstrode's story, and the indignant responses in each social stratum. In keeping with George Eliot's commitment to organic heterogeneity, the chapter concludes, not with Bulstrode, but with Dorothea, fervently asserting her faith in Lydgate. Though the majority of characters in this chapter scarcely know of each other's existence, they are all linked together by the connecting chain of opinion.

An example of the principles of lateral construction is furnished by chapter 56 which moves from a general discussion of the coming of the railway to trace its effects on individual lives. George Eliot enumerates in this chapter the three social issues she employs to unite the disparate elements of Middlemarch existence: 'In the hundred to which Middlemarch belonged,' she observes, 'railways were as exciting a topic as the Reform Bill or the imminent horrors of Cholera, and those who held the most decided views on the subject were women and landholders' (ch. 56, III, 30). Though the three issues of railways, Reform, and Cholera engross the social organism, their unifying force lies less in their material effects than in their mobilisation of public opinion. Individual psychology is defined, in accordance with Lewes' theories, both by the accumulated beliefs and prejudices stored within language, and the contemporary functions of gossip. Indeed, the processes of gossip constitute both the dominant principles of chapter construction, and one of the novel's major themes. As George Eliot demands, in reference to Bulstrode, 'Who can know how much of his inward life is made up of the thoughts he believes other men to have about him, until that fabric of opinion is threatened with ruin?' (ch. 68, III, 238). Public opinion cannot be ignored; it actively enters into the creation of both mind and self-identity. George Eliot explores through the plot and formal structure of her novel the implications of this principle of organic interdependence.

The constant shifts in perspective within the chapters, from the social whole to the individual parts, accord with George Eliot's conception of organic form which she outlined in her notebook essay 'Notes on Form in Art' (1868). Form, she argued, 'must first depend on the discrimination of wholes & then on the discrimination of parts'.[18] Lydgate, translating this premise into biological practice, believed that 'there must be a systole and diastole in all inquiry'. Unlike Lydgate, George Eliot actually follows this method; her novel is 'continually expanding and shrinking between the whole human horizon and the horizon of an object glass' (ch. 63, III, 163). Both the chapter construction and larger structure of the work reinforce this process. Book titles, like 'Old and Young' or 'Waiting for Death', draw attention away from the continuity of plot to suggest a wider unity of theme, while the epigraphs, which often hold an enigmatic relation to the following material, similarly disrupt linear narration to establish a framework of expectations for the ensuing chapter. The jumps in perspective reflect the heterogeneous structure of the social organism itself, for, as George Eliot argued in her essay, 'The highest Form ... is the highest organism, that is to say, the most varied group of relations bound together in a wholeness which again has the most varied relations with all other phenomena.'[19] Her definition follows Spencer's theory that the highest form of art will be 'not a series of like parts simply placed in juxtaposition, but one whole made up of unlike parts that are mutually dependent'.[20] The universal principle of development from homogeneity to heterogeneity to which Spencer refers here is one, George Eliot suggests in the essay, that governs equally the development of organic life, or poetic form, and the growth of mind, both in the individual and in the race.[21] Within the form of her novel she attempts to capture the organic principles that govern both historical growth and social interdependence.

In a recent study, which points to the connections between notions of organic form, narrative conventions, and 'the system of assumptions which is associated with the idea of history in Western culture', Hillis Miller argues that in *Middlemarch* 'in place of the concept of elaborate organic form, centered form, form organised around certain absolute generalizable themes, George Eliot presents a view of artistic form as inorganic, acentered, and discontinuous'.[22] He mistakenly identifies all 'Western ideas of history' with a Hegelian teleological organicism, ignoring the fact that the 'unlikeness and difference' of *Middlemarch* crystallises George Eliot's conception of organic form and development. Yet in stressing the discontinuity, and the 'contradictory struggle of individual human energies' within the novel, Hillis Miller does locate a source of internal narrative tension. The historical process of differentiation could, for Spencer, only be one of progress; the mutual dependence of unlike parts would necessarily be harmonious. Theoretically, according to George Eliot's own definition of organic form, the *differentiation* of opinion would actually unite Middlemarch. Her study reveals, however, the destructive functions of gossip. Mrs Bulstrode learns to her cost the meaning of 'candour' in the Middlemarch vocabulary, while the dinners required to feed gossip about her husband and Lydgate suggest a decidedly cannibalistic interpretation of the social organism. The narrator's early observation that Middlemarch 'counted on swallowing Lydgate and assimilating him very comfortably' (ch. 15, I, 274) proves to be disturbingly accurate.

At every level, the interdependence of Middlemarch life seems to be based not on harmony, but on conflict. Thus Mr Brooke learns, during his lamentable experience as a political candidate, that Middlemarch is not the cosy paternalist society of his imaginings: 'the weavers and tanners of Middlemarch . . . had never thought of Mr. Brooke as a neighbour' (ch. 51, II, 349). Economically, indeed, Middlemarch society reveals the worst vices of capitalism. We discover, for instance, from Mr Vincy that Bulstrode is associated with Plymdale's house which employs dyes liable to rot the silk, while Mr Vincy himself is identified by Mrs Cadwallader as 'one of those who suck the life out of the wretched handloom weavers in Tipton and Freshitt' (ch. 34, II, 82). Though the narrator refers at one stage to the 'stealthy convergence of human lots', thus seeming to offer a moral rebuke to Lydgate and Dorothea for their 'mutual indifference', the description of social interaction which follows is scarcely suggestive of harmonious integration:

> Old provincial society had its share of this subtle movement: had not only its striking downfalls, its brilliant young professional dandies who ended by living up an entry with a drab and six children for their establishment, but also those less marked vicissitudes which are constantly shifting the boundaries of social intercourse, and begetting new consciousness of interdependence.
>
> (ch. 11, I, 142)

Social interdependence is defined primarily by vicissitudes, while the actual process of change is marked by darwinian elements of competition. The inhabitants of Middlemarch are displaced by successful settlers who 'came from distant counties, some with an alarming novelty of skill, others with an offensive advantage in cunning'. In the darwinian battle for survival, success belongs to those with the highest powers of adaptation. Middlemarch life exhibits all the characteristics of a vital organism, for movement of each part affects the whole. Thus, even those who stand 'with rocky firmness amid all this fluctuation' are by the surrounding changes themselves transformed, 'altering with the double change of self and beholder'. Yet despite this evident interdependence, town life displays none of the peaceful unity of the organic social ideal.

George Eliot adheres, in *Middlemarch*, to the moral ideal of organic unity while simultaneously demonstrating the social impossibility of attaining this goal. Such an internal contradiction does not lead her, however, to deconstruct notions of historical unity and continuity as Hillis Miller, for rather different reasons, has suggested. Though innovatory in form, *Middlemarch* is a solidly nineteenth-century text, constructed in the light of contemporary social and scientific debates concerning historical growth. In true realist fashion, the novel poses a social and moral problem which the narrative seeks to resolve. George Eliot is committed, ultimately, not to openness and discontinuity but to narrative closure. The difficulties she encounters in moving towards the desired resolution are clearly exacerbated, however, by her recognition of the social conflict which the myth of social heterogeneity actually conceals.

On a more fundamental level, her difficulties are also increased by the model of individual development to which she subscribes. Though the function of her 'experiment in time' is to assess the relative claims of the individual and the social organism, she actually adheres to a dynamic theory of organic process which undermines conceptions of individual autonomy upon which such judgements must necessarily be based. Thus, Lewes, outlining the psychological implications of Lydgate's theory of organic interdependence, argued that the division between self and not-self is false; it is analytic rather than real. The individual cannot be isolated out and defined apart from the organic process, for the individual, he concludes, *is* its relations.[23] This model suggests a fluidity and openness incompatible with the traditional realist demand for moral closure. If character is treated as flux, or process, there can be no fixed points of value, no grounds for assessing individual moral responsibility for action. Nor can the narrative draw to a defined close. The dynamic theory of organic order in fact undercuts the terms of the original organic problematic. George Eliot strives in *Middlemarch* to resolve this contradiction: to reconcile the idea of individual fluidity with the need for fixed moral judgement.

The opening chapter of *Middlemarch* clearly reveals George Eliot's organicist premises. Characters are introduced not in terms of fixed personal attributes, but in terms of their social effects. Dorothea, we learn in the opening paragraph, 'was usually spoken of as being remarkably clever'. Public opinion defines each character: thus Mr Brooke 'was held in this part of the county to have contracted a too rambling habit of mind', while 'The rural opinion about the new young ladies, even among the cottagers, was generally in favour of Celia'. We discover, furthermore, that Mr Brooke, though blamed by neighbouring families for not securing a companion for Dorothea, was yet 'brave enough to defy the world – that is to say, Mrs. Cadwallader the Rector's wife, and the small group of gentry with whom he visited in the north-east corner of Loamshire' (ch. 1, I, 7–13). The increased particularisation draws attention to the specificity of their environment. To comprehend Dorothea or Mr Brooke, one must bring knowledge, not of the world, but rather of that particular 'north-east corner of Loamshire' which determines their lives.

Our understanding of each character is formed through the medium of his neighbours' eyes. The narrator's protest against the reader's possible response to Casaubon draws attention to her own technique:

> I protest against any absolute conclusion, any prejudice derived from Mrs Cadwallader's contempt for a neighbouring clergyman's alleged greatness of soul, or Sir James Chettam's poor opinion of his rival's legs,—from Mr Brooke's failure to elicit a companion's ideas, or from Celia's criticism of a middle-aged scholar's personal appearance.
>
> (ch. 10, I, 125)

Character cannot be defined apart from social opinion, for each individual is only the sum of his, constantly changing, relations with the social organism. Such relativism, however, is more apparent than real; it is clearly undercut by the text's claim to offer authoritative judgement. We rest in little doubt concerning the 'absolute conclusion' we should draw about each character. Through analysis of the three histories of Lydgate, Bulstrode, and Dorothea I will try to suggest the different ways in which George Eliot actually used the premises of organicist theory to achieve this moral closure. Drawing on the assumption, which she outlined in 'Notes on Form in Art', that the same principles of organic life govern physiological, psychological, and social development, she mediates constantly between these different levels of analysis in *Middlemarch* in an attempt to impose structural and moral order on the text.

Introducing Lydgate, George Eliot observes that 'character too is a process and an unfolding' (ch. 15, I, 226). This admission of fluidity is not borne out, however, by the narrative. The statement is immediately followed by a detailed account of Lydgate's history which functions to define his character independently of his life within the social organism of Middlemarch. In the case of Lydgate, plot, or the patterning of social events, does not trace a process of dynamic interaction between the individual and the social whole. It functions, rather, as a structural analogue of the predefined composition of his mind. The history of Lydgate's association with Laure illustrates his 'two selves'; his relations with Middlemarch are but an external enactment of this fixed internal contradiction. The 'spots of commonness' in his nature find their reflection in the petty judgements of the Middlemarch mind, while his other, idealistic, self finds its social correlative in Dorothea's willing faith. But as the 'spots of commonness' predominate in his nature, so the judgement of Middlemarch ultimately prevails. The social drama is merely that of his psychological constitution writ large. Reflecting on Lydgate's failure, George Eliot observes that 'It always remains true that if we had been greater, circumstance would have been less strong against us' (ch. 58, III, 82). Sympathy is linked to firm moral judgement, thus suggesting a strong sense of order in the world. This stance is possible, however, only because George Eliot did not adhere firmly to a fluid model of character. It is, in the final instance, Lydgate's intrinsic moral flaws, his lack of innate greatness, and not the circumstances of his interaction with Middlemarch, that create his downfall.

The need to offer moral judgement also determines the representation of Bulstrode. At its simplest level, George Eliot wants to suggest that crime does not pay. If organic social harmony is to be preserved, wrongdoing must be shown to have undesired consequences for the perpetrator. In order to enforce this moral George Eliot departs once more from the fluid model of character. Bulstrode is the only other character apart from Lydgate who is given a detailed history outside his incorporation within Middlemarch life; relations with Middlemarch can similarly be defined as the gradual unfolding or revelation of the prior structure of his mind. The history of Bulstrode is the only one in which coincidence strains credibility; Will's presence in Middlemarch, and Raffles' re-emergence conform more to a desired moral configuration than to the laws of realistic probability. In order to naturalise these occurrences George Eliot turns once more to physiology, to the idea of a physical basis for memory:

> The terror of being judged sharpens the memory: it sends an inevitable glare over that long-unvisited past which has been habitually recalled only in general phrases. Even without memory, the life is bound into one by a zone of dependence in growth and decay; but intense memory forces a man to own his blameworthy past. With memory set smarting like a reopened wound, a man's past is not simply a dead history, an outworn preparation of the present: it is not a repented error shaken loose from the life: it is a still quivering part of himself, bringing shudders and bitter flavours and the tinglings of a merited shame.
>
> (ch. 61, III, 125–6)

The final term 'merited' reveals the moral bias of the whole description. George Eliot uses physiology to suggest that for the individual, as much as for the society or culture, there is a vital interdependence in history. Past history can never be 'dead', never be discarded; shame must inevitably occur. All the terms employed reinforce the idea of a physical basis of memory; whether the 'shudders' and 'tinglings' of the sensations aroused, or the quivering vibrations which constitute the physiological response. The zone of dependence in growth and decay recalls de Blainville's theory upon which Lewes based his theory of mind: that organic life is a process of composition and decomposition in interaction with the environment.[24] George Eliot employs this physical theory, as she did with Tito in *Romola*, to suggest a moral conclusion which is by no means sure: that a man will always be called to account for his past actions. The apparent transitory nature of social experience is referred to the constancy of physiological composition.

Raffles' social ostracism mirrors his status in Bulstrode's mind. George Eliot employs the operations of the unconscious as a model for the plot and social events, thus proposing a form of homology between the social and psychic realms that appears to offer a grounding within nature for the moral patterning of the narrative. She draws, however, on contemporary theories of unconscious life which do not simply reinforce ideas of a linear, cumulative history. Thus Bulstrode:

> felt the scenes of his earlier life coming between him and everything else, as obstinately as when we look through the window from a lighted room, the objects we turn our backs on are still before us, instead of the grass and the trees. The successive events inward and outward were there in one view: though each might be dwelt on in turn, the rest still kept their hold in the consciousness.
>
> (ch. 61, III, 126)

This superb image presents a model of the mind which, departing from the linear model of associationist theory, admits the simultaneity of different levels of consciousness. The analysis of Bulstrode's mental processes focuses strongly on duality, whether of past and present, or the simultaneous existence of the 'theoretic phrases' he had used to justify his actions, and his actual experience of egoistic terror (ch. 53, II, 385). Both modes are captured in Lewes' theory of the psychological subject:

> He lives a double life and has a double world – the world of Feeling and the world of Thought, that of sensations and images and that of abstract ideas. The Present is to him a complex web, with threads of the Past and threads of the Future inextricably interwoven.[25]

The web image recalls Bulstrode's inability to 'unravel' his confused promptings (ch. 70, III, 271), while the distinction between thought and image is that which occurs when he attempts to pray: 'through all this effort to condense words into a solid mental state, there pierced and spread with irresistible vividness the images of the events he desired; (ch. 70, III, 262). Although Bulstrode has interpreted history as one unified Providential order, his psychological experience of duality and contradiction exposes the falsity of this model. The representation of Bulstrode's consciousness clearly challenges linear models of the *cogito*. Yet, his experience is used, not to subvert, as Hillis Miller suggests, but rather to reinforce the continuum of history. The physiological coherence of his body appears to offer a guarantee of cumulative social order.

Bulstrode and Lydgate were both defined by their histories before they entered Middlemarch. George Eliot tries, however, in the case of Dorothea, to follow more closely her theory of dynamic development. We witness a reciprocal interaction between social organism and individual: social contradiction becomes personal. Dorothea is introduced in terms of two conflicting value systems and forms of language, suggesting two different temporal schemas. Her plain garments 'by the side of provincial fashion gave her the impressiveness of a fine quotation from the Bible,—or from one of our elder poets,—in a paragraph of to-day's newspaper' (ch. 1, I, 7). The long-standing cultural and religious traditions expressed in poetry or the Bible are contrasted with the pragmatic, ephemeral prose of a newspaper, the voice of contemporary social values. Dorothea is caught between the two. The reasons given for her dress clearly suggest this conflict; they are firstly those of economic class and status, and only secondly those of religion. The reader should not be fooled by Dorothea's self-image. She is not the embodiment of ahistorical religious values, but rather the product of a conflict between historically established religious tradition, and the rising values of her social class. The discussion of her religious proclivities is thus placed in the context of her marriageability: the two are intimately related.

Analysis of Dorothea's thoughts and actions clearly reveals her internalisation of external social contradictions. Though she enjoys riding in a 'pagan sensuous way' she looks forward to renouncing it. Her religious values are revealed to be primarily social constructs that actually denature sensuous response. Indeed her imitation of Madame Poinçon betrays the role-playing her 'religion' demands. In the episode with the jewels Dorothea's internal contradiction emerges as semi-conscious duplicity, finally erupting in her angry defence of her decision to keep the jewels she had earlier scorned. We are left with Celia's verdict: 'But Dorothea is not always consistent' (ch. 1, I, 19). Whereas Lydgate's inconsistencies appeared due to innate flaws in his character, Dorothea's are shown to be socially produced.

In portraying the history of Bulstrode George Eliot employed the physiological coherence of his mind as a seeming guarantee of historical continuity and social unity. Dorothea's unity of consciousness, by contrast, reflects the strange association of dissonant elements that actually constitutes the social organism. In the sole connection drawn between Dorothea and Featherstone she glances from her window at his funeral. The scene, aloof as it seemed to be from the tenor of her life, always afterwards came back to her at the touch of certain sensitive points in memory, just as the vision of St. Peter's at Rome was inwoven with moods of despondency. Scenes which make vital changes in our neighbours' lot are but the background of our own, yet, like a particular aspect of the fields and trees, they become associated for us with the epochs of our own history, and make a part of that unity which lies in the selection of our keenest consciousness.

(ch. 34, II, 79–80)

George Eliot draws on contemporary theories of physiological psychology to illuminate the composition of the social organism.[26] Her model of mind is not, however, that of the rational intelligence which, for Spencer, best explained the harmonious distribution of functions within the social organism. Middlemarch is best represented by the confused associations of the mind which are established and recalled without obvious functional reason, far beyond the control of rationality. Although the physiological unity of mind determines the selection of consciousness, there is no order or harmony in that unity. George Eliot explicitly relates this mode of association to Dorothea's position within the social organism:

The dream-like association of something alien and ill-understood with the deepest secrets of her experience seemed to mirror that sense of loneliness which was due to the very ardour of Dorothea's nature. The country gentry of old time lived in a rarefied social air: dotted apart on their stations up the mountain they looked down with imperfect discrimination on the belts of thicker life below. And Dorothea was not at ease in the perspective and chilliness of that height.

(ch. 34, II, 80)

Dorothea's situation at the window, isolated and looking down, is paradigmatic of her social position; the dream-like associations of her mind capture the inharmonious connections of Middlemarch life. The Middlemarchers may be bound together in relations of vital organic interdependence but they remain 'alien and ill-understood' to each other. Social unity need not be harmonious; it can equally well be founded on conflict and contradiction.

In portraying the three histories of Lydgate, Bulstrode, and Dorothea, George Eliot shifts constantly between physiological, psychological, and social levels of explanation attempting, in the case of the first two, to resolve social problems metonymically by reference to psychic structure. Only in the case of Dorothea does she portray a truly dynamic relationship between the individual and society, or employ physiology to suggest the dissonance, rather than the order, of the social organism. Yet this image of social and psychological confusion is implicitly contrasted with its ideal forms: free flow of energy on the psychic level and harmonious integration on the social. The thrust of the novel is still towards resolution, whether of historical, social, or psychological disorder. George Eliot poses the problem of integration on each of these three levels; she also supplies, however, a structure of imagery which enables her to mediate between these different levels of analysis.

Following Lewes' conviction that science is based on Ideal Construction, George Eliot employs a controlling idea, or hypothesis, to structure her experiment. The ruling idea of *Middlemarch* is that of a labyrinth. Fundamentally, a labyrinth is a structure that dissipates energy, impedes the free flow of force. With the rise of physiological psychology it was a concept that could be applied equally to social, mental, or physiological structure. Drawing on contemporary developments in scientific theory, George Eliot employs the idea of channelled, free-flowing energy to establish a value framework for her novel. The image of a labyrinth first occurs to describe Dorothea's ardour, impeded by the entanglements of Middlemarch society: 'and with such a nature struggling in the bands of a narrow teaching, hemmed in by a social life which seemed nothing but a labyrinth of petty courses, a walled-in maze of small paths that led no whither, the outcome was sure to strike others as at once exaggeration and inconsistency' (ch. 3, I, 39). Contorted social channels are reduplicated in the mind. Dorothea's natural energy is blocked, dissipated by socially created friction. Her case is like that of Lydgate whose progress towards greatness is halted by the 'retarding friction' of 'small temptations and sordid cares' (ch. 15, I, 221–2). In accordance with Lewes' theory that psychology was based on the physiological flow of energy, the tendency of sensation to 'discharge itself through the readiest channel', the way through the social and psychological labyrinth of Middlemarch is to establish clear channels of transmission.[27]

The central question in *Middlemarch* is whether, as the Prelude despairingly suggests, Dorothea's energy will be 'dispersed among hindrances' or will attain, in the words of the Finale, 'fine issues', 'channels' of positive social effect. The recurrent imagery of flowing water and streams in the novel is not simply metaphoric in origin but is grounded in contemporary social and psychological theories of energy flow.[28] As Spencer remarks in the second edition of *The Principles of Psychology*:

> when describing how discharges of molecular motion go along lines of least resistance, and by recurring render them lines of less resistance, it was pointed out that in this respect there is an analogy between the flow of molecular motion and the flow of a liquid; for a stream, in proportion as it is strong and continued, cuts for itself a large and definite channel.[29]

The comparison between the 'full current' of Dorothea's mind and the 'shallow rills' of Casaubon's has significant scientific implications. Both Spencer and Lewes were working concurrently on questions concerning the relationship between force and cause, psychological feeling and physiological motion. Their assumptions help structure George Eliot's narrative; social and psychological action is interpreted as the movement of force.

In one of her direct scientific analogies George Eliot observes: 'In watching effects, if only of an electric battery, it is often necessary to change our place and examine a particular mixture or group at some distance from the point where the movement we are interested in was set up' (ch. 40, II, 190). The image is possibly drawn from William Grove's *On the Correlation of Physical Forces* which George Eliot records rereading 'with new interest, after the lapse of years' in May 1870.[30] The voltaic battery, Grove observes, 'affords us the best means of ascertaining the dynamic equivalents of different forces'.[31] Grove's thesis, and George Eliot's own marginal comments in the book, concern the inseparability of cause and effect, force and motion. As a scientist examining the dynamic interdependence of the social organism George Eliot analyses action in terms of the play of force. Those convenient authorial spokesmen, the two 'gents' of the epigraphs, confirm this reading; they appear twice to discuss the nature of causality. Chapter 34, which contains Featherstone's funeral, opens with their observations:

1st Gent.   Such men as this are feathers, chips, and straws,
            Carry no weight, no force.
2nd Gent.   But levity
            Is causal too, and makes the sum of weight:
                                    (ch. 34, II, 75)

In a deliberate pun, George Eliot suggests that, in the complex interdependent network of the social organism, the seeming 'feather' has the causal force of a weighty stone. The domestic relations of the Lydgates receive comparable analysis. To the suggestion in chapter 64 that blame lies with power the second Gent replies that power is relative:

> All force is twain in one: cause is not cause
> Unless effect be there;
>
> (ch. 64, III, 173)

Lydgate's action is inseparable from Rosamond's response, just as his social effect on Middlemarch is determined not by his avowed intentions but by a balance of social forces. As Lewes observes, 'In a vital organism every force is the resultant of *all* the forces: it is a disturbance of equilibrium, and equilibrium is the equivalence of convergent forces.[32] Each action in Middlemarch can only be comprehended in terms of the convergence of social forces.

Psychological behaviour is also interpreted in terms of the movement of force. Thus George Eliot observes of Mr Casaubon's disappointment concerning his lack of delight in his forthcoming marriage: 'It is true that he knew all the classical passages implying the contrary; but knowing classical passages, we find, is a mode of motion, which explains why they leave so little extra force for their personal application' (ch. 10, I, 126–7). Though light-hearted in tone, the passage confirms George Eliot's adherence to Lewes' theory that 'Motion is a mode of Feeling'.[33] Close scrutiny of the novel reveals the frequency with which action is interpreted as the discharge and channelling of energy. Chapter 37 furnishes two apparently trivial examples. The first refers to Will: 'He did not shrug his shoulders; and for want of that muscular outlet he thought the more irritably of beautiful lips kissing holy skulls and other emptinesses ecclesiastically enshrined' (ch. 37, II, 137–8). The second refers to Mr Casaubon: 'In uttering the last clause, Mr. Casaubon leaned over the elbow of his chair, and swayed his head up and down, apparently as a muscular outlet instead of that recapitulation which would not have been becoming' (ch. 37, II, 145–6). Unimportant in themselves, the passages yet demonstrate the degree to which George Eliot has departed from the traditions of the realist novel, and the model of the rational actor in full control of his own actions. The 'Thinking Principle', Lewes argues, 'is not an antecedent but a resultant, not an entity but a convergence of manifold activities'.[34] The self in *Middlemarch* is not a predefined entity that determines action, but, like the social organism, is only a product of the convergence of forces.

Principles of energy transmission thus establish the foundation for a theory of psychology, and of social interaction which undermines conceptions of individual autonomy and control. The same principles, however, also underpin the novel's rather conservative inheritance plot. The labyrinth is equally one of impeded ardour and misman-aged estates. In each of the separate strands of plot concerning Featherstone, Bulstrode, Will, Casaubon, and the Brookes, George Eliot explores the moral question of how the future channel of property is to be determined. The term 'channel' occurs explicitly in relation to the Bulstrode inheritance plot: if the lost daughter were found 'there would be a channel for property—perhaps a wide one, in the provision for several children' (ch. 61, III, 130). Questions of issue and transmission relate not simply to abstract qualities of soul, but also to the material realm of social order. Dorothea's story, we learn in the opening chapter, is not only that of a would-be St Theresa but also that of a potential heiress for 'if Dorothea married and had a son, that son would inherit Mr. Brooke's estate' (ch. 1, I, 10). In the history of her Puritan ancestor who served under Cromwell but emerged from political troubles as 'the proprietor of a respectable family estate' (ch. 1, I, 8) one can see an encapsulation of Dorothea's own history. Her 'hereditary strain of Puritan energy' (ch. 1 I, 10) leads her into unfortunate entanglements but ultimately enables her to bequeath a respectable family estate. The story is a more prosaic version of the St Theresa problem presented in the Prelude: native energy confronted with a labyrinth must strive to create some issue, not degenerate into formlessness like the childless Mr Brooke who 'will run into any mould', but 'won't keep shape' (ch. 8, I, 103).

In her marriage to Casaubon Dorothea can produce no issue, she experiences a 'nightmare of a life in which every energy was arrested by dread' (ch. 37, II, 155). Entangled in the labyrinth of history, the impotent Casaubon can produce neither Key nor child. By violating in his will, however, the rules of social propriety (a term which shares a common root with property), he releases Dorothea from her bond, thus freeing her will or energy. Significantly, it is in marriage to the vital Will that she produces the desired heir. The pun is clearly deliberate. Though Will has twice been the victim of irresponsible inheritance Dorothea, in marrying him, returns him to his rightful role of property owner. Vitality is thus restored to the social organism and history established, once more, on its true course.

The question of property is linked to both the continuity and

solidarity of the social organism; just inheritance ensures the per-
petuation of social order, while just administration establishes
organic harmony amongst the different social strata. Unlike Mr
Brooke, or Featherstone, Dorothea, on accession to her estates,
demonstrates responsible administration: she appoints Mr Farebrother, releases Lydgate from his debt to Bulstrode, and engineers
the reappointment of Caleb Garth. Looked at with a jaundiced eye,
Caleb, preserving Mr Brooke's rule by mending his broken fences,
could be seen to be patching up a broken system. The text, however,
gives no explicit confirmation of this reading. Caleb's activities
receive nothing but praise, while even Sir James emerges as a model
figure. Dorothea had 'to resolve not to be afraid of him—all the more
because he was really her best friend' (ch. 72, III, 309). The
organicism of benevolent paternalism would appear to be the
political stance of the novel. *Middlemarch*, however, conforms
neither to the social vision nor the methodology of *Adam Bede*.
Acting as a creative scientist, George Eliot offers, through the
controlling experimental conception of a labyrinth, many levels of
analysis of Middlemarch life. From the materialist analysis of
property transmission she moves, through levels of ascending complexity, to consider questions of psychological and social structure,
offering, at the highest level, an interrogation of the nature of
historical understanding and mythic creation.

Though, on one level, the inheritance plot might appear to confirm
Carlylean conceptions of organic harmony, the narrative is also
clearly critical of the 'labyrinth of petty courses' which inhibits the
flow of Dorothea's 'full current of sympathetic motive' (ch. 10, I,
128). Trapped within the literal confines of Middlemarch society,
Dorothea is also imprisoned mentally by her own confused notions.
During courtship she gazes into the 'ungauged reservoir' of Mr
Casaubon's mind and sees 'reflected there in vague labyrinthine
extension every quality she herself brought' (ch. 3, I, 32). She
discovers on her honeymoon, however, that the work which had
originally seemed of 'attractively labyrinthine extent' is literally
without issue: 'the large vistas and wide fresh air which she had
dreamed of finding in her husband's mind were replaced by ante-
rooms and winding passages which seemed to lead nowhither' (ch.
20, I, 300). The restricted channels of Middlemarch social life have a
psychic replica in the contorted passages of Casaubon's mind. The
question originally posed by the narrative concerned Dorothea's
relations to her social surroundings, but this shift in imagery subtly

transposes the problem to one of historical understanding. Casaubon is imprisoned, primarily, by his inability to understand the historical process.

This change in emphasis is accompanied by a change in scene; the narrative moves from the narrow world of Middlemarch to Rome, and to a wider historical perspective. While Middlemarch life in 1829 represents one moment in the historical development of the social organism, Rome is itself the embodiment of history. The bewildered Dorothea encounters 'the city of visible history, where the past of a whole hemisphere seems moving in funeral procession with strange ancestral images and trophies gathered from afar' (ch. 20, I, 295). A deliberate parallel is drawn between her relationships to Casaubon and to Rome, for the 'stupendous fragmentariness heightened the dreamlike strangeness of her bridal life' (ch. 20, I, 295). Rome becomes the material, external expression of Casaubon's historical confusion, and of Dorothea's frustration in marriage.

The impact of Rome on Dorothea is described in physiological terms:

> all this vast wreck of ambitious ideals, sensuous and spiritual, mixed confusedly with the signs of breathing forgetfulness and degradation, at first jarred her as with an electric shock, and then urged themselves on her with that ache belonging to a glut of confused ideas which check the flow of emotion.
>
> (ch. 20, I, 296)

Like Middlemarch, Rome impedes the free flow of energy. By casting the problem of the labyrinth in terms of physiological response, however, George Eliot is able to offer an apparent source of resolution – the tendency of Dorothea's mind to flow in a unified current: 'But in Dorothea's mind there was a current into which all thought and feeling were apt sooner or later to flow—the reaching forward of the whole consciousness towards the fullest truth, the least partial good' (ch. 20, I, 311). Innate physiological constitution seems to hold the key to the problem of historical understanding.

George Eliot's use of physiology here is in accordance with Spencer's belief that it was both possible, and necessary, to interpret mental evolution in terms of a redistribution of Matter and Motion:

> If from a corollary to the Persistence of Force we can legitimately draw the conclusion that, under certain conditions, lines of nervous communication will arise, and, having arisen, will become lines of more and more easy communication in proportion to the number and

strengths of the discharges propagated through them; we shall have found a physical interpretation which completes the doctrine of psychical evolution.[35]

Spencer employs the principle of the persistence of force to demonstrate necessary psychic evolution, and thus to support his theory of history as unified progress. Mental evolution occurs as wider and wider channels of communication are carved in the mind. The same argument is offered by Lewes in *The Foundations of a Creed*. 'The evolution of Mind', he observes, 'is the establishment of definite paths: this is the mental organisation, fitting it for the reception of definite impressions, and their co-ordination with past feelings.'[36] In *Middlemarch* the problem of the social and historical labyrinth becomes one of psychic coordination as cultural confusion is set against Dorothea's physiological tendency towards unity.

Spencer based both his social and political theories on the principle of the persistence of force. Thus in *Social Statics* he argued against government interference in the workings of the country for the administrative mechanism would only dissipate social force in friction.[37] Even in his late work *The Data of Ethics* (1879), he still maintained that 'Ethics has a physical aspect; since it treats of human activities which, in common with all expenditures of energy, conform to the law of the persistence of energy: moral principles must conform to physical necessities.'[38] Lewes, however, though acknowledging a physiological basis to psychology, also recognised that social interaction introduced a higher level of complexity that did not conform to the principles of energy exchange. Men, he believed, were separated from mere animal life by 'the Language of symbols, at once the cause and effect of Civilisation'.[39] A study of the 'redistribution of Matter and Motion' could never, for Lewes, give full insight into mental evolution since human development and interaction are primarily determined by the linguistic social medium: 'The Language we think in, and the conceptions we employ, the attitude of our minds, and the means of investigation, are social products determined by the activities of the Collective Life.'[40] Language both determines individual moral and cultural development and offers a symbolic system which functions, like scientific construction, to reveal connections and relations not evident to sense.

George Eliot follows Lewes' pattern, considering Dorothea's relations to the social labyrinth on both an initial physiological level, and on the more complex level of language. Dorothea's passage through the labyrinth is from the darkness of Middlemarch life and ignorance to the light of historical and linguistic comprehension. Thwarted by her lack of any sense of connection with or understanding of the people who surround her in Middlemarch, Dorothea remarks, 'I don't feel sure about doing good in any way now: everything seems like going on a mission to a people whose language I don't know' (ch. 3, I, 40). Her cultural confusion is reinforced by that miniature version of Rome, her uncle's study; his 'severe classical nudities and smirking Renaissance-Correggiosities' were, to her, 'painfully inexplicable' (ch. 9, I, 109). Through her marriage to Casaubon, Dorothea hopes to find a language that will enable her to make sense of surrounding Middlemarch life, and the developing cultural history of the world. It is Will, however, who is to offer this illumination. On first meeting Will Dorothea refuses to offer judgement on his sketch, for pictures ' "are a language I do not understand. I suppose there is some relation between pictures and nature which I am too ignorant to feel—just as you see what a Greek sentence stands for which means nothing to me" ' (ch. 9, I, 117). The analogy is suggestive. While Casaubon imprisons his young bride in his labyrinthine research, forcing her to transcribe alien Greek characters she is not permitted to understand, Will brings a language that illuminates the unity lying beneath the surface chaos of history, embodied for Dorothea in the inexplicable art of Rome. Under his tuition Dorothea begins to gather.

> quite new notions as to the significance of Madonnas seated under inexplicable canopied thrones with the simple country as a background, and of saints with architectural models in their hands, or knives accidentally wedged in their skulls. Some things which had seemed monstrous to her were gathering intelligibility and even a natural meaning; but all this was apparently a branch of knowledge in which Mr. Casaubon had not interested himself.
>
> (ch. 22, I, 327–8)

Will breaks through Dorothea's narrow Puritanic conceptions, arousing within her an understanding of the evolving cultural language of the social organism that presages her later 'awakening' to the true relations of Middlemarch life.

Amidst the chaos of Rome, Casaubon can aid Dorothea only by making a spurious distinction between 'a genuine mythical product' and 'the romantic invention of a literary period' (ch. 20, I, 302). He is trapped by his theory that history is only a process of degeneration, that 'all the mythical systems or erratic mythical fragments in the world were corruptions of a tradition originally revealed' (ch. 3, I,

33). Will, on the other hand, is concerned less with origins than with the vital organic processes of historical growth; he would 'prefer not to know the sources of the Nile' (ch. 9, I, 120). His attitude corresponds to that outlined by Lewes, in a passage later praised by George Eliot, in which he likens the investigation of any phenomenon to the exploration of the sources of a river. Lewes stresses, however, not the importance of the source, but the 'individuality at each stage' of the river:

> the thread of light, the cloud of spray, the floating mist, and leaping cataract, the snow-flake, and the breaker, are embodied histories. Each successive form is a succession of events, each event having been determined by some prior group. This is the circulation of Cause. Causation is immanent Change.[41]

Emphasis is placed on the dynamic process of change; even seemingly static forms are in reality 'successions of events', 'embodied histories' in the process of 'immanent Change'.

Will's response to Rome partakes of this dynamic conception. While Casaubon's energy is trapped and impeded, 'lost among small closets and winding stairs' (ch. 20, I, 302), Will's, on the contrary, is released. He enjoys the miscellaneousness 'which made the mind flexible with constant comparison, and saved you from seeing the world's ages as a set of box-like partitions without vital connections' (ch. 22, I, 325). He confesses 'that Rome had given him quite a new sense of history as a whole: the fragments stimulated his imagination and made him constructive' (ch. 22, I, 325). Will's creative energy uncovers the vital organic life of history. Like George Eliot in her construction of *Middlemarch*, he reveals through constant comparison the vital interdependence of apparently fragmented parts, offering release from the labyrinth through the language of historical understanding.

Unlike Casaubon, George Eliot was actually up-to-date in her mythological research; she believed, in accordance with Feuerbach, that the creation of myth was a continual process, inseparable from the writing of history.[42] Her story of the labyrinth is thus cast on the three ascending levels of physiology, social history, and universal myth. In the mythic vision of the novel Will is presented as a solar deity. The history of Will, Dorothea, and Casaubon in fact accords with the dominant contemporary school of thought, established by Max Muller, which interpreted all myth in terms of solar symbolism.[43] Descriptions of Will centre on his irradiation of light: 'The first impression on seeing Will was one of sunny brightness ... his hair seemed to shake out light ... Mr Casaubon, on the contrary, stood rayless' (ch. 21, I, 320–1). The deliberate juxtaposition is indicative of the process by which Dorothea's struggles with Middlemarch are turned into a mythic battle between the forces of light and dark. Echoes of the myths of Dis and Persephone, and Orpheus and Eurydice, recur throughout the tale. Casaubon is surprised that the matrimonial path, which should have been bordered with flowers, did not 'prove persistently more enchanting to him than the accustomed vaults where he walked taper in hand' (ch. 10, I, 126). Casaubon's feelings as a husband are inseparable from his inability to find his way through the labyrinth of history. Dorothea, as the fair flower-gatherer Persephone, is imprisoned by her Dis in a tomb of dead languages, trapped at Lowick, whose very name suggests the absence of light and energy.[44] Will offers the only hope of light and release. The chance of seeing him acted 'like a lunette opened in the wall of her prison, giving her a glimpse of the sunny air' (ch. 37, II, 134). As Eurydice, Dorothea sees her final hope of social integration fade as her Orpheus turns towards her as he retreats:

> She longed for work which would be directly beneficient like the sunshine and the rain, and now it appeared that she was to live more and more in a virtual tomb, where there was the apparatus of a ghastly labour producing what would never see the light. To-day she had stood at the door of the tomb and seen Will Ladislaw receding into the distant world of warm activity and fellowship—turning his face towards her as he went.
>
> (ch. 48, II, 307)

Dorothea's desire for beneficent activity links the classical myth of renewal to the social ideal of organic integration. Will, as fertility god, brings the sun and rain, and thus the possibility for organic social growth.

Casaubon's incorporation within contemporary myth acts as an implicit condemnation of his belief that all myths were corruptions of one original source. Locked within the confines of this theory, ignoring even contemporary developments in his field, he refuses to acknowledge history as a constant process of organic growth and change: 'in bitter manuscript remarks on other men's notions about the solar deities, he had become indifferent to the sunlight' (ch. 20, I, 303). Will, by contrast, actively embodies the spirit of creative renewal. In talking to Dorothea he shows 'such originality as we all share with the morning and the spring-time and other endless renewals' (ch. 22, I, 342). Will shares in the mythic process of the novel, casting himself as the rescuer of Dorothea from 'fire-breathing dragons' (ch. 47, II, 299), and giving voice to the narrative's implied underlying myth of Ariadne. George Eliot's use of the term 'monstrous' to describe Dorothea's responses to Catholic art prefigures Will's own formulation of Dorothea's imprisonment:

> It is monstrous—as if you had had a vision of Hades in your childhood, like the boy in the legend. You have been brought up in some of those horrible notions that choose the sweetest women to devour—like Minotaurs. And now you will go and be shut up in that stone prison at Lowick: you will be buried alive.
>
> (ch. 22, I, 337)

As Gillian Beer has pointed out, 'Ladislaw's verbal energy readily shifts dead metaphor into myth: (monstrous becomes Minotaur)'.[45] Will's creative vision suggests how the labyrinth of classical myth becomes the imprisoning network of nineteenth-century language and beliefs.

The key to Will's role in the novel lies in the flexibility of his responses. He possesses the qualities he attributes to a poet: 'a soul in which knowledge passes instantaneously into feeling, and feeling flashes back as a new organ of knowledge' (ch. 22, I, 341–2). Knowledge does not become a 'lifeless embalment' but is fully integrated within the current of feeling. In accordance with the value structure established by physiology, energy is neither blocked nor dissipated but directly channelled.

Will's mode of expression differs markedly from that of the surrounding Middlemarch characters, whose inadequacies in social response are reflected in their choice of linguistic forms.[46] Mr Brooke's syntactic incoherence, for example, replicates his confusion in the realm of history and his social irresponsibility as a landlord; Mr Casaubon, taken on a 'severe mental scamper' by Mr Brooke, remains mindful that 'this desultoriness was associated with the institutions of the country', and that his host was a 'landholder and custos rotulorum' (ch. 3, I, 35–6). The frigid rhetoric of Casaubon's own address reflects his own particular failings in historical understanding. Thus his memory 'was a volume where a vide supra could serve instead of repetitions, and not the ordinary long-used blotting-book which only tells of forgotten writing' (ch. 3, I, 36).[47] In accordance with his model of history, Casaubon's mind and language proceed by a linear chain of association which denies any vital organic or emotional connections.

Both Rosamond Vincy and Mrs Garth are also guilty of unnecessary rigidity in their approach to language. In a judgement which reflects the neat propriety of her egoistic vision, Rosamond distinguishes between 'correct English' and 'slang' thus associating the constantly transforming social medium of language with the narrow values of her own class (ch. 11, I, 148). The worthy Mrs Garth, for her part, displays too strict an adherence to the rules of the grammar of the past. The *Lindley Murray* which, in the wreck of society, she would hold above the waves is discarded by her daughter.

Language, George Eliot reveals, need not necessarily act as a medium for vital communication but, like the pier glass of her parable, it can act directly to enforce egoistic vision. Thus Bulstrode hides behind his language of divine intention, whilst Rosamond had 'no consciousness that her action could rightly be called false' for, as George Eliot observes, 'We are not obliged to identify our own acts according to a strict classification, any more than the materials of our grocery and clothes' (ch. 65, III, 203–4). Language, when misused, actually blocks communication, creating a self-sufficient system that can remain, as Rosamond clearly shows, impervious to outside challenge or change.

In contrast to these models of language, Will's dynamic interchange between knowledge and feeling suggests a response hindered neither by egoism nor rigidity of thought. His language does not just reflect the inner world, entrapping energy like a labyrinth, but turns outwards, actively creating bonds and connections. Through conversations with Naumann, Will relates his commitment to language to his theory of history. While Casaubon believes there is only one origin to history, Naumann believes there is only one end. He assumes, in Will's words, '"that all the universe is straining towards the obscure significance of your pictures"' (ch. 19, I, 290). Imposing his own preconceptions on the historical process, Naumann ignores dynamic connections, and, like Casaubon, transforms history into a series of box-like partitions. Will, however, objects to the static air of finality such paintings carry. More experimental biologist than natural historian, he insists that the changing processes of life cannot be captured through external form: '"As if a woman were a mere coloured superficies!"' He defends, instead, language as a 'finer medium' which 'gives a fuller image, which is all the better for being vague' (ch. 19, I, 292). Since women 'change from moment to moment', only within the flexible medium of language could one hope to capture this process.

Under Will's creative vision Dorothea is revealed as the perfect enbodiment of art and language; she is 'a poem—and that is to be the best part of a poet—what makes up the poet's consciousness in his best moods' (ch. 22, I, 342). Will shifts the definition of a poem from a static form to a continuing process of effect; Dorothea, with her unified current of thought and feeling, has the integrative effect of art on the life of her fellow Middlemarchers. She holds the key to the labyrinth of art and history. Painting, Will believed, could never capture the changing timbre of a voice; Dorothea's impact on Middlemarch is described in terms of her voice—the external expression of the inner channels of the mind. For Caleb, who hears 'sublime music' in the sounds of integrated labour, Dorothea's voice recalls the 'mighty structure of tones' of parts of the *Messiah* (ch. 56, III, 29). For Lydgate, Dorothea's voice confirms the unity of history: 'That voice of deep-souled womanhood had remained within him as the enkindling conceptions of dead and sceptred genius had remained within him' (ch. 58, III, 91). Dorothea offers a resolution to social and historical fragmentariness. As Will illuminated the chaos of Rome for her, so she illuminates the life of Middlemarch: 'The presence of a noble nature, generous in its wishes, ardent in its charity, changes the lights for us: we begin to see things again in their larger, quieter masses, and to believe that we too can be seen and judged in the wholeness of our character' (ch. 76, III, 352). Dorothea breaks through the narrowing egoism of Lydgate's vision to suggest order where he perceives only chaos. Her ardent faith leads her past the stumbling block of insular perception to a wider, integrated vision of the social whole. Dorothea follows, in fact, the unifying processes of both art and science, creating the 'ideally illuminated space' of Lydgate's scientific vision.

In revealing the underlying unity of the social organism Dorothea fulfils, on a scientific plane, her mythic role of Ariadne.[48] Bernard used the image of Ariadne's thread to describe the complex interdependence of organic life which rendered experimentation, and thus scientific medicine, possible.[49] Lewes extends the image to encompass the fundamental processes of science:

> It is the greatness of Science that while satisfying the spiritual thirst for knowledge, it satisfies the pressing desire for guidance in action: not only painting a picture of the wondrous labyrinth of Nature, but placing in our hands the Ariadne-thread to lead us through the labyrinth.[50]

Dorothea, with her desire for a life both 'rational and ardent' is the narrative's Ariadne thread. It is she, not Lydgate, who is the novel's true physician; instead of searching for origins she offers, through her vision of social interconnections, actual 'guidance in action'. Dorothea fulfils, within the novel, her creator's fictional goal for, as George Eliot observed in a letter of 1868, 'the inspiring principle which alone gives me courage to write is, that of so presenting our human life as to help my readers in getting a clearer conception and a more active admiration of those vital elements which bind men together and give a higher worthiness to their existence'.[51]

As creative experimenter, George Eliot weaves together the materials of history, science and myth, attempting to find a resolution to the social problem posed in the Prelude. Through the play of metaphor the social labyrinth is transposed into one of mind, and then of history, resolvable, on a physiological level, through flexibility of response, and on a conceptual level, through the light of historical understanding. Yet, though Dorothea shows Lydgate things 'in their larger, quieter masses', he is still judged by the petty Middlemarch mind. Will might irradiate light, but Dorothea, in marrying him, becomes only 'a wife and mother'. On a material level, the labyrinth is successfully traversed once property is correctly channelled; but Dorothea's son, though inheriting the estates, declines the stifling possibility of representing Middlemarch. Though George Eliot moves into the realm of myth and symbol, using the ideal hypothesis of a labyrinth to construct the moral framework of her novel, she is still committed to a traditional realist form of narrative resolution.

The complexities and internal contradictions within *Middlemarch* can be traced, in large part, to the relationship between the moral and epistemological aspects of contemporary organicist theory. Thus Lewes, defining his dynamic theory of organic social composition observed: 'the search after the *thing in itself* is chimerical: the thing being a group of relations it *is* what these are. Hence the highest form of existence is Altruism, or that moral and intellectual condition which is determined by the fullest consciousness – emotional and cognitive – of relations.'[52] The passage could be taken as a scenario for *Middlemarch*. The moral climax of the novel occurs, as Paris has noted, when Dorothea, arising from her night of sorrow, sees the far-off figures in the field: 'she felt the largeness of the world and the manifold wakings of men to labour and endurance. She was a part of that involuntary, palpitating life, and could neither look out on it from her luxurious shelter as a mere spectator, nor hide her eyes in selfish complaining' (ch. 80, III, 392).[53] Dorothea transcends the narrowing limitations of egoism to accept the full responsibilities of her social role. In thus recognising her membership of that 'palpitating' she attains the emotional and cognitive understanding of relations which, for Lewes, constitutes the state of Altruism.

There is, however, a logical jump in Lewes' argument. No essential connection exists between the epistemological statement that a thing *is* its relations, and the moral conclusion that full knowledge of these relations would create a state of altruism.[54] Lewes, in fact, assumes that the relations of mutual dependence within the social organism are, in essence, harmonious, and that increased understanding of these social relations will necessarily lead to augmented good will, and not hostility. Yet Middlemarch, as George Eliot clearly reveals, is not a harmonious whole; it possesses all the vices of a capitalist economy, and the social antagonisms of a class-ridden society. Indeed, the analysis of the functions of that primary connecting medium, language, or gossip, does not augur well for a Middlemarch blessed in the future with increased understanding of mutual relations. George Eliot's ambivalent response to organic theory is reflected in the novel in her treatment of Dorothea. Although Dorothea ardently desires full social integration her stature as heroine in fact arises from her social aloofness, her blindness to the petty courses of the Middlemarch mind. Following her awakening George Eliot promptly removes her from the town. The theory of growing social altruism is not put to the test.

Like Lewes, George Eliot is torn between intellectual allegiance to a radical, dynamic theory of organic life, and emotional commitment to a moral vision of social order. Although Lewes formulated a model of organic life which could encompass conflict and contradiction, he yet attempted to wed this conception to his moral belief in evolving social harmony. George Eliot adopts, in Lydgate's biological theories of organic interdependence, a theoretical model which forms the basis, in the novel, for a dynamic social theory, and a radical conception of fictional method. Yet her commitment to fluidity and ideal construction is undercut by her simultaneous allegiance to the idea of narrative resolution. Thus, as I argued earlier, in portraying the histories of her characters she employs physiology to create moral closure. The admission that 'character is process' is counteracted by the fact that Lydgate's relations with Middlemarch are merely the analogue of his prior psychic structure.

In the case of Bulstrode, George Eliot uses the physiological unity of the unconscious mind to suggest moral order and coherence in external social events. Although more openness is evident in the representation of Dorothea, her innate physiological constitution, the one ardent channel of her mind, functions as a locus of value. Flexibility is over-ruled amidst the imperative need for a fixed basis for moral judgement.

George Eliot's dual allegiances are clearly revealed in the Finale which opens with the observation that the fluidity of social life actually prohibits narrative closure for 'Every limit is a beginning as well as an ending'. There can be no final moral judgements since the fragment examined will not be necessarily 'the sample of an even web'. Yet this statement of continuing process is immediately followed by an atemporal vision of Fred and Mary's future: 'On inquiry it might possibly be found that Fred and Mary still inhabit Stone Court—that the creeping plants still cast the foam of their blossoms over the fine stone-wall into the field where the walnut-trees stand in stately row' (III, 459). Instead of organic process we are presented with a vision of life in which there is no possibility of change. The technique recalls the Epilogue of *Adam Bede* where apparent changes were referred to the constants of light, and the unchanging house. Here again we are referred to the solidity of objects in a natural landscape; the eternal natural rhythms guarantee the unchanging order of Fred and Mary's style of life. This ending is in keeping with the treatment of the Garths throughout the novel for, within the harsh social world of Middlemarch, they seem to repre-sent an enclave of pastoral organicism. Caleb, with his worship of the divinity of labour, is a later embodiment of Adam Bede. Despite references to mechanisation and the encroaching town, he still seems to live within an unchanging rural order. Indeed the Garths' house, 'a homely place with an orchard in front of it' (ch. 24, I, 369), clearly belongs to the world of Hayslope. *Middlemarch*, however, differs fundamentally from the earlier novel. While the Epilogue of *Adam Bede* merely reaffirmed the values and model of society which ran throughout the book, the Finale of *Middlemarch* creates internal contradiction. The atemporality and affirmation of pastoral organ-icism which characterises the portrait of Fred and Mary's future lives consorts strangely with the dynamic representation of society, where constant changes create fresh difficulties for social integration.

George Eliot cannot escape, in *Middlemarch*, the fundamental problem that her moral vision of organic interdependence is clearly at odds with her analysis of the harmful, destructive effects of social

integration. In *The Mill on the Floss* this problem was resolved by the
two endings: the idealistic, atemporal vision of Tom and Maggie's
union, and the realistic assessment of the ravages of nature. A similar
contradiction gives rise to a dual ending in *Middlemarch*. In marked
contrast to the idyll of Fred and Mary the Finale also covers the
future histories of Lydgate and Dorothea. Lydgate's future, in which
he experiences an absolute contradiction between the report of his
inner senses and that of the outer world, is the direct antithesis of the
sentimentalised picture of Fred and Mary. The treatment of Dorothea
is more complex. On the one hand, there is a tone of regret, an
admission, almost, of failure: 'Many who knew her, thought it a pity
that so substantive and rare a creature should have been absorbed
into the life of another, and be only known in a certain circle as a
wife and mother' (III, 461). But, on the other hand, there is an
attempt to integrate this vision of Dorothea's future with the organic
ideal. The birth and inheritance of Dorothea's son is given a
commanding position in the concluding paragraphs thus suggesting
the continuity of the social organism on a material level. George Eliot
also draws upon the psychological and social implications of the
term channel to demonstrate Dorothea's impact on evolving social
order: 'Her finely-touched spirit had still its fine issues, though they
were not widely visible. Her full nature, like that river of which
Cyrus broke the strength, spent itself in channels which had no great
name on the earth' (III, 465).

This concluding passage was clearly resonant for George Eliot;
echoes of its imagery appear in her work eight years later. In
preparing for publication the final volume of Lewes' *Problems of
Life and Mind* she added the following section to explain his theory
that consciousness of social interdependence awakens sympathy, 'till
we finally see in many highly wrought natures a complete submerg-
ence (or, if you will, a transference) of egoistic desire, and an habitual
outrush of the emotional force in sympathetic channels'.[55]
Dorothea, with her 'finely-touched spirit' literally embodies this
organic ideal. Sympathy, not egoism, clearly determines the outrush
of her feeling into external social channels. George Eliot draws on
the organic principle of interdependence, by which movement of
each part effects the whole, to suggest that Dorothea's life will
determine the future development of the entire social organism.

A less positive conclusion, however, is implied by the reference to
Cyrus, whose history George Eliot recorded in her 'Middlemarch
Miscellany': the breaking of the river's strength staved off the fall of

Babylon, but only for one year.[56] George Eliot is torn, finally, between an idealistic commitment to the organic ideal, and a realistic assessment of possibilities. Her references to the vital 'growing good of the world' are counteracted by the final image of the novel: 'unvisited tombs'. Associations with Casaubon are immediately provoked, summoning images of death in life, and casting the gloomy shadow of Casaubon's sterility over the conclusions of the novel. In the mythological battle between light and dark, the forces of darkness remain unvanquished.

From Sally Shuttleworth, *George Eliot and Nineteenth-Century Science: The Make-Believe of a Beginning* (Cambridge, 1984), pp. 142–74.

NOTES

[Like Suzanne Graver in the previous essay, Sally Shuttleworth sets George Eliot in her Victorian context, judging her novels against systems of belief and ideas at the time. The focus here is on nineteenth-century science. We begin to appreciate the relevance of this to George Eliot's work when we see that what is focused on is organic theory, which raises questions about the relationship of the part to the whole. Shuttleworth explores the far from simple nature of such ideas in Victorian England, and how George Eliot's novel, rather than expounding a single position, is complex and uncertain. The whole of Shuttleworth's long chapter on *Middlemarch* has been reprinted as the detail of the chapter underlines the complexity of George Eliot's project in the novel, and the intricacy and subtlety of her achievement. We are offered a powerful picture of the text as a product of its period, and of the text, in its sophistication as a work of art, living up to Shuttleworth's description of George Eliot as a 'creative experimenter [who] weaves together the materials of history, science and myth, attempting to find a resolution to the social problem posed in the Prelude'. The chapter refers frequently to G. H. Lewes, the man George Eliot lived with from 1854 until his death in 1878; they were unable to marry as he could not divorce his wife. Ed.]

1. George Eliot, *Middlemarch*, Cabinet Edition, 3 vols (Edinburgh, 1878–80), Prelude, I, p. 2. All references to this edition are cited hereafter in the text.

2. In Lewes' *The Study of Psychology* (London, 1879), which George Eliot prepared for publication, there occurs the observation that we may 'term History an experiment instituted by Society, since it presents conspicuous variations of mental reactions under varying social conditions' (p. 152). In writing the history of *Middlemarch*, George Eliot

was instituting her own experiment, creating her own experimental conditions.

3. My interpretation of George Eliot's fictional methodology differs from that of Bernard J. Paris (*Experiments in Life* [Detroit, 1965]) who views her as a 'militant empiricist' throughout her career (p. 73). I would argue that the theory of realism which she defined in her review of Ruskin's *Modern Painters* (see Paris, p. 26 and ch. 4) only applies to her earlier work. Although Paris views all George Eliot's novels as 'experiments', I would suggest that the term should perhaps be more narrowly applied to *Middlemarch* and *Daniel Deronda* in order to distinguish the radical changes which occur in her methodology in these works.

4. For discussion of this point see Michael York Mason, '*Middlemarch* and Science: Problems of Life and Mind', *Review of English Studies*, 22 (1971) 151, 162; Gillian Beer, 'Plot and the Analogy with Science in later Nineteenth-Century Novelists', *Comparative Criticism: A Yearbook*, ed. E. S. Shaffer, 2 (1980), pp. 138, 144–5; George Levine, 'George Eliot's Hypothesis of Reality', *Nineteenth-Century Fiction*, 35 (1980), 12–13.

5. Claude Bernard, *Leçons de physiologie expérimentale appliquée à la médicine*, vol. 2 (Paris, 1855–6), p. 12.

6. G. H. Lewes, *The Foundations of a Creed*, vol. 1 (London, 1874), p. 296. Lewes was working on this volume while George Eliot was writing *Middlemarch*.

7. Claude Bernard, *An Introduction to the Study of Experimental Medicine*, trans. Henry C. Green (New York, 1949), p. 18.

8. G. H. Lewes, *The Foundations of a Creed*, vol. 1 (London, 1874), p. 26.

9. Claude Bernard, *An Introduction to the Study of Experimental Medicine*, trans. Henry C. Green (New York, 1949), p. 26.

10. Ibid., p. 34.

11. G. H. Lewes, *The Foundations of a Creed*, vol. 1 (London, 1874), p. 296; vol. 2 (London, 1875), p. 28.

12. G. H. Lewes, *Sea-side Studies* (Edinburgh, 1858), p. 153.

13. George Eliot observes, in a letter to Mrs Gaskell written in 1859, that, 'I was conscious, while the question of my power was still undecided for me, that my feeling towards Life and Art had some affinity with the feeling which had inspired *Cranford* and the earlier chapters of *Mary Barton*' (G. S. Haight, *The George Eliot Letters*, vol. 3 [New Haven and London, 1954–5], p. 198). The spirit of *Cranford*, which George Eliot read for the first time in 1857, lies behind *Scenes of Clerical Life* and *Adam Bede*.

14. G. H. Lewes, *The Foundations of a Creed*, vol. 2 (London, 1875), p. 18.

15. G. H. Lewes, *The Foundations of a Creed*, vol. 1 (London, 1874), p. 128.

16 G. H. Lewes, *The Foundations of a Creed*, vol. 1 (London, 1874), p. 124.

17. For an extended analysis of chapter construction in *Middlemarch* see John Holloway, 'Narrative Process in *Middlemarch*', in *Narrative and Structure: Exploratory Essays* (Cambridge, 1979), pp. 38–52.

18. George Eliot, 'Notes on Form in Art (1868)', in Thomas Pinney (ed.), *Essays of George Eliot* (London, 1963), pp. 431–6 (p. 432).

19. Thomas Pinney (ed.), *Essays of George Eliot* (London, 1963), pp. 433.

20. This theory was first outlined in 'The Philosophy of Style', published in the *Westminster Review*, 58 (October, 1852), 234–47, whilst George Eliot was editor. Herbert Spencer, *Essays: Scientific, Political and Speculative, First Series* (London, 1858), p. 261.

21. Thomas Pinney (ed.), *Essays of George Eliot* (London, 1963), pp. 435–6.

22. J. Hillis Miller, 'Narrative and History', *English Literary History*, 41 (1974), 455–73 (p. 468).

23. G. H. Lewes, *The Foundations of a Creed*, vol. 2 (London, 1875), p. 27.

24. Lewes had adopted De Blainville's definition from Comte. See G. H. Lewes, *Comte's Philosophy of the Sciences* (London, 1852–3), pp. 171–3.

25. G. H. Lewes, *The Foundations of a Creed*, vol. 2 (London, 1875), pp. 122–3.

26. See G. H. Lewes, *The Physiology of Common Life*, vol. 2 (London, 1859–60), p. 68.

27. Ibid., p. 58.

28. In his article 'Optic and Semiotic in *Middlemarch*', J. Hillis Miller traces the 'family of intertwined metaphors and motifs – the web, the current, the minutely subdivided entity' which occurs in the novel and enquires in a footnote, 'What, exactly, is the nature of the resemblance which binds together the members of this family and makes it seem of one genetic stock? Why, if Eliot's goal is to describe what is 'really there', objectively, must there be more than one model in order to create a total picture?' (*The Worlds of Victorian Fiction*, ed. J. H. Buckley [Cambridge, 1975]). I would suggest that all these metaphors can be traced back to the same source in contemporary physiological and psychological theory. [Hillis Miller's essay is reprinted in this collection – see p. 65. Ed.]

29. Herbert Spencer, *The Principles of Psychology*, 2nd edn, 2 vols (London, 1870–2), vol. 1, p. 585.

30. Diary entry for 30 May 1870; Manuscript diary, July 1861–December 1877, no. 3, Beinecke Rare Book and Manuscript Library, Yale University.

31. William Grove, *On the Correlation of Physical Forces*, 3rd edn (London, 1855), p. 211.

32. G. H. Lewes, *The Foundations of a Creed*, vol. 1 (London, 1874), p. 114.

33. G. H. Lewes, *The Foundations of a Creed*, vol. 2 (London, 1875), p. 457.

34. G. H. Lewes, *The Foundations of a Creed*, vol. 1 (London, 1874), pp. 144–5.

35. Herbert Spencer, *The Principles of Psychology*, 2nd edn, 2 vols (London, 1870–2), vol. 1, p. 509.

36. G. H. Lewes, *The Foundations of a Creed*, vol. 1 (London, 1874), p. 121.

37. Herbert Spencer, *Social Statics* (London, 1850), p. 279.

38. Herbert Spencer, *The Data of Ethics* (London, 1879), p. 62.

39. G. H. Lewes, *The Foundations of a Creed*, vol. 1 (London, 1874), p. 156.

40. Ibid., p. 174.

41. Ibid., p. 360.

42. George Eliot, or rather, Marian Evans, had published her translation of Feuerbach's *The Essence of Christianity* in 1854, before she embarked on her career as novelist. All her novels, however, as Paris (*Experiments in Life* [Detroit, 1965]) has argued, reveal the impact of Feuerbach's ideas.

43. For an analysis of the role of myth in *Middlemarch* see Gillian Beer, 'Myth and the Single Consciousness: *Middlemarch* and "The Lifted Veil"', in Ian Adam (ed.), *This Particular Web: Essays on 'Middlemarch'* (Toronto, 1975), pp. 91–115; Brian Swann, '*Middlemarch* and Myth', *Nineteenth-Century Fiction*, 28 (1973–4), 210–14; and U. C. Knoepflmacher, 'Fusing Fact and Myth: The New Reality of *Middlemarch*', in Adam (ed.), *This Particular Web: Essays on 'Middlemarch'* (Toronto, 1975), pp. 43–72. I am indebted to all these articles in my discussion of myth.

44. A point made by Brian Swann, '*Middlemarch* and Myth', *Nineteenth-Century Fiction*, 28 (1973–4), 213.

45. Gillian Beer, 'Myth and the Single Consciousness', in Ian Adam (ed.), *This Particular Web: Essays on 'Middlemarch'* (Toronto, 1975), p. 105.

46. For a good analysis of the function of language and dialogue in *Middlemarch* see Robert Kiely, 'The Limits of Dialogue in *Middle-*

march', in J. H. Buckley (ed.), *The Worlds of Victorian Fiction* (Cambridge, 1975), pp. 103–24.

47. Lewes, in describing his conception of the mind, used the image of the palimpsest.

48. Dorothea, when first encountered in Rome, is standing next to a statue of Ariadne (ch. 19, 1, 288).

49. See Claude Bernard, 'Du Progrès dans les sciences physiologiques', *Revue des Deux Mondes*, 58 (1865), 653.

50. G. H. Lewes, *The Foundations of a Creed*, vol. 1 (London, 1874), p. 26.

51. G. S. Haight (ed.), *The George Eliot Letters*, vol. 4 (New Haven and London, 1954–5), p. 472.

52. G. H. Lewes, *The Foundations of a Creed*, vol. 2 (London, 1875), p. 27.

53. See Bernard J. Paris, *Experiments in Life* (Detroit, 1965), p. 190.

54. My interpretation of the Lewes passage differs from that of George Levine in 'George Eliot's Hypothesis of Reality', *Nineteenth-Century Fiction*, 35 (1980), 8, who seems to follow Lewes and Eliot in imposing a moral interpretation on an epistemological principle.

55. K. K. Collins, 'G. H. Lewes Revised: George Eliot and the Moral Sense', *Victorian Studies*, 21 (1978), 491.

56. See John Clark Pratt and Victor A. Neufeldt (eds), *George Eliot's 'Middlemarch' Notebooks* (Berkeley and Los Angeles, 1979), p. 101, n. 4.

8

'Middlemarch': Vocation, Love and the Woman Question

KATHLEEN BLAKE

Eliot shows that one of Lydgate's 'spots of commonness' contributes heavily to the failure of the marriage. This spot is indeed common; if it were less so Rosamond would not be what she is. Lydgate completely fails to imagine that she resembles himself in needing something to do, and that he himself becomes her work by default. 'It had not occurred to Lydgate that he had been a subject of eager meditation to Rosamond, who had neither any reason for throwing her marriage into distant perspective, nor any pathological studies to divert her mind from that ruminating habit, that inward repetition of looks, words, and phrases, which makes a large part in the lives of most girls' (p. 123). In the same scene in which Lydgate expresses his deep need to act and to be recognised for his accomplishments – 'What good is like to this, / To do worthy the writing, and to write / Worthy the reading and the world's delight?' – he wonders why Rosamond displays no ambition. He conceives of a woman's ambition as her wanting her husband to achieve great things (pp. 319–20). This conception of women as beings providentially framed to live in and through their husbands meets the refuting irony of Rosamond's failure to identify with him at all, as becomes clear during his troubles. Lydgate expects that women should find fulfilment through a vicariousness that his own experience, indeed all of *Middlemarch*, puts in question.

For when women fulfil their need for vocation through men, they do so through their impact on the men, not through the men's independent achievements. Rosamond knows that she does not make a great deal of difference to Lydgate's scientific research. When he ruminates on it, 'Rosamond's presence at that moment was perhaps no more than a spoonful brought to the lake, and her woman's instinct in this matter was not dull' (p. 334). She can achieve more measurable effect in gaining a home and furniture than in aiding in the discovery of the primitive tissue, and if we are not charmed to see her aiming at these things and forcing Lydgate to go along, we can hardly feel the surprise necessary for outrage. When women have no work but men, and men fail to realise it, a husband may well find the romance of vocation disrupted by the romance of the sexes.

*

Rosamond thrives and Lydgate succumbs, while Dorothea is released by Casaubon's death. Yet she emerges only into 'another sort of pinfold than that from which she had been released' (p. 361). Does Dorothea escape from this pinfold when she takes the initiative and marries Will despite Middlemarch? I think not entirely, for the tone of regret sounds strongly in the 'Finale', at the same time that the novel reconciles itself to what could hardly be helped. The end balances gains and losses. Dorothea and Will are dear to each other, and she finds some scope for achievement in her marriage, and yet their union represents some sacrifice too, only less sad than might have been (p. 612). Eliot says that 'many . . . thought it a pity that so substantive and rare a creature should have been absorbed into the life of another . . . but no one stated exactly what else that was in her power she ought rather to have done' (p. 611).

Dorothea does not gain the stature of a nineteenth-century Saint Theresa. The blocking of the channels to deeds also diffuses or deflects the character which might have performed them, hence the 'inconvenient indefiniteness' of even the most impressive women, or their lapse into 'the common yearning of womanhood'. Dorothea achieves the definite at the expense of her highest potential, which remains too vague to do much good to her or to the world. In explaining her decision to marry Will she says, 'I might have done something better, if I had been better. But this is what I am going to do' (p. 601). *Middlemarch* shows that Dorothea would have *been* better if she had been in a position to *do* better. Eliot does not allow us the sentimental contemplation of great souls trapped in an indifferent universe; souls that do not contribute significantly lose some of their greatness. Lydgate apprehends this in his own case (p. 473). The same holds for Dorothea, though she bears less blame for her fate. In her essay on Margaret Fuller and Mary Wollstonecraft, Eliot commends the two feminists for refusing to idealise women. Indeed, women's standing below the level of their potential argues the need for emancipation.

While generally recognising that Dorothea hardly liberates herself from Middlemarch to the extent of undertaking epic action, opinion varies as to the scope of her pinfold and the amount of satisfaction we should feel in it. At the centre of this debate stands Will Ladislaw. Dorothea's marriage to Will disappointed many early reviewers, as it did early readers like those Eliot describes in a letter to John Blackwood. Two ladies came up to her at Oxford; one wondered how she could let Dorothea marry that Casaubon, while the other found Ladislaw just as bad.[1]

Will is often criticised on the grounds of inadequacy for his impressive wife. Henry James, Leslie Stephen, Lord David Cecil and Walter Allen speak for the view that Eliot is carried away by her own fondness for him. Jerome Thale blames her for a lapse in artistic control rather than a lapse in her taste in men. Not so much authorial indulgence as insufficient development accounts for Will's weakness, he says. Patricia Beer reverses the analysis by finding distaste for Will as a conceited dilettante the sentiment Eliot 'cannot help' venting, though she intends otherwise, and Jean Kennard joins those assuming that the author means Will to be a match for Dorothea but fails to convey it.[2]

Some critics take the other, I think wrong, course of concluding that since Eliot ends her book with a second marriage better than the first, we must view Will with full favour. Foremost among these are believers in marriage and the family and the woman's finding her man. But Eliot's ironies at the expense of the third-volume marriage in 'Silly Novels by Lady Novelists' indicate that she did not always regard marriage as 'that desirable consummation'.[3]

I place myself among the small number of critics for whom R. H. Hutton in the *British Quarterly Review* of 1873 may speak: 'one feels, and is probably meant to feel acutely, that here too, it is the "meanness of opportunity" and not intrinsic suitability, which determines Dorothea's second comparatively happy marriage.'[4] Will seems a slight creature beside her. Surely Eliot means us to sense this when she follows the climactic chapter on Dorothea's noble resolve in going to Rosamond by opening the next chapter with Will's flimsier kind of resolve – 'a state of mind liable to melt into a minuet with other states of mind, and to find itself bowing, smiling, and giving place with polite facility' (p. 586).

Will adds to his own limitations certain assumptions about women's limitations which create a sometimes uncomfortable resemblance to Mr Brooke, Sir James, Lydgate and Casaubon. He can be as put off by Dorothea's power and eloquence as any of them. Eliot says of him, 'A man is seldom ashamed of feeling that he cannot love a woman so well when he sees a certain greatness in her: nature having intended greatness for men' (p. 285). He cherishes Dorothea's innocent shortsightedness and her inaccessibility. He would almost rather do without her love than that she be sullied by recognising the obvious fact of his devotion and the implications of Casaubon's jealousy. Also, 'what others might have called the futility of his passion, made an additional delight for his imagination' (p. 344). His pedestal theory – Dorothea sits 'enthroned in his soul' according to the dictates of the 'higher love poetry' (p. 344) – sometimes produces problems for her. In her carriage, passing him as he walks on foot, she 'felt a pang at being seated there in a sort of exaltation, leaving him behind' (p. 465). One wonders whether she might not lose a bit of her charm for him in delivering herself from the pedestal into his arms, just as she does in speaking with unfeminine greatness.

Will shares some of the attitudes that contribute to the meanness of a woman's opportunity, but at the same time, the very irresoluteness and flexibility that make him slight, make him impressionable. He can take the pressure of other people's thoughts (p. 364). And Dorothea certainly needs to make a mark somewhere. She will be able to find some vocation in influencing his work.

Any estimation of Dorothea's final lot should take account, not only of her husband's character, but of his work toward political reform, for we know that she gives him wifely help in it. The magnitude of the undertaking to which she contributes is too seldom considered. Eliot's readers had just witnessed the passage of the second Reform Bill, and though *Middlemarch* ends with the defeat of the first Reform Bill, they would have recognised this as a temporary setback. An historical perspective informs the novel. Setting the story in 'ante-reform times' (p. 20) locates it in relation to the ultimate passage of Reform. Helping a husband who works for this passage, Dorothea helps forward a movement that would eventually prevail and that bears comparison to Saint Theresa's reform of a religious order as a 'far-resonant action'. The importance of Reform is, I think, a given. To understand it forms part of the necessary equipment for reading the novel. In her notebook Eliot ranks it as one of the momentous events of the period. We can take Felix Holt as a spokesman for her political views, more than is usually safe when it comes to fictional characters, since she uses his persona in a separate non-fictional political article for *Blackwood's* in 1868. Felix Holt advocates Reform. He says he would despise any man not interested in the great political movement of the time. His friend and fellow-Radical calls it a 'massive achievement'.[5] In *Middlemarch* Will Ladislaw emerges with the upper hand in contending against Lydgate that the Bill must be passed, if necessary even without immaculate political tools. Whatever Eliot's reservations about some of the tactics for passing Reform, she surely judges it part of 'the growing good of the world' (p. 613). While our hopefulness in response to the end of *Middlemarch* should be somewhat dashed in contemplating Will, we may find something heartening in the prospect of Reform.

*

Women's writing on feminine accommodation or failure presents a problem for feminist criticism, as we have seen in the chariness of response to Christina Rossetti. Thus feminist critics are often discouraged by the end of *Middlemarch* – more than they need be. Neither Abba Goold Woolson in the 1880s nor Lee Edwards, Patricia Beer, Jean Kennard, Patricia Stubbs, or Jenni Calder nearly a hundred years later pays any attention to Reform. Woolson reproaches Eliot for suggesting that a heroine must fail when some real women do not; Edwards and Beer point out that Eliot did not. Kennard thinks the author fell into the trap of a literary convention that demands a marriage, however it might shortchange the heroine. Stubbs thinks Dorothea comes to too little, and Calder that Eliot cheats us of Dorothea's success.[6]

When Harriet Rosenstein excoriates Elizabeth Hardwick's book *Seduction and Betrayal* for seeming to endorse a literary tradition that dignifies women by measure of their tragic calamity, she implies a contrary ideal for women's writing. Woolson supplies a description of the ideal, to which, in less Victorian terms, some modern feminists seem to subscribe: 'From the fictitious scenes upon [the female author's] pages, her gifted sisters will gather inspiration and hope, to quicken all their brave endeavours after good. For she will picture their advancing life, not as a gloomy valley, into which their pathways must descend through ever deepening shades, till existence closes in endless night, but as a broadening upland, along whose sweet ascents they are summoned to pass, with bounding steps and uplifted gaze.' Eliot does not summon her heroine to an altogether sweet ascent, but to supply such a satisfactory summons would endanger realism. Ruth Yeazell and Zelda Austen chide critics for expecting pictures of strong women succeeding in the literature of a period that didn't make them likely in life. Feminist criticism has now gone beyond the stage of a simple insistence on positive role models. Still, Patricia Stubbs challenges the realistic tradition of the novel as one confined to diagnosing existing contradictions and suffering, and she prefers a utopian strain. Finding little to please her in Eliot, she takes an attitude reminiscent of Lee Edwards' – Edwards decides that *Middlemarch* 'can no longer be one of the books of my life'.[7]

If I examine my own feelings upon finishing *Middlemarch*, I don't find depression predominant. As a reader I respond to the fact that if the main characters all slip below their own intentions, the novel doesn't. I venture here an explanation that may seem to stretch thin because it can be made to cover so much. What great work cannot be said to redeem sad content by the inspiration of its artistry? But then again, does not form triumph palpably in a work so acutely concerned with dispersal?

A strong narrative control has traditionally been recognised in Eliot's works. Studies of the composition of *Middlemarch* by Ann Theresa Kitchel and Jerome Beaty show its highly systematic construction. Here is a control that not only operates but makes itself felt. In fact, a standard complaint directs itself against Eliot's insistence as a narrator. She generalises, she judges, she philosophises, she aphorises, she moralises. Those who resist this intrusive narrative persona, which they would rather see disappear behind the characters, attest to its power. The word power figures often in commentary on Eliot. A commonplace of critical discourse, certainly, in this case it often takes on a rather literal meaning. Sidney Colvin's essay in the *Fortnightly Review* offers a good example. He keeps coming back to the 'overwhelming power', the 'potency', and 'trenchancy' of the style. Likewise, finding Eliot's narrator the most fully realised of the characters, Quentin Anderson remarks, 'when one is reading

Middlemarch there are many moments when one looks up and says, "How intelligent, how penetrating this woman is!" [8]

And yet there are those who question Eliot's controlling intelligence. Notably, Will Ladislaw seems to some to escape his creator's designs. Calvin Bedient boldly avers that *Middlemarch* 'has written itself', that the theme holds Eliot 'helplessly and almost mindlessly in its spell'. A development in feminist criticism takes a similar direction. It derives, I think, from the feminist quandary in dealing with a literature of compromised heroines. For example, Sandra Gilbert and Susan Gubar find a 'compensatory and conservative' element in the credit Eliot gives to the feminine fate of making something of very little. But instead of judging this harshly (as they sometimes do Rossetti's work) they deploy a theory that allows for more sympathy. Boldly provocative, this theory grows out of Harold Bloom's Oedipal explanation of literary influence, with its ultimate roots in Freud, and it gives large scope to the unconscious workings of the author's mind and text. 'What literary women have hidden or disguised' becomes essential, what they have covered, evaded, veiled, submerged. Working 'consciously or unconsciously', a repeated phrase, they subvert their own ostensible messages of accommodation. Due to the strain of their 'anxiety of authorship', they write less consciously and objectively than male writers. Gilbert and Gubar concentrate on a subversive strain of rage throughout nineteenth-century literature by women, and this they find in Eliot's novels, especially in plots that punish male characters who symbolise patriarchal power (Casaubon, even Lydgate). They find violent meanings at odds with Eliot's professed purposes. [9]

A related character of thought informs the philosophically sophisticated work of Mary Jacobus. She builds on the linguistic theory of Jacques Lacan and the theory of textual deconstruction of Jacques Derrida, both indebted to Freud, and she makes use of French feminist revisions of these positions. She locates feminism in gaps of coherence and awkward spots, such as in the very ill-fittingness of the original lines of indictment in *Middlemarch*'s 'Finale', later 'self-censored' by Eliot. Deconstruction offers attractions to those feminists who, in the manner of Lacan, conclude that language itself and, with this, the structures of thought are 'phallocentric'. If one is willing to accept that to make sense is masculine, it follows that what is most feminist, most subversive, must emerge from the subtext, from below thought. Whether in feminist or other deconstructions, attention goes to the unintended, the unconscious, the unassimilated, disproportionate, uncontrolled. And as Jacobus says, 'the rift [in the text] exposes the fiction of authorial control and objectivity'. Whatever this approach has to offer, it tends to take away the author as a disciplined maker of meaning, an artist. Thus in work akin to Jacobus' Nancy K. Miller uses a Freudian theory of daydreaming to comment on Eliot's literary creation. Just as I am affronted by Bedient's picture of a helpless and mindless Eliot whose book writes itself, I find myself dismayed by feminist post-Freudian deconstructions, deauthorisations of women authors. I look to the past to discover and celebrate female striving and accomplishment and hesitate to let go a belief in women's power of conscious shaping. Derrida himself recognises a common nostalgia for presence, origin, authority, producer, subject. As a student of an age when people sought to bring forth self and product by work, I feel a certain nostalgia for the producing subject, and, as a feminist literary critic, I feel especially nostalgic for the authority of women writers. Not denying the artist her spontaneity, still, with Simone de Beauvoir, I want to suppose her 'witting' and well-considering. Derrida recognises that we all use language and ideas that serve us, though we can admit them to be problematical. So deconstructionists speak of the anonymity of textuality, but I choose to speak of George Eliot.[10]

If anyone exerts authority, George Eliot does. Her power draws attention to itself. While Mr Brooke's discourse flows out in a manner desultory and glutinous, this does not happen in the narration of *Middlemarch*. The unfolding of the eighty-six chapters, the 'Prelude', and the 'Finale' follows a principle of human speech different from the usual one, which dictates saying what one has said before (p. 28). How can Eliot keep up for so long the eloquent incisiveness of her images and phrases? – memory resembles 'the ordinary long-used blotting-book which tells only of forgotten writing'; 'in bitter manuscript remarks on other men's notions about the solar deities, Casaubon had become indifferent to the sunlight'; in Rosamond's petty mind 'there was not room enough for luxuries to look small in' (pp. 19, 147, 514). The spectacle of Rome is like 'a disease of the retina'; to be sensitive to ordinary human suffering would mean to 'die of that roar which lies on the other side of silence' (p. 144). Something noticeably strenuous informs these expressions. George Eliot is as strenuous as her characters.

From this point of view, the narrator plays counterpoint to the characters. Where they fail, she succeeds, and we sense it on every page. We see how the constraints of Middlemarch frustrate a woman's impulse toward vocation, turning her toward love and, in turn, turning love into self-postponement. We see how a man's failure, too, derives indirectly from the common view identifying women with love to the exclusion of other vocations. At the same time the text of *Middlemarch* itself affirms the possibility of 'far-resonant action' and 'long recognizable deed'. No feminist need feel disappointed.

From Kathleen Blake, *Love and The Woman Question in Victorian Literature* (Brighton, 1983), pp. 44–53.

NOTES

[Traditional criticism of *Middlemarch* tended to stress the unity and coherence of George Eliot's vision. Some critics, however, found it easy to dismiss this as narrowness and conservatism. More recently critics have focused on the contradictory nature of *Middlemarch*. Nowhere are these issues more clearly seen than in considerations of George Eliot's presentation of women characters. The first wave of feminist criticism had little patience with George Eliot, condemning her for showing the defeat of female characters and for seeming to argue that characters should suppress their individual needs for the general good of the community. There has been a move away from this negative view of George Eliot. In this extract from a chapter about *Middlemarch*, for example, Kathleen Blake stresses how George Eliot can understand and express the frustrations of a character such as Dorothea living in a patriarchal society. At the same time, however, Blake distances herself from those feminist critics who see *Middlemarch* as a subversive text, and from views of *Middlemarch* as a text full of 'unintended' meanings. She stresses George Eliot's authority as narrator, her role as a 'disciplined maker of meaning'. In a sense, whilst offering a feminist reading of *Middlemarch*, Blake approaches the novel in a fairly traditional way; some other feminist critics, several of whom Blake discusses in this extract, would argue that the 'feminine strain' in the novel is unavoidably question-ing and unassimilated, that it must be at odds with the text's movements towards social and aesthetic unity. All quotations from *Middlemarch* in this essay are from the Riverside edition, edited by G. S. Haight [Boston, 1956]. Ed.]

1. See Barbara Hardy (ed.), *Middlemarch: Critical Approaches to the Novel* (London, 1967), pp. 128–9; 19 September 1873, *The George Eliot Letters*, vol. 5, ed. G. S. Haight (New Haven and London, 1954–5), p. 441.

2. James and Cecil, cited in G. S. Haight, *A Century of George Eliot Criticism* (London and New York, 1965), pp. 83, 204–5; L. Stephen,

George Eliot (London, 1902), pp. 178–80; W. Allen, *George Eliot* (London, 1964), pp. 159–60; J. Thale, *The Novels of George Eliot* (New York, 1959), p. 119; Patricia Beer, *Reader, I Married Him* (London, 1974), pp. 207–11; Jean Kennard, *Victims of Convention* (Hamden, 1978), p. 127.

3. George Eliot, 'Silly Novels by Lady Novelists', *Westminster Review*, 66 (1856), 442–61, in *Essays of George Eliot*, ed. Thomas Pinney (New York, 1963), p. 308.

4. R. H. Hutton, *British Quarterly Review*, 57 (1873), 407–29, in Barbara Hardy (ed.), *'Middlemarch': Critical Approaches to the Novel* (London, 1967), p. 142.

5. 'More Leaves from George Eliot's Notebook', ed. Thomas Pinney, *Huntington Library Quarterly*, 29 (1966), 372; George Eliot, 'Address to the Working Man, By Felix Holt', *Blackwood's*, 103 (1863), 1–11; George Eliot, *The Works of George Eliot*, vol. 7 (*Felix Holt*), (Edinburgh and London, 1877–80), chap. 95, pp. 262–3.

6. Abba Goold Woolson, *George Eliot and Her Heroines* (New York, 1886), pp. 99–102; Lee R. Edwards, 'Women, Energy, and *Middlemarch*', *Massachusetts Review*, 13 (1972), 236; Patricia Beer, *Reader, I Married Him* (London, 1974), p. 181; Jean Kennard, *Victims of Convention* (Hamden, 1978), p. 128; Patricia Stubbs, *Women and Fiction: Feminism and the Novel, 1880–1920* (Brighton, 1979), p. 36; Jenni Calder, *Women and Marriage in Victorian Fiction* (New York and Oxford, 1976), p. 158.

7. Harriet Rosenstein, 'A Historic Booby Prize', *Ms* (July 1974), 35–7, 85–7; Abba Goold Woolson, *George Eliot and Her Heroines* (New York, 1886), p. 176; Ruth Yeazell, 'Fictional Heroines and Feminist Critics', *Novel*, 8 (1974), 35; Zelda Austen, 'Why Feminist Critics Are Angry With George Eliot', *College English*, 37 (1976), 552; see Virginia Woolf, 'George Eliot', *The Common Reader* (London, 1925), pp. 241–2; Lee R. Edwards, 'Women, Energy, and *Middlemarch*', *Massachusetts Review*, 13 (1972), 238.

8. Ann Theresa Kitchel, *George Eliot's Quarry for 'Middlemarch'* (Berkeley and Los Angeles, 1950); Jerome Beaty, *'Middlemarch' from Notebook to Novel: A Study of George Eliot's Creative Method* (Urbana, 1960); Sidney Colvin, in J. Holstrom and L. Lerner (eds), *George Eliot and Her Readers* (London, 1966), p. 100; Quentin Anderson, 'George Eliot in *Middlemarch*', in *The Pelican Guide to English Literature*, vol. 6, ed. Boris Ford (Harmondsworth, 1958), in *Discussions of George Eliot*, ed. Richard Stang (Boston, 1960), p. 90.

9. Calvin Bedient, *Architects of Self: George Eliot, D. H. Lawrence, E. M. Forster* (Berkeley and Los Angeles, 1972), pp. 94, 86; Sandra Gilbert and Susan Gubar, *The Madwoman in the Attic* (New Haven and London, 1979), pp. 499, 75, 86, 491, 479.

10. Mary Jacobus, 'The Difference of View', in *Women Writing and Writing About Women* (London, 1979), p. 17. Jacques Lacan, *Speech and Language in Psychoanalysis*, trans. Anthony Wilden (Baltimore and London, 1968); and Jacques Derrida, *Of Grammatology*, trans. Gayatri Spivak (Baltimore and London, 1974). Jacobus' frame of reference also includes Lucy Irigaray, Julia Kristeva, and Hélène Cixous, whose work is available in English translations in *New French Feminisms*, ed. Elaine Marks and Isabelle de Courtivron (Brighton, 1981), and in the *Signs* issue on French Feminist Theory, 7 (1981). Nancy K. Miller, 'Emphasis Added: Plots and Plausibilities in Women's Fiction', *PMLA*, 96 (1981), 36–48; Simone de Beauvoir, *The Second Sex* (1949), trans. H. M. Parshley (New York, 1961), pp. 664–5.

9

'Middlemarch' and 'The Woman Question'

GILLIAN BEER

'Since I can do no good because a woman,
Reach constantly at something that is near it'.
Beaumont and Fletcher, *The Maid's Tragedy*
(Epigraph to *Middlemarch*, ch. 1)

The period in which George Eliot grew to adulthood was one which
saw an increasing number of studies of the condition of women,
some of which had outcome in action. In the 1840s the emphasis in
England was on realising fully the special moral influence of women.
The route towards liberation, such as it was, was still based on their
mothering role. As Françoise Basch formulates it:

> Any activity deriving from woman's specific role of mother, exercising
> an ennobling and purifying influence in the natural framework of her
> family, alleviating suffering and sacrificing herself to others, was
> recognized as legitimate.[1]

This role could be extended 'to encompass society at large, seen now
as a vast family'. Bonnie Zimmerman remarks,

> Shattering the dichotomy of home and world was one way to increase
> power in the nineteenth century. Extending the home to *encompass*
> the world was another, and far more common, way.[2]

Works such as the anonymous *Woman's Rights and Duties* took a
somewhat more militant line than that of Louis Aimé-Martin, *The*

Education of Mothers of Families; or *The Civilization of The Human Race by Woman* (1842). Reading Martin 'electrified' the young Marian Evans. She had already read Ellis's *Woman's Mission*, the work whose contradictory message is attacked by Anna Jameson in ' "Woman's Mission" and Woman's Position' (1846). Sydney Owenson Morgan's *Woman and Her Master* (1840) looked in historical terms at the treatment of women by men; Mrs Hugo Reid wrote *A Plea for Woman: being a vindication of the importance and extent of her natural sphere of action* (1843). As Anna Jameson commented, 'The press has lately teemed with works treating of the condition, the destiny, the duties of women. . . . The theme, however treated, is one of the themes of the day.'[3] Catchpenny titles, as well as serious works, continued to teem through the 1850s, like Steven Fullom's *The History of Women, and her Connexion with Religion, Civilization and Domestic Manners, From the Earliest Period* (1855) which Marian Evans/George Eliot denounced in the *Westminster Review* in 1855.

But despite the degree of discussion in the 1840s and 1850s, the state of legislation concerning women was still primitive:

> Man's legislation for woman has hitherto been like English legislation for Ireland: it has been without sympathy; without the recognition of equality; without a comprehension of certain innate differences.[4]

The connection with oppressed races, with 'operatives' and with slaves, were all essential to the vocabulary of Victorian feminism. The fascination in George Eliot's novels and poems with gypsies and Jews – races excluded from the dominating culture – also owes something to this discourse. Fedalma in *The Spanish Gypsy* compresses the figure of the woman trapped between dominant culture and tribal descent and oppressed by both.

The state of legislation, about property rights and about divorce, held women in a state of dependency. This was completed by their lack of education and their economic dependence on the home either of husband or father. The author of *Woman's Rights and Duties* had compared the enforced fecklessness of women and slaves. If they sustained 'natural buoyancy of spirit it was assumed that slaves' condition was good enough. The same shallow view is sometimes taken of the condition of women.' But 'the want of liberty destroys all motives for exertion'. Barbara Bodichon, travelling through Mississippi in 1858, writes ironically of the emphasis given to religious differences:

To believe in transubstantiation or the divinity of the Virgin is not so perverting to the mind as to believe that women have no rights to full development of all their faculties and exercise of all their powers, to believe that men have rights over women, and as fathers to exercise those pretended rights over daughters, as husbands exercising those rights over wives. Every day men acting on this false belief destroy their perception of justice, blunt their moral nature, so injure their consciences that they lose the power to perceive the highest and purest attributes of God. Slavery is a greater injustice, but it is allied to the injustice to women so closely that I cannot see one without thinking of the other and feeling how soon slavery should be destroyed if right opinions were entertained upon the other question.[5]

In *Felix Holt*, and even more in *Daniel Deronda*, George Eliot explores the condition of women, apparently at ease, living privileged lives, and yet atrophied by their condition of slavery. Mrs Transome, Mrs Glasher and Gwendolen all share this imagery. In *Middlemarch* Rosamond Vincy is a woman entrapped so completely that she is hardly aware of it, so smoothly does her compliance fit. And that 'type of woman' most traps men into mutual delusion:

Lydgate thought that after all his wild mistakes and absurd credulity, he had found perfect womanhood—felt as if already breathed upon by exquisite wedded affection such as would be bestowed by an accomplished creature who venerated his high musings and momentous labours and would never interfere with them; who would create order in the home and accounts with still magic, yet kept her fingers ready to touch the lute and transform life into romance at any moment; who was instructed to the true womanly limit and not a hair's-breadth beyond—docile, therefore, and ready to carry out behests which came from beyond that limit.

(II, ch. 36, pp. 120–1)

When in 1855 Barbara Bodichon drew up a petition in support of the Married Women's Property Bill, she wrote that the aim of the Bill was 'that in entering the state of marriage, they no longer pass from freedom into the condition of a slave'.[6] George Eliot signed this petition and distributed sheets for it. Also in 1855 there was a commission on the law of mortmain. 'The Dead hand' in *Middlemarch*, as Book V is titled, refers to 'mortmain': the impress of Mr Casaubon's will on Dorothea's subsequent life and of Featherstone's on that of Mary Garth and Fred Vincy.

Throughout her writing career, George Eliot was notably interested in legal problems. She increasingly researched not only the immediate effects on women's position, but also the ideological assumptions embedded in the laws of inheritance and of kin. The patriarchal nature of law became clearer with the increase in historical and anthropological studies of women's position. As George Eliot worked through Lecky's *History of European Morals* she particularly noted such material. This concern links her with the pressing interests of her friends active in the women's movement. Divorce, child custody, married women's property rights – all figure constantly in *The English Woman's Journal*.

George Eliot uses the pivot of the unwritten years in *Middlemarch* – the years between setting and composition – to register some changes in women's circumstances, but rather small change in the actual conditions of women's lives. One of the sad speculative movements of the book is to bring into question the extent to which any real enfranchisement had been achieved between 1830 and 1870.

In George Eliot's novels 'independence' implies money, but money does not guarantee independence. Dorothea is beset by the problems of her money and by her ignorance of how best to use it. She asks Casaubon to compensate Ladislaw for the exclusion of his grandmother from her rights of inheritance: She wants to use her money wisely. At the end of the book she leaves behind Casaubon's money, which has become loaded with his jealous will. Mary Garth alone maintains independence without money, and her integrity is rescued and pastoralised by the novel's events, which conspire to free her from the consequences of her refusal to connive with Featherstone. Maggie Tulliver's predicament was in part that her independence of mind was not matched by independent means: much of the narrative, after all, is concerned with the drop in her family's fortunes. Gwendolen goes into marriage with Grandcourt as a way of recouping her family funds and providing for her mother.

Marrying for money, when the alternative is to live in the woman's land of governessing, seamstressing, or even aimless genteel poverty, is a real alternative. It may give a woman some form of independence, a household to manage, funds to dispense, a career of a kind. The forlorn passivity of the unmarried daughter, even when her parents are alive, was a constant theme of Victorian feminist writing. If only, say the Shirreff sisters, or Emily Faithfull, or Barbara Bodichon, women were educated in such a way that they could earn their own living and achieve independence. Idleness eats away vitality or leaves it ricocheting without control. So the campaigns for education, work and independent property rights are very closely and coherently connected.

In *Middlemarch* education and money 'greatly determine' the characters, and George Eliot takes as her central topic the unfit preparation of women for life's opportunities. This is a theme as crucial for understanding Rosamond as it is for understanding Dorothea.

The obverse of the same problem is shown in the experience of Lydgate. Lydgate is imaginative in relation to science, tender in his impulses, and yet utterly untrained to treat with analytical serious-ness the emotional business of life. The emphasis on women's 'special province' of feeling is shown to disable even those men talented in emotion. Lydgate has never been led to evaluate his own ignorance. Casaubon – a great believer in the separate spheres principle – cannot experience emotion except as fear and anger.

Will Ladislaw, son of two generations of rebellious women, is shown as lucid about his own feelings and responsive to women. He is not shut up in his own masculinity. He is not much oppressed by guilt. His failure for a long time to find a role in the world sets him alongside women's experience. He is outside the educational hege-mony. His problem is to find a use for himself. His attachment to Dorothea is sound and yet for much of the book a little dilettante, like his opinions. It thrives on delicacy and distance, on the edge of commitment. It is hard for him, after all, to *do* anything, except gently to seduce her to criticise her husband. He feels grandeur, though he does not feel grandly. It is that quality of the aspirant which distinguishes him. He hopes for much. He delights in many things. He is kin to women, not polarised against them. Ladislaw's position, outside money inheritance, sharing the awkward financial dependency more often associated with women, does have the effect of reinforcing his feminisation. It also shows that not only women suffer from dependency and powerlessness. At the same time, Will is much freer than a woman in an equivalent position would be – and that is a pointer to another of his uses. He exactly focuses what is peculiar to women's predicament by sharing many of their con-ditions, and yet living a liberated life. This liberation depends upon his being a man, with freedom to travel, to live where he will, and to make his own friends.

Throughout *Middlemarch* the multiple points of comparison and divergence between characters in the text enable George Eliot to draw more and more exactly the focus of her experiments.

Dorothea finds it hard to distinguish between love and learning: this is a problem which bears particularly hard on women. The mentor–pupil relationship in its male–female form presents the man as teacher and the woman as pupil. The pattern traditionally extends across intellectual and sexual experience. Men teach women sexually and intellectually. To Dorothea, passion and knowledge are identified. She seeks to *know* more than her meagre education has so far allowed her, and thereby to *do* more than her society designates as appropriate to her. At the beginning of the book, Casaubon is irradiated for her by the light of his imagined knowledge. His great project suggests a world of interconnection and exploration which satisfies her heart. Dorothea clearly figures partly as a chastened re-reading of the writer's own early experience; in particular, her attraction to learned older men who seemed to offer access to an intensified world of ideas. In her relationship with Herbert Spencer, Marian Evans had been forced to the point of understanding that the power of intellectual synthesis does not guarantee emotional power or sexual feeling.

But Dorothea is not utterly wrong about Casaubon. He does represent a way out of safety. She needs risks as well as usefulness and her enclosed environment has not taught her to recognise worse imprisonment. Casaubon's devoted commitment to a large intellectual project, though it has turned into a search which simplifies all complexity back into a single form, does yet represent an aspiration which remains with Dorothea throughout the work. The proper and liberating task proves in the course of the book to be that of making connections, not seeking origins. So she learns to do without the masculine as father. She grows out of her belief that men father knowledge, are its origin and its guardian: 'The really delightful marriage must be that where your husband was a sort of father, and could teach you even Hebrew, if you wished it' (I, ch. 1, p. 12). She is herself an orphan and by the death of Casaubon is released from the oppressive demands of another 'sort of father'.

Her attraction to Will grows through the play of spirit and learning between them: they teach each other. He frees her from desiring martyrdom; she gives him a great project. The rapidity of interconnection in their conversation is reinforced by the narrative discourse; spontaneity and danger, innovation and scepticism, are all represented in the dialogues at Rome. The work beautifully records the extent to which falling in love *is* conversation, the passionate discovery and exchange of meanings. Will is, as Mr Brooke sagely remarks, 'a kind of Shelley', absolutely at home in the world of ideas, yet uncertain how to use this knowledge. He and Dorothea educate each other, abandoning the model of mentor and pupil as a kind of father and daughter. The book itself resists the usual punitive outcome for lovers who educate each other which is shown in the stories of Francesca and Paulo, Abelard and Heloise, Julie and St Preux.

But lovers cannot be relied on as educators. Institutions are essential. One of the principal areas in which it was possible to doubt improvement between 1830 and 1870 was in the nature of women's education. In the 1860s the *Alexandra Magazine* emphasised the need for women to take part in examinations, because they would otherwise never be tested or qualified alongside men. In an article on 'A Comparison between the Education of Girls in France and England' we find that

> Englishwomen have now the advantages of the extended education desired for them; they do sympathize largely in the progress of the world of ideas, but the superficial nature of the instruction which they receive, is making itself felt in every matter in which they are concerned.[7]

The unsympathetic nature of women's education and training had been commented on by the Shirreff sisters in *Thoughts on Self-Culture*:

> In general, there has been everything to thwart and nothing to encourage in women the desire to study. The more pompous enumeration of school-room learning in the present day makes no real difference in this respect; in that chaos of laborious trifling, it would be vain to expect that the mind should be trained to any serious method of study; and, therefore, when a woman becomes convinced of the value of mental pursuits, and desires to cultivate them, she is at a loss to know how or what to begin; she is aware how superficial is all her previously acquired information, but how to learn better, and what to seek first, are points concerning which she feels perplexed and helpless.[8]

The situation described – the sense of ineffectual striving and discouragement – is close to that more metaphorically represented for Dorothea:

> For a long while she had been oppressed by the indefiniteness which hung in her mind, like a thick summer haze, over all her desire to make

her life greatly effective. What could she do, what ought she to do?—she, hardly more than a budding woman, but yet with an active conscience and a great mental need, not to be satisfied by a girlish instruction comparable to the nibblings and judgments of a discursive mouse.

(I, ch. 3, p. 39)

Immediately after, the narrative condenses imagery which thrives on allusions beyond Dorothea's reach:

The intensity of her religious disposition, the coercion it exercised over her life, was but one aspect of a nature altogether ardent, theoretic, and intellectually consequent: and with such a nature struggling in the bands of a narrow teaching, hemmed in by a social life which seemed nothing but a labyrinth of petty courses, a walled-in maze of small paths that led no whither, the outcome was sure to strike others as at once exaggeration and inconsistency.

(Ibid.)

The allusion to Blake's infant in the *Songs of Experience* summons a primal energy imprisoned by society and kin: part of the poignant intensification lies in the awareness that Dorothea cannot cross the transition into the metaphors of the commentary not because of any lack of intelligence, but because of a lack of education. Labyrinths have become petty garden mazes. Mr Brooke, with his own delightfully unreconstructed eclecticism, speaks out frankly the assumptions about women which result in such frittering of potentiality:

'But there is a lightness about the feminine mind—a touch and go—music, the fine arts, that kind of thing—they should study those up to a certain point, women should; but in a light way, you know'.

(I, ch. 7, p. 94)

The implicit comparison between conditions in the 1830s and 70s is used to show not how much things have improved, but how little.

In *Aurora Leigh* (1857) Elizabeth Barrett Browning describes a relatively thoroughgoing girl's education:

I learnt my complement of classic French
(Kept pure of Balzac and neologism)
And German also, since she liked a range
Of liberal education,—tongues, not books.
I learnt a little algebra, a little
Of the mathematics,—brushed with extreme flounce
The circle of the sciences, because
She disliked women who are frivolous.

(Bk I, ll. 399–405)

All this was to prepare her to be a wife of the kind that would exactly
have suited Mr Casaubon:

> I read a score of books on womanhood
> To prove, if women do not think at all,
> They may teach thinking, (to a maiden aunt
> Or else the author)—books demonstrating
> Their right of comprehending husband's talk
> When not too deep, and even of answering
> With pretty 'may it please you,' or 'so it is,'—
> Their rapid insight and fine aptitude,
> Particular worth and general missionariness,
> As long as they keep quiet by the fire
> And never say 'no' when the world says 'ay',
> For that is fatal,—their angelic reach
> Of virtue, chiefly used to sit and darn,
> And fatten household sinners,—their, in brief,
> Potential faculty in everything
> Of abdicating power in it.
>
> (Bk I, ll. 426–41)

In her enthusiastic review of *Aurora Leigh* in 1857, George Eliot
quoted approvingly another such passage in which Aurora refuses
'To show a pretty spirit, chiefly admired/Because true action is
impossible'.[9]

In the *Report on the Committee of Council* (1869–70) Mr
Allington reports:

> Girls fail much more frequently than boys in all subjects and in all
> standards. It does not necessarily follow that they are inferior to boys
> in capacity, but as a matter of fact, owing partly to previous neglect
> and partly to the comparative indifference with which even sensible
> parents still regard the education of their daughters, the girls . . . are as
> a rule far below the boys in attainments.[10]

Maria Grey, in *The Education of Women*, comments in a style which
exactly describes the outcome of Rosamond's lady-like education:

> They are *not* educated to be wives, but to get husbands. They are *not*
> educated to be mothers; if they were, they would require and obtain
> the highest education that could be given, in order to fit them for the
> highest duties a human being can perform. They are *not* educated to
> be the mistresses of households; if they were, their judgment would be
> as sedulously trained, habits of method and accuracy as carefully
> formed, as they are now neglected. They would not give, as Mr Bryce

calculates, 5,520 hours of their school life to music against 640 to arithmetic; and social and political economy, which are scarcely thought of in their course of instruction now, would take the foremost place in it.[11]

Joshua Fitch, among the most enlightened of Victorian workers for women's education, wrote in his report to the Schools Inquiry Commission an account of intellectual estrangement in marriage which runs alongside that of Lydgate and Rosamond:

> It would not be difficult to point to thousands of instances of men who have started in life with a love of knowledge and with a determination to master at least some department of honourable thought or inquiry; yet who have gradually sunk into habits of mental indolence, have allowed all their great aims to fade out of view, and have become content with the reading supplied by Mudie and the newspapers, simply from a dread of isolation.... There is no hope for the middle classes, until the range of topics which they care about includes something more than money making, religious controversies, and ephemeral politics.[12]

Starting from this relativist position of considering women in relation to men's good he reaches a position still rare, then and since, of asserting a woman's right to knowledge:

> When they come to consider this, they will set as great a value on intellectual power or literary taste when they are put forth by a girl as by a boy; and they will feel that the true measure of a woman's right to knowledge is her capacity for receiving it, and not any theories of ours, as to what she is fit for or what use she is likely to make of it.[13]

These are some of the predicaments that George Eliot enters in *Middlemarch*: Lydgate's 'allowing his great aims to fade out of view'; Rosamond 'being from morning till night her own standard of a perfect lady' (I, ch.16, p. 253); Dorothea's sense of the 'chaos of laborious trifling ... at a loss to know how or where to begin', misinterpreting Mr Casaubon as a possible way out of her 'walled-in maze of small paths that led no whither' (p. 39). The mind of the young woman 'bewildered and overcome ... can neither understand its own wants, nor frame a method to meet them'.[14]

George Eliot's piercing sarcasm in the first books of *Middlemarch* works at the expense of the 1870s reader's easy developmental assumption of distance from the material of 1830s life. How far have things changed? The comments of her concerned contemporaries show how little. Although conditions have changed again, modern readers are likely to recognise a process of attrition and exclusion in the predicaments of Rosamond and of Dorothea, even of Mary Garth, which is still a crucial concern for all those concerned with the education of women and of men in the present day.

George Eliot, then, did engage with issues vital in the life of the women's movement. The kind of comment we often encounter that 'she always sought to be free of any close involvement with the feminist movement of her time either in life or in literature'[15] is simply not true. Nor is Ellen Moers' flat assertion that George Eliot was 'no feminist' to be accepted. We do not need to convert her into a radical feminist: it would be pointless to pretend to do so. What is demonstrable is that she was intimately familiar with the current writing and actions of the women's movement and that in *Middlemarch* particularly, she brooded on the curtailment of women's lives in terms drawn from that movement and in sympathy with it.

*

But uncertainty does remain. Where precisely *did* George Eliot stand on the women's movement and women's rights? Did she, in Dorothea, praise women's 'potential faculty in everything of abdicating power in it'? (*Aurora Leigh*). She is not, as Zelda Austen makes clear, a woman writer who writes solely 'about women from a woman's point of view, and, more narrowly, about liberated women from a liberated woman's point of view'.[16] So far as her life went, we know that although she was a subscriber to the *English Woman's Journal* she was never a contributor, and that Bessie Rayner Parkes grudged her refusal to write for them. Her life will not take us all the way into her writing. Up to now in this chapter I have been indicating ways in which her writing engaged with the vocabulary and the ideas of the women's movement, and the extent to which she concurred with Barbara Bodichon's position. Later in this chapter I shall consider an issue which may allow us to reach further. This is the function of metaphor and of organisation in extending *Middlemarch*'s questioning of history and of 'natural law'.

It would be a mistake to accept George Eliot's 'realism' as a purely descriptive or a socially confirming method, or to interpret *Middlemarch* solely in terms of its empirical relations to current writing and events. But I hope I have already demonstrated the speculative energy that went into her reading and interpretation, an energy which drives her out into *possibilities*, an enterprise akin to that oft-quoted passage on Lydgate's imagination with its significant and momentary doubling of the sense of 'relation' as relationship and narrative: 'he was enamoured of that arduous invention which is the very eye of research, provisionally framing its object and correcting it to more and more exactness of relation' (I, ch. 16, p. 249). Possibilities are recognised as coherence of relations.

Before we leave the biographical question of that figure 'George Eliot', so authoritatively inscribed on the title-page and bearing so tortuous, yet ungainsayable, a relationship to Mrs Lewes, let us consider the evidence of the life and letters for what light they may cast on unresolved questions of allegiance and default.

Almost every one of the women with whom George Eliot was intimate from the mid-1850s was actively involved in the women's movement. One such was Clementia Doughty (Mrs Peter Taylor), a worker for women's suffrage; another less active was the positivist Maria Bury (Mrs Richard Congreve). Bessie Rayner Parkes and Barbara Bodichon we have already discussed. Edith Simcox we shall come to. When periods of estrangement with Barbara came – as they will come in long relationships – they were over questions other than the women's movement: issues such as personal immortality and George Eliot's determined abandonment of the idea. The socially more daring and active Barbara Bodichon writes to Bessie in 1861:

> Since Pater's death the hopelessness of life without immortality has made me quite lean off from Marian . . . fond as I am of her. . . . I told Marian if I felt *convinced* as she professes to be of *utter annihilation*, I should not have power to live for this little scrap of life'.[17]

Courage takes diverse forms. George Eliot's own affirmed lifestyle, living unmarried with a still-married man, meant that it was probably inevitable that all her close women friends should be active in the women's movement, since they were the only ones who would visit her and accept her fully. Only in her late years did her home become a fashionable intellectual centre; and even then most visitors were men. Bessie Rayner Parkes describes a visit where she found Marian Lewes surrounded by men and felt her relief at the arrival of women. We should not condescendingly assume that Bessie was mistaken.

One of the most impressively courageous workers for women's rights among George Eliot's intimates was Edith Simcox, the young and learned woman who fell in love with George Eliot during the last years of her life. Edith Simcox has been harshly treated by biographers of George Eliot. By extracting for quotation from her journal only those passages which have bearing on George Eliot, she has been transformed into a lap-dog. Her lesbianism has been a source of acute unease to writers who have misread as 'sentimental effusion' what are often courageous statements of attachment and self-recognition. Edith Simcox was an international socialist and on the national committee of the first International Working Men's Association. She founded the first trade union for women, and was one of the first two women delegates at the Trades Union Congress. She organised a collective of women workers in the exploited clothing trade, hence the title of her journal 'Autobiography of a Shirtmaker'. She was an excellent Germanist, wrote a philosophical work on *Natural Law* (1877), and a perceptive essay on *Middlemarch*.

Because she is pictured only at George Eliot's feet, it is insufficiently understood how far her passion for George Eliot and for her writing liberated Edith Simcox into action. In the midst of a vivid account of a packed women workers' meeting and of the conditions in which they work, she comments, 'It is very mysterious the way all my mental energies are stimulated by a touch from her.' On another Sunday she leaves George Eliot, attends the 'Shirtmakers' Committee', then, 'I walked home—crossing Hyde Park for the first time in the dark.' This is testimony to set over-against the debilitating view of Lynn Linton, or the oppressed awareness of George Eliot's life and writing which weighs on Mrs Oliphant. Neither Mrs Linton nor Mrs Oliphant were in sympathy with the women's movement. The people to whom George Eliot offered energy prove almost to a woman to have been so. How then do we interpret her peripheral and equivocal role?

So far as her own life went there was one obvious tactical reason why it might be sound sense for George Eliot to remain a counsellor and friend behind the scenes. Her 'irregular' life might jeopardise more than it gained for the movement if she were an open and active supporter. This reason may not suffice, but it should not be discounted. It is very easy from our point of advantage to underestimate the enormous step George Eliot took in committing herself to a relationship which put her outside society. It made it necessary for her to renegotiate every other relationship. Some of the most valued, like that with her brother, foundered.

Law-breaking may make us law-abiding. We carefully conform in order to make room for sustained resistance. (It will be remembered that what her brother Isaac blamed her for was her 'secrecy'.) The massive caution of her later behaviour and expressions of opinion should be seen in the light of this doubling. The 'studied restraint' and counteractive 'temperament' which Lynn Linton described with jealous shrewdness issued from 'her endeavour to harmonise two irreconcilables – to be at once conventional and insurgent'.[18]

George Eliot herself, late in life, claimed that her function was 'that of the *aesthetic*, not the doctrinal teacher. . . . If I had taken a contrary decision, I should not have remained silent till now.'[19] She is replying to Mrs Peter Taylor's request to her to speak out, though we do not know on what subject. The heaviness of statement in such letters lies oddly alongside the more complicated activity of the fiction. When in this letter she speaks of her enterprise as 'the rousing of the nobler emotions, which make mankind desire the social right', the effect is altogether less convincing than that which we encounter as reading process in the novels. The experience of relation, delay, pain, resolve, irresolution, that we participate in as readers, is both more engrossing and more disquieting than this passage suggests. But George Eliot correctly emphasises the *affective* nature of her fiction and the grounding of its claims to social action in that quality.

No commentary can replicate or enlarge, for example, the effect of chapter 74 of *Middlemarch* in which Mrs Bulstrode sets out to discover what has happened to her husband by visiting her friends, at last hears the truth from her brother, and at the chapter's end moves to her husband's side. We enter experience here through the play of dialogue, wit, free indirect discourse, metaphor, recounting, unsaid statement. That is, we enter experience not only alongside the characters but *as reading*. The chapter may move us to tears because the language allows us 'to conceive with that distinctness which is no longer reflection but feeling—an idea wrought back to the directness of sense, like the solidity of objects' (I, ch. 21, p. 323). The impossibility of *foreseeing* either Mrs Bulstrode's behaviour, or our experience, as readers, bears out George Eliot's claim that her best work is done in silence, the silence of writing.

Within that silence, insurgence and conformity can both take their place. Dorothea is not obliged to call upon the divorce laws: Casaubon conveniently dies. But her resistance to him remains, so that she is even driven to write him a letter after his death explaining that she cannot bind herself to complete his project. In an early review Marian Evans had noted sardonically that in novels 'deaths always happen thus opportunely'.[20] In *Middlemarch* the 'opportuneness' of death is employed in the figure of Casaubon; it is sceptically surveyed as the central knot of the plot in the death of Raffles (so opportune for Bulstrode, so disbelieved in by the community who know that such opportune deaths happen only in romances); while in the subsequent life of Lydgate no release is offered, until the sad opportuneness of his own early death releases Rosamond into a wealthy second marriage when she 'often spoke of her happiness as "a reward"' (II, Finale, p. 460). This complicated use of 'opportune' death marks George Eliot's particular quality as a writer. The novel's enabling scepticism towards fictional and social orders never diminishes strong feeling. But the same mixture of feeling and scepticism made it difficult, perhaps increasingly so, for her to feel much confidence in the power of specific social measures to rectify women's lot. In the Cabinet edition she removed sentences from the Finale which include: 'society smiled ... on modes of education which make a woman's knowledge another name for motley ignorance—on rules of conduct which are in flat contradiction with its own loudly-asserted beliefs'.

Did she feel that the overdetermination of women's predicament made any such local symptoms inadequate as explanation, and therefore too comforting to the reader? Or had she lost faith in the potential for change of the women's movement? I take the former view, but I do not think that we can look for a single position. She needed and sustained contradiction, and, even more multiplied positions than contradiction.

The 'nature of women' troubled her as an idea, and as an experience, throughout her life. We have seen how the image of the mother as originator moves through her relationship to her own writing. She wrote in 1869 that she 'profoundly rejoiced that I never brought a child into the world', and yet is 'conscious of having an unused stock of motherly tenderness'. She wrote admiringly to Harriet Beecher Stowe: 'you have had longer experience than I as a writer, and fuller experience as a woman, since you have borne children and know the mother's history from the beginning.' The sense of 'the mother's history' as a narrative reserved from her and to be discovered only laboriously, only enigmatically as art, fuels much of the intensity of *Daniel Deronda* where the characters must seek absent mothers, as Deronda and Mirah do; or learn to live with mothers who cling to and threaten them, as Gwendolen must with her own mother and with Mrs Glasher.

George Eliot was writing in a period before women could readily control their own fertility. Childbearing, therefore, peculiarly marks women and opposes them to men. We have seen how the problem of generalising the mothering role across society, and across class, preoccupied the women's movement and was the source of many divisions within it. It is in the light of such arguments that we should read George Eliot's letter to John Morley, written while she was working on *Middlemarch*. Morley was at the time publishing articles in *The Fortnightly* supporting the movement for women's franchise and, in this month of May, John Stuart Mill moved an amendment to Gladstone's Reform Bill to permit women to vote:

> Your attitude in relation to Female Enfranchisement seems to be very nearly mine. If I were called on to act in the matter, I would certainly not oppose any plan which held out any reasonable promise of tending to establish as far as possible an equivalence of advantages for the two sexes, as to education and the possibilities of free development. I fear you may have misunderstood something I said the other evening about nature. I never meant to urge the 'intention of Nature' argument, which is to me a pitiable fallacy. I mean that as a fact of mere zoological evolution, woman seems to me to have the worse share in existence. But for that very reason I would the more contend that in the moral evolution we have 'an art which does mend nature'—an art which 'itself is nature'.[21]

George Eliot denies the 'intention of Nature' argument, which argues that women's current role is immutable and fixed by nature, but affirms that in terms of zoology (their childbearing?) women have the worse share. Yet, she declares, quoting *The Winter's Tale* with its fructifying argument that the discoveries of culture (including the 'artificial') are aspects of the natural order which is thus open to change, women have 'an art which does mend nature'.

In 'Armgart' four years later, the contrary possibilities of art and nature are divided differently. Armgart declares:

> I am an artist by my birth—
> By the same warrant that I am a woman: ...
> I need not crush myself within a mould
> Of theory called Nature: I have room
> To breathe and grow unstunted.[22]

But that is possible to Armgart only because of her exceptionalness. Once her splendid voice is gone, she finds herself trapped in the common lot of disregarded women, though she recovers herself through teaching, not through marriage and children. The letter paragraph ends thus:

> It is the function of love in the largest sense, to mitigate the harshness of all fatalities. And in the thorough recognition of that worse share, I think there is a basis for a sublimer resignation in woman and a more regenerating tenderness in man.

Here she comes out tentatively in favour of 'sublimer resignation' for women and 'more regenerating tenderness' for men. 'I do not trust very confidently to my own impressions on this subject.'

The argument continues:

> The one conviction on the matter which I hold with some tenacity is, that through all transitions the goal towards which we are proceeding is a more clearly discerned distinctness of function (allowing always for exceptional cases of individual organisation) with as near an approach to equivalence of good for woman and for man as can be secured by the effort of growing moral force to lighten the pressure of hard non-moral outward conditions.

Women and men have distinct functions. But what those functions may be are here obscure, as is the tone. Is this separatism or apartheid? That women are to be left at the mercy of their pro-creativity, caught between that and 'hard non-moral outward conditions' seems a melancholy upshot to her brooding. Yet how else can we read this letter?

*

One way is to look ahead to the activity of *Middlemarch* which brings into question again the idea of what is 'natural' in function and in attitude for women. The Victorian fascination with the concept of natural law – a reconstitution within the physical order of the older concept of design – had many consequences in the culture. It could be used to ratify socially-determined practices as if they were part of nature. Even Marx fell into this trap with his treatment of the family as a 'prior' and natural organisation. Once things are 'natural', they are seen as inevitable. And we feel, even in the letter just discussed, a tension between the repudiation of 'nature' and the embrace of 'function'.

The concept of natural law bore hard on women since it based their role on the precondition of procreativity. Moreover, as Edith

Simcox observed in her study, *Natural Law*, it restored the idea of providence as 'order'. In a passage which may have George Eliot's 'pier-glass' image behind it, Edith Simcox writes of this teleological problem:

> Every one instinctively and, in a manner necessarily, regards the incidents which concern himself as really grouped in the manner in which they present themselves to his feeling—as of course they really are—though not less really in a thousand different ways, visible with equal clearness to other centres of consciousness.[23]

But though 'each several mode of stringing together the actual occurrence is true – from an arbitrarily narrowed point of view', they are 'worthless as a formula for the general relations among all the things concerned'.

Is *Middlemarch* seeking 'general relations', a reconstitution of the text as natural law? The book opens by bringing into question any easy definitions of 'the nature of women'. *Middlemarch* is a novel which calls into play the 'range of relevancies called the universe', all the more so for its ironic insistence that it must forgo doing so, to concentrate on the interweaving of a few 'lots'. 'Lot', with its doubled emphasis on chance and on overdetermined outcome, its entwining of the magical and the humdrum, is a crucial word for George Eliot, particularly in her later career. Silas is cast out of his community as the result of the drawing of lots. *Middlemarch* turns on that modern equivalent, voting in committee, and *Daniel Deronda* opens with Gwendolen at play.

The chanciness of propinquity and intimacy is admirably summarised in the initiating remark on the frozen stare with which we greet our neighbours at dinner. Chance meeting may become intimate involvement over time. It is a social parallel to that earlier comment on the sadness of 'the family face' in Adam Bede. In *Middlemarch*, in particular, the action of the novel reminds us that families are made by acts of choice (or what appear to the people involved to be acts of choice). Courtship and wedding is the coming together of people linked only by social acquaintance into a knitting-up of flesh and blood in childbearing.

Is the multiformity of 'lots' within the work designed ultimately to reveal a taxonomy which conditions individual women and men according to 'laws of nature'? Or is the enterprise rather that of irradiating differences, extending distinctions, and bringing under our survey the impossibility of reaching that full interpretation which must precede any attempt to describe law? 'Differences are form,' she wrote in 'Notes on Form in Art'. Can fiction allow everything to be known? Is the narrative discourse that of a privileged, all-embracing mother? Or does it display a series of 'experiments' without reaching a 'binding theory', such as Dorothea herself always hopes to discover? Is the search for 'binding theory' itself a kind of acquiescence?

Middlemarch works through explanation – passionate explanation which produces some of the same intensity as the gossip of lovers or of intimate friends, a sustained conversation which secures and surprises. But such explanation is not end-stopped, but endless. It is no wonder that she needs the focusing metaphors of microscope and telescope. The compunction bred in the reader by the long interpenetrations of Middlemarch may make us forget before the end of the novel the brilliant play of spirit with which the novel opens. In the first chapters we begin to read the characters through gossip, pithy cross-comments, ironic situation, and physical details of appearance. This 'coming to know' dramatises our role as that of a privileged newcomer, reading the social scene. Not only are we getting to know people, but they are getting to know each other, a process which is intensified and restricted in courtship: Sir James Chettam courts first Dorothea, then Celia; Dorothea and Casaubon ineptly try to fit each other to prior images and, somewhat later, in the already mitigated light of accumulating interconnection, we watch the courtship of Lydgate and Rosamond. The action of the novel corresponds to the reader's entry into the fiction – particularly to that subtle wooing intrinsic to George Eliot's organisation of discourse. We participate in the initiating events because they coincide with our simultaneous experiences as readers.

In the early books of Middlemarch there is an edge of treason in that intimacy offered by the insistent voice of the narrative. The league of reader and writer, the 'we', sometimes inveigles us into admissions we had not foreseen. At other times it forms an allegiance which deflates the characters. The contrast of reader and writer appears to be between equals, yet reserves to the writing an authority beyond whose span it is not possible for the reader to function. In Comte's Catechism (1858) the debate is divided between the woman who enquires and the priest who answers. Here woman and priest are combined in the narrative discourse. Precisely because so many different kinds of explanation are afforded, it is hard for the reader to counter-interpret.

George Eliot's imagination, however, works in a mode which

allows her to evade factitious authority and the peremptoriness of willed sequence: metaphor creates lateral understanding, the primary participation of the reader. 'Images are the brood of desire'; that image itself multiplies images, creating a familial order (images are the children or outcome of desire) summoning equally the idea of desire brooding on possibilities, or images realising desire. The urgency of metaphor, which does not so much sort as condense, gives the reader multiple routes to knowledge. It disturbs stereotypes and the fixity of 'natural law'. Our passionate coming to consciousness in the act of realising metaphor repeats the ideal activity enjoined by the book. The unforeseen discharge of new affinity which is central to metaphor is a pleasure crucial to George Eliot's language and to her narrative ordering. Metaphor is a means of 'reaching constantly at something that is near it', at qualities which elude or strain, or poignantly are debarred to us. Her significant placing as epigraph to chapter 1 of the passage from *The Maid's Tragedy* with which I began this chapter, has its bearing on her uses of metaphor.

Clichés and tropes which bind up experience stir again into meaning. Words yield at their boundaries. Fugitive kinship is discovered in metaphor: affinity proves to be real without needing to be permanent. George Eliot's moral sense of connectedness is eased by metaphor's double motion, towards and away from present objects and feelings. Her intensely metaphorical style offers multiple routes beyond the world of *Middlemarch* itself, discovering at once connection and difference. In that sense, metaphor can act as an alternative mode of classification, one that makes more space for divergence and possibility. Her method is different from the encyclopaedism of Rabelais or Joyce, though it calls on as full a range of learning. The gigantism of lists has little appeal for her, nor does the collapse of puns. Instead she emphasises relations.

George Eliot's impress of knowledge gives us range and freedom. Elsewhere I have discussed ways in which in *Middlemarch* the writings of Darwin and of Jameson are related in a releasing perception of lateral connections.[24] We are not, as readers, obliged to carry the burden of her characters' disappointment without relief. We have access to a world compacted of meaning, yet so profuse that we need not even expect to raise all connections into consciousness. This quality of latency means that the exhaustiveness of explanation does not enclose or imprison text and reader. Explanation is preceded and surpassed by the condensed form of image. The drama of analysis is supplemented by the suffusive action of imagery, and the sources of that imagery range wide across human knowledge. By this means she is able to discover the intense particularity of experience in what is common. Simultaneously she uses that particularity as the ground of generalisation, dwelling on the common physical conditions of our life (the body, the material world) as the matter of metaphor.

Some of the novelty of her method has vanished for us now, as the up-to-date range of scientific allusions sinks into familiarity or vanishes out of sight. It is with some surprise that a present-day reader comes upon Hutton's objection to her early description of Dorothea:

> Signs are small measurable things, but interpretations are illimitable, and in girls of sweet, ardent nature every sign is apt to conjure up wonder, hope, belief, vast as a sky, and coloured by a diffused thimbleful of matter in the shape of knowledge, (by the way, should George Eliot assume in the mind of her readers a knowledge of the results of Professor Tyndall's speculations as to the cause of the blueness of the sky?)[25]

The 'imaginative' for her means the mind's primary power of 'swift images' which register desire's entry into consciousness: 'We are all of us imaginative in some form or other, for images are the brood of desire' (Bk II, p. 77). Images cross bounds, and first of all the bound between the unconscious and language: 'these fine words . . . are not the language in which we think. Deronda's thinking went on in rapid images of what might be'.[26] Barriers are needed for naming, but must be broken for experience. Her realism uses not only the sub-sets of classification in which categories more and more closely divide and articulate, but also the traversing of categories in ways which measure 'the subtlety of those touches which convey the quality of soul as well as body' (ch. 39).

At the beginning of chapter 37 she gives a practical demonstration of how words subtly shift their signification according to the case they refer to. She cites as epigraph Spenser's noble sonnet which she had earlier written out in her commonplace book.

> Thrice happy she that is so well assured
> Unto herself, and settled so in heart,
> That neither will for better be allured
> Ne fears to worse with any chance to start,
> But like a steddy ship doth strongly part
> The raging waves, and keeps her course aright:

> Ne aught for tempest doth from it depart,
> Ne aught for fairer weather's false delight.
> Such self-assurance need not fear the spight
> Of grudging foes; ne favour seek of friends;
> But in the stay of her own stedfast might
> Neither to one herself nor other bends.
>   Most happy she that most assured doth rest.
>   But he most happy who such one loves best.

The sonnet is placed immediately after the chapter in which Rosamond has declared to Lydgate 'I never give up anything that I choose to do' and he has thought how adorable is such constancy of purpose. The wedding is brought forward. The chapter ends:

> Lydgate relied much on the psychological difference between what for the sake of variety I will call goose and gander: especially on the innate submissiveness of the goose as beautifully corresponding to the strength of the gander.
>
> (II, ch. 36, p. 216)

Heading the page immediately after that conclusion, the poem is ironised: the 'stay of her own stedfast might' is now suspect. Lydgate misreads along the lines of traditional values. Yet the tranquillity of the sonnet also endures and offers a possibility of recuperating a fuller meaning for words which their setting demeans. Dorothea is less 'well assured' and 'settled', but the ensuing chapter suggests a new reading of the sonnet inspired by her troubled sense of justice.

The disadvantage of words, as George Eliot noted in her journal in a passage from Victor Hugo, is that they have a stricter outline than do ideas. Truth, she quoted elsewhere in her Commonplace Book, lies in nuances. In *Middlemarch* she seeks ways beyond this difficulty by means of permeating metaphors, which enact knowledge shared by author and reader. The multiplying of narratives and the manifold comparisons and divergences of human lots take us beyond dualism or the 'hierarchised opposition', as Cixous calls it, of the 'two-term system, related to the couple man/woman'.[27] The constant metaphoric activity 'incorporates' the reader. One of Donne's letters, which she read as she worked on *Middlemarch*, chimed in with her own creative activity as well as with the problems that she was creating for her characters:

> Therefore I would fain do something: but that I cannot tell what, is no wonder. For to choose, is to do: but to be no part of any body, is to be

nothing. At most, the greatest persons, are but great wens, and excrescences; men of wit and delightful conversation, but as moles for ornament, except they be so incorporated into the body of the world, that they contribute something to the sustenation of the whole . . . [I] was diverted by the worst voluptousness, which is an hydroptic immoderate desire of human learning and languages.[28]

The 'hydroptic immoderate desire of human learning' is the mole-ridden Casaubon's failing perhaps, except that he does not with *sufficient* voluptousness desire full 'human learning'. It is even more a danger for George Eliot whose polymathic discourse in *Romola* had ornamented rather than sustained the whole. In *Middlemarch*, where the crucial topic of the whole is finding satisfying work to do, George Eliot finds a way of escaping 'excrescence'. Her work is the text. She is a professional writer; but rather than setting that self apart, the novel as reading-process incorporates the activity of writing into the society of Middlemarch, from which it would otherwise be excluded. The narrative discourse does not dramatise its own 'exceptionalness': it ranges tranquilly across shared worlds. It presents its telling as reminding; it discovers insight in the reader. There is no opposition between the 'ordinary' and the 'exceptional' in this work, between Cixous's poles: 'Nature/History, Nature/Art, Nature/Mind, Passion/Action'. Both metaphor and generalisation here emphasise what is held in common: the human body, human emotions and the physical conditions of the material world which sustain and hold them in check. Her hard recognition of the shared material world is also at times playfully reversed to yield improbable connections: Mrs Cadwallader's mind is 'as active as phosphorus, biting everything that came near into the form that suited it'. The forced connection of chemical and psychological action is witty and temporary. The full physical intensity of interconnected mental and bodily life counterweights the next passage:

> And now she pictured to herself the days, and months, and years which she must spend in sorting what might be called shattered mummies, and fragments of a tradition which was itself a mosaic wrought from crushed ruins—sorting them as food for a theory which was already withered in the birth like an elfin child. Doubtless a vigorous error vigorously pursued has kept the embryos of truth a-breathing: the quest of gold being at the same time a questioning of substances, the body of chemistry is prepared for its soul, and Lavoisier is born. But Mr Casaubon's theory of the elements which made the seed of all tradition was not likely to bruise itself unawares

against discoveries: it floated among flexible conjectures no more solid than those etymologies which seemed strong because of likeness in sound until it was shown that likeness in sound made them impossible: it was a method of interpretation which was not tested by the necessity of forming anything which had sharper collisions than an elaborate notion of Gog and Magog: it was as free from interruption as a plan for threading the stars together.

(II, ch. 48, pp. 312–13)

The imagery of childbirth, of alchemical transformation and of necessary questioning, of comparative grammar and etymology, of Grimm's law, of embryos, bodies and soul, here suggests the possibility that Casaubon's enterprise of seeking a key to lock stories together, may have some worth. But the loss of contact with human sense and human sexuality (that vigorous connection between knowledge and desire which Donne and George Eliot both know) reveals Casaubon's enfeebled imagination: 'but the seed of all tradition was not likely to bruise itself unawares.' No hard surfaces, no collisions, no necessary connections: he floats like embryo or traveller in a space of purely fanciful connection: 'a plan for threading the stars together'.

The idea that meant so much to George Eliot, 'incarnation' – the word made flesh – takes some of its particular intensity and difficulty for her from childbirth. 'Incorporation' in *Middlemarch* is also a crucial image: as Donne says, 'to be no part of any body is to be nothing.' Sexual love and commitment to community share in this work the same energy. 'Contributing something to the sustenation of the whole' must be a limiting as well as a satisfying endeavour. Lydgate ends by feeling that 'he had not done what he once meant to do', (III, Finale, p. 495) and Dorothea by feeling 'that there was always something better which she might have done, if she had only been better and known better' (p. 461). The conditions of their education, of the false relations created socially between men and women, bear a large responsibility for their sense of inadequacy or failure. But it is also a measure of the enlargement of our expectations created by the book's activity that we perceive the true power of their aspirations.

We experience the successful doctor, Lydgate, and the Member of Parliament's wife, Dorothea Ladislaw, not according to such social labels, but as mitigated failures precisely because of the high value that they have placed upon themselves. This value is sustained by the activity of the text which, through imagery and imagination, makes us join in understanding that the 'ordinary' is freighted with fullest potential. To have rescued Dorothea – or any other of her characters – from the social conditions which unyieldingly contain, would have been to sentimentalise, and to allow her readers to feel satisfied that conditions have changed sufficiently since 1830. As it is, the book forces us still to recognise exclusion, false consciousness and atomism as part of daily experience for women, and for men and women in their relations with each other. At the same time the activity of the writing incarnates human potentiality; a potentiality which here has its diffused 'origin' in a woman, Mary Ann Evans, Mrs Lewes, who has found her work: George Eliot.

From Gillian Beer, *George Eliot* (Brighton, 1986), pp. 166–99.

NOTES

[The previous essay, by Kathleen Blake, reconsiders *Middlemarch* from a feminist perspective but employs a fairly traditional critical approach. Gillian Beer's approach is more innovatory. For a start, she looks again at the Victorian period, looking at evidence, including writing by and about women, which critics have tended to ignore. She establishes connections between the evidence of the period and the evidence of the text. Her re-examination of the past leads to a shifting of the angle of assessment, which leads to a new sense of the text, a reading that need not defer to received critical opinion. The whole essay (which is the second half of a chapter on *Middlemarch*), is characterised by Beer's readiness to think about how the Victorians perceived and thought about their world. She provides a sense of the complexity of George Eliot's stance: as much as George Eliot might desire connectedness she is always aware of difference: as much as she values independence, she also values interdependence. What comes across, as in much recent criticism, is a view of George Eliot asking questions, and expressing an astonishingly subtle sense of the dilemmas that shaped and dominated the lives of the people of her time. The stress falls on the openness of the text rather than its resolutions. All quotations from the text are from the Cabinet edition (Edinburgh and London, 1877–80). Ed.]

1. Françoise Basch, *Relative Creatures: Victorian Women in Society and the Novel, 1837–67*, tr. A. Rudolf (London, 1974), p. 115.

2. Bonnie Zimmerman, ' "The Mother's History" in George Eliot's Life and Political Ideology', in *The Last Tradition: Mothers and Daughters in Literature*, ed. Cathy N. Davidson and E. M. Booner (New York, 1980), p. 91.

3. Anna Jameson, *Memoirs and Essays: Illustrative of Art, Literature, and Social Morals* (London, 1846), pp. 15–16.

4. Steven W. Fullom, *The History of Woman, And Her Connexion with Religion, Civilization, and Domestic Matters, from the earliest Period*, 2 vols (London, 1855), pp. 214–15.

5. Barbara Bodichon, *An American Diary, 1857–8*, ed. J. Reed (London, 1972), p. 63.

6. Hester Burton, *Barbara Bodichon, 1827–91* (London, 1949), p. 71.

7. *The Alexandra Magazine* (March, 1865), p. 133.

8. Emily Shirreff and Maria G. Grey (nee Shirreff), *Thoughts on Self-Culture: Addressed to Women* (2 vols, 1850; London, 1854), p. 262.

9. *Westminster Review*, 67 (1857), p. 308.

10. Maria G. Grey, 'On the Education of Women' (London, 1871), p. 19.

11. Ibid., p. 20.

12. Ibid., pp. 56–7.

13. Ibid.

14. Emily Shirreff and Maria G. Grey (née Shirreff), *Thoughts on Self-Culture: Addressed to Women* (2 vols, 1850; London, 1854), p. 263.

15. Rosalind Miles, *The Fiction of Sex: Themes and Functions of Sex Difference in the Modern Novel* (New York, 1974), p. 52.

16. Zelda Austen, 'Why Feminist Critics are Angry with George Eliot', *College English*, 37 (1976), 556.

17. Bessie Rayner Parkes, V, 178, MS Girton.

18. Eliza Lynn Linton, *My Literary Life* (London, 1899), p. 97.

19. Gordon Haight (ed.), *The George Eliot Letters*, vol. 6 (New Haven and London, 1954–78), p. 44.

20. *Westminster Review*, 67 (1857), 306–10.

21. Gordon Haight (ed.), *The George Eliot Letters*, vol. 8 (New Haven and London, 1954–78), p. 402.

22. George Eliot, *Poems*, Cabinet edition (Edinburgh and London, 1877–80), p. 98.

23. Edith Simcox, *Natural Law* (London, 1877), p. 156.

24. Gillian Beer, *Darwin's Plots* (London, 1983).

25. R. H. Hutton, in *George Eliot: The Critical Heritage*, ed. D. R. Carroll (London, 1971), p. 287.

26. George Eliot, *Daniel Deronda*, Cabinet edition (Edinburgh and London, 1877–80), Bk 1, ch. 19, p. 308.

27. Hélène Cixous, in *New French Feminisms*, ed. Elaine Marks and Isabelle de Courtivron (Brighton, 1981), p. 91.

28. Henry Alford (ed.), *The Works of John Donne, D. D., Dean of Saint Paul's, 1621–1631, With a Memoir of His Life* (London, 1839), p. 321.

Further Reading

The obvious approach in a bibliography is to list those books and articles about an author which have contributed most to an understanding and reinterpretation of her or his work. This bibliography will, therefore, mention the recent critical work on *Middlemarch* which (along with the material collected in this anthology) has had the most interesting things to say about George Eliot. But to present the critical work of the last two decades in such a straightforward way would be to ignore a fact which has been crucial in determining the whole shape and direction of this anthology. This is the fact that critics do not suddenly and unexpectedly deliver a new reading of *Middlemarch*. Criticism is always shaped by the period within which the critic writes, and in the last two decades criticism of specific works has been influenced consistently by broader debates in the field of critical theory. Some may regret this and recall a time of critical innocence, as recently as the 1960s, when critics offered their own personal theories about a text. Of course, criticism never was this 'innocent': critical views have always been shaped by broader cultural and political views. But it is only in the last twenty years that criticism has become consistently self-conscious about its stance. Even those critics who reject theory, and who see themselves as maintaining a traditional approach, are now self-conscious in a way that would not have been the case in the past, as they see themselves defending a threatened position. Criticism today is, whether one likes it or not, consistently influenced by theory.

The effect of this for a student of literature can be rather frightening. It might seem as if it is necessary to approach a book via theory rather than directly. It is, therefore, worth repeating a standard piece of advice: it is always better to read the text than read a critic, and when you have read the text, the most rewarding thing you can do is read it again. But there will come a time when students want to know what other readers think, a time when they will become curious about available perspectives on a text. The problem here is that a great deal of recent criticism moves so far away from traditional assumptions that it can prove difficult to understand. In this collection, for example, it is likely that many readers will find a number of the essays puzzling and, as such, rather disappointing. The difficulty is that they offer unconventional approaches, and sometimes employ an unfamiliar critical language. To an extent it is necessary to absorb the pattern of thinking of recent criticism before one can see fully why it focuses on certain questions in certain kinds of ways. For this reason I have decided to start this reading list with a number of general books about current critical theory. Most of these books barely mention George Eliot, but it is quite possible that you might see how the ideas they present are relevant to the ways in which we might discuss George Eliot. I should add that many students find these books hard to grasp, at least to begin with. But if you persevere you are likely to find that, suddenly, everything drops into place. There are, of course, far too many books listed here to make it feasible to read them all, but it is well worth looking at two or three which take your fancy or which you can get hold of.

The list starts with three introductions to structuralism (although they also consider developments beyond pure structuralism):

Terence Hawkes, *Structuralism and Semiotics* (London: Methuen, 1977).
Jonathan Culler, *Structuralist Poetics* (London: Routledge & Kegan Paul, 1975).
John Sturrock, *Structuralism* (London: Paladin, 1986).

Beyond structuralism, we encounter poststructuralism and deconstruction:

Catherine Belsey, *Critical Practice* (London: Methuen, 1980).
John Sturrock, *Structuralism and Since* (Oxford: Oxford University Press, 1979).
J. Hillis Miller, *Fiction and Repetition* (Oxford: Blackwell, 1982).
Christopher Norris, *Deconstruction: Theory and Practice* (London: Methuen, 1982).
Christopher Butler, *Interpretation, Deconstruction and Ideology* (Oxford: Clarendon Press, 1984).

There are also many excellent introductions to feminist criticism, such as:

Catherine Belsey and Jane Moore (eds), *The Feminist Reader* (London: Macmillan, 1989).
Mary Eagleton (ed.), *Feminist Literary Theory: A Reader* (Oxford: Blackwell, 1986).
Gayle Greene and Coppélia Kahn (eds), *Making a Difference: Feminist Literary Criticism* (London: Methuen, 1985).
Elaine Showalter (ed.), *The New Feminist Criticism: Essays on Women, Literature and Theory* (London: Virago, 1986).

The final category here is Marxist and historicist criticism:

Terry Eagleton, *Literary Theory: An Introduction* (Oxford: Blackwell, 1983).
Raymond Williams, *The English Novel from Dickens to Lawrence* (London: Chatto and Windus, 1970).
Frank Lentricchia, *After the New Criticism* (London: The Athlone Press, 1980).
H. Aram Veeser (ed.), *The New Historicism* (London: Routledge, 1989).

As a complement to the works listed above, the following book takes a broad look at the current state of literary theory:

Ralph Cohen (ed.), *The Future of Literary Theory* (London: Routledge, 1989).

Turning now to works which deal directly with George Eliot, the three most widely available collections of essays are:

Patrick Swinden (ed.), *Middlemarch* (London: Macmillan, 1972).
George Creeger (ed.), *George Eliot: A Collection of Critical Essays* (Englewood Cliffs NJ: Prentice-Hall, 1970).
Kenneth Newton (ed.), *George Eliot* (London: Longman, 1990).

Other interesting collections are:

Ian Adam (ed.), *This Particular Web: Essays on Middlemarch* (Toronto and Buffalo: University of Toronto Press, 1975).
Barbara Hardy (ed.), *Critical Essays on George Eliot* (London: The Athlone Press, 1970).
Anne Smith (ed.), *George Eliot: Centenary Essays and an Unpublished Fragment* (London: Vision Press, 1980).

Beyond these collections, there is a mass of recent criticism on George Eliot and on *Middlemarch* in particular. The list that follows is therefore very selective, and the way in which it is divided up might not be entirely accurate (as obviously no critic confines her or his attention to just one aspect of the novel). None the less, there does seem some advantage in dividing the material into groups, although the first section in particular is a very broad group indeed. It consists of general and wide-ranging books about George Eliot (and, sometimes, other authors):

Calvin Bedient, *Architects of the Self: George Eliot, D. H. Lawrence, E. M. Forster* (Berkeley and Los Angeles: University of California Press, 1972).
Simon Dentith, *George Eliot* (Brighton: Harvester, 1986).
Elizabeth Deeds Ermarth, *Realism and Consensus in the English Novel* (Princeton NJ: Princeton University Press, 1983).
Elizabeth Deeds Ermarth, *George Eliot* (Boston: Twayne, 1985).
Peter K. Garrett, *The Victorian Multiplot Novel* (New Haven: Yale University Press, 1980).

A thoroughly up-to-date book on *Middlemarch* alone is:

T. R. Wright, *Middlemarch* (London: Routledge, 1990).

Critic after critic focuses on George Eliot's language, but the three essays below are particularly stimulating:

Janet Gezari, 'The Metaphorical Imagination of George Eliot', *English Literary History*, 45 (1978), 93–106.
Robert Kiely, 'The Limits of Dialogue in *Middlemarch*', in *The Worlds of Victorian Fiction*, ed. Jerome Buckley (Cambridge Mass.: Harvard University Press, 1975), pp. 103–23.
Rachel Trickett, 'Vitality of Language in Nineteenth-Century Fiction', in *The Modern English Novel*, ed. Gabriel Josipovici (London: Open Books, 1976), pp. 37–53.

The following articles and books reveal something of the variety of feminist approaches to George Eliot. To draw attention to the emphases of two of the most recent books in the list, Dorothea Barrett questions the traditional image of George Eliot and finds in her work elements of 'anger, feminism, subversiveness, revenge, iconoclasm, wit, and eroticism – elements that we have been taught not to expect'; Kristin Brady considers George Eliot's writing as 'a site of conflict between the conventional plot or voice and the contradictory desires fostered by the work's detailed attention to sexual difference':

Zelda Austen, 'Why Feminist Critics are Angry with George Eliot', *College English*, 37 (1976), 549–61.

Dorothea Barrett, *Vocation and Desire: George Eliot's Heroines* (London: Routledge, 1989).

Penny Boumelha, 'George Eliot and the End of Realism', in *Women Reading Women's Writing*, ed. Sue Roe (Brighton: Harvester, 1987), pp. 15–35.

Kristin Brady, *George Eliot* (London: Macmillan, 1989).

Christina Crosby, *The Ends of History: Victorians and 'The Woman Question'* (London: Routledge, 1990).

Sandra Gilbert and Susan Gubar, *The Madwoman in the Attic* (New Haven: Yale University Pres, 1979).

Barbara Hardy, '*Middlemarch*: Public and Private Worlds', *English*, 25 (1976), 5–26.

Mary Jacobus, *Reading Woman: Essays in Feminist Criticism* (London: Routledge, 1986).

Judith Lowder Newton, *Women, Power and Subversion: Social Strategies in British Fiction, 1778–1860* (London: Methuen, 1981).

Elaine Showalter, 'The Greening of Sister George', *Nineteenth-Century Fiction*, 35 (1980), 292–311.

This last group is fairly miscellaneous but covers primarily books and articles that look at George Eliot in a nineteenth-century context, seeing her work in relation to cultural and social developments and problems of the time:

Rosemary Ashton, 'The Intellectual "Medium" of *Middlemarch*', *Review of English Studies*, 30 (1979), 154–68.

Gillian Beer, *Darwin's Plots* (London: Routledge & Kegan Paul, 1983).

Gillian Beer, 'Beyond Determinism: George Eliot and Virginia Woolf', in *Women Writing and Writing About Women*, ed. Mary Jacobus (London: Croom Helm, 1979), pp. 80–100.

Catherine Gallagher, *The Industrial Reformation of English Fiction* (Chicago: Chicago University Press, 1985).

Hugh Witemeyer, *George Eliot and the Visual Arts* (New Haven: Yale University Press, 1979).

T. R. Wright, 'George Eliot and Positivism: A Reassessment', *Modern Language Review*, 76 (1981), 257–72.

I must stress that not all of the books and articles listed above deal directly with *Middlemarch*; indeed, some only include a few pages about George Eliot. But I hope that by now it is apparent that the way to arrive at your own understanding of a novel is less a matter of accumulating information and ideas about that particular novel than of becoming aware of the reading strategies offered by a variety of critical approaches. These books and articles are recommended for the same reason that essays were selected for inclusion in this anthology: they do not save you the effort of reading and thinking about the novel but suggest various ways in which you might want to read and think about the novel. Rather than criticism providing a short-cut to understanding it should start to alert you to the almost endless possibilities open to you as a reader – and therefore critic – of the novel.

Notes on Contributors

Gillian Beer is Professor of English, Girton College, University of Cambridge. Her books include *Meredith, A Change of Masks* (London, 1970); *Darwin's Plots* (London, 1983); and *Arguing With the Past* (London, 1989).

Kathleen Blake is Professor of English, University of Washington. Her publications include *Play, Games, and Sport: The Literary Works of Lewis Carroll* (Cornell, 1974); *Love and the Woman Question in Victorian Literature: The Art of Self-Postponement* (Brighton, 1983); and *Approaches to Teaching George Eliot's 'Middlemarch'* (Chicago, 1990).

Terry Eagleton is Professor of English, Wadham College, Oxford. His books include *Marxism and Literary Criticism* (London, 1976); *The Rape of Clarissa* (Oxford, 1982); *Literary Theory: An Introduction* (Oxford, 1983); *William Shakespeare* (Oxford, 1986); a novel, *Saints and Scholars* (London, 1987); and a play, *Saint Oscar* (London, 1989).

Suzanne Graver is Professor of English, Williams College, Massachusetts. Her publications include *George Eliot and Community: A Study in Social Theory and Fictional Form* (Berkeley, 1984).

David Lodge was formerly Professor of English at Birmingham University. He is a novelist as well as a critic. His critical works include *Language of Fiction* (London, 1966); *The Modes of Modern Writing* (London, 1977); and *Working With Structuralism* (London, 1981). Three of his more recent novels are *Changing Places* (London, 1975); *Small World* (London, 1984); and *Nice Work* (London, 1988).

Kerry McSweeney is Molson Professor of English, McGill University. His publications include *Tennyson and Swinburne as Romantic Naturalists* (Toronto, 1981); *Four Contemporary Novelists* (Montreal, 1983); *'Middlemarch'* (London, 1984), *Moby-Dick: Ishmael's Mighty Book* (Boston, 1986); and an edition of Carlyle's *Sartor Resartus* (Oxford, 1987).

D. A. Miller is Professor of English, Harvard University. His publications include *Narrative and its Discontents: Problems of Closure in the Traditional Novel* (Princeton, 1981); and *The Novel and the Police* (Berkeley and Los Angeles, 1987).

J. Hillis Miller is Professor of English and Comparative Literature, University of California, Irvine. His publications include *Fiction and Repetition* (Cambridge, Mass., 1982); *The Linguistic Moment* (Princeton, 1985); *The Ethics of Reading* (New York, 1987); and *Versions of Pygmalion* (Cambridge, Mass., 1990).

Sally Shuttleworth is Lecturer in the School of English, University of Leeds. Her publications include *George Eliot and Nineteenth-Century Science* (Cambridge, 1984); and a critical edition of *The Mill on the Floss* (London, 1990). She is joint editor, with John Christie, of *Nature Transfixed: Science and Literature, 1700–1900* (Manchester, 1989); and, with Mary Jacobus and Evelyn Fox Keller, of *Body Politics: Women and the Discourses of Science* (London, 1989).

Index